The Status of Protection Programs for Endangered, Threatened, and Depleted Marine Mammals in U.S. Waters

Michael L. Weber
David W. Laist

2007

One of a series of reports prepared in response to a directive from Congress to the Marine Mammal Commission to examine the biological viability and cost–effectiveness of protection programs for the most endangered marine mammals in U.S. waters

CONTENTS

List of Tables

List of Figures

I.   INTRODUCTION AND PURPOSE OF STUDY

As part of its fiscal year 2004 Omnibus Appropriations Act, Congress directed the Marine Mammal Commission to "review the biological viability of the most endangered marine mammal populations and make recommendations regarding the cost-effectiveness of current protection programs." Pursuant to this directive, the Marine Mammal Commission sought to address four basic questions:

1.   What are the most endangered marine mammal populations in U.S. waters?
2.   What is their biological viability?
3.   What is the biological effectiveness of current protection programs?[1]
4.   What is the cost-effectiveness of expenditures to implement those programs?

This report reviews protection programs for the 22 taxa listed under the Endangered Species Act (ESA) and the Marine Mammal Protection Act (MMPA) and is intended to complement other parts of the Commission's response to Congress, including—

- The report of a workshop to examine population viability analyses (PVAs) conducted to date on marine mammals in U.S. waters and ways to improve their usefulness for management (Marine Mammal Commission 2007).
- A report to examine systems for classifying marine mammals under the ESA, the MMPA, and IUCN–The World Conservation Union's Red List of Threatened Species, including a review of information on the current biological condition of each listed species (Lowry et al. 2007).
- A more in-depth review of the cost-effectiveness of recovery efforts for the North Atlantic right whale (Reeves et al. 2007).

These reports provide background information for use by the Commission as it prepares its findings and recommendations for submission to Congress.

This report is divided into three major sections. The first discusses provisions of the MMPA and the ESA that form the foundation for most marine mammal protection programs. The second profiles protection programs for all 22 listed taxa. Each profile summarizes information on the taxon's status, major threats, management framework, critical habitat, recovery planning, major management actions, and staffing and funding levels. The third summarizes overall trends in protection programs for the listed species and populations, based on those profiles. Appendices include tables and charts with estimates of expenditures for related conservation programs, additional details regarding key provisions of the MMPA and the ESA, and information on the status of the various taxa.

With regard to the allocation of funding levels related to recovery, the species profiles present cost data from four principal sources. First, they include actual funding spent by various federal

---

[1] For purposes of the study, the terms "protection" and "protection program" encompass all activities undertaken under the auspices of federal programs to reverse a population's decline and restore the population to its former abundance. This definition includes, but is not limited to, research and regulatory and other management actions, including enforcement, public outreach, and recovery planning.

and state agencies as reported to the U.S. Fish and Wildlife Service for its annual reports to Congress on federal and state expenditures for listed species, a report required by the ESA. Second, the profiles include information on species-specific research and management actions reported to the Marine Mammal Commission as part of its annual surveys of federally funded marine mammal research. Third, funding levels listed in agency budget documents are identified to the extent that line items clearly focus on an individual species. And fourth, the profiles present projected annual funding needs set forth in recovery plans at the time of their adoption. In almost all cases, funding projections in recovery plans are substantially higher than actual allocations.

Although these were the best available sources of funding data and provide a general picture of funding levels provided or believed necessary to foster a species' recovery, readers also should be aware that accounting practices used by the reporting agencies often differ greatly among agencies and even within agencies between years. Thus, funding levels reported here from different sources are not always consistent, and aggregate funding levels should be considered as general approximations at best.

II.   MAJOR FEDERAL STATUTORY PROTECTION MEASURES

Provisions of the MMPA and the ESA form the foundation and framework for most marine mammal protection activities. Those provisions are summarized briefly below and in greater detail in Appendix A.

THE MARINE MAMMAL PROTECTION ACT

When it was passed in 1972, the MMPA fundamentally changed the management of human activities affecting marine mammals and their ecosystems. The Act sets as its primary objective "…to maintain the health and stability of the marine ecosystem." Consistent with this objective, it calls for maintaining marine mammals at their "optimum sustainable population keeping in mind the carrying capacity of the habitat."

The Secretary of Commerce, acting through the National Marine Fisheries Service (NMFS), has primary authority for all cetaceans (i.e., whales and dolphins) and pinnipeds (i.e., seals and sea lions) except walruses. The Commerce Secretary also implements the MMPA's provisions for managing incidental take of all marine mammals in commercial fisheries. The Secretary of the Interior, acting through the U.S. Fish and Wildlife Service (FWS), has authority for managing all manatees, dugongs, polar bears, sea and marine otters, and walruses. The Act also established the Marine Mammal Commission, whose primary responsibility is to provide an independent source of advice and oversight to the Services and other federal agencies on implementation of the Act's provisions. The MMPA preempts state laws or regulations relating to the taking of marine mammals unless authorized through a formal process by which management authority can be transferred to individual states. However, states are not prevented from cooperating with NMFS and FWS in conservation efforts consistent with the Act's objectives, and in many cases they are vital partners in this regard.

Other important features of the MMPA include the following:

- Moratorium on taking: The Act imposed a moratorium on taking that includes both intentional and unintentional capture, killing, and harassment (including potential injury) of marine mammals. Subject to certain limitations or requirements, exemptions and exceptions to the moratorium are authorized for the following purposes:

    - Non-wasteful taking by Alaska Indians, Aleuts, or Eskimos when the taking is for subsistence purposes or for the purpose of creating authentic handicrafts and clothing;
    - Taking for scientific research, public display, enhancement, or commercial or educational photography;
    - Taking of small numbers of marine mammals incidental to activities other than commercial fishing;
    - Taking of non-depleted marine mammals under the Act's waiver provisions;
    - Deterring marine mammals from damaging fishing gear and catch or private property;
    - Taking by government officials for the protection and welfare of a marine mammal, the protection of public health and welfare, or relocation of nuisance animals; and
    - Taking in defense of one's self or another person in immediate danger.

- Depleted species: The Act directs the responsible agencies to designate a species as "depleted" if its abundance declines below its optimum sustainable population (OSP) level. This level is defined as a range between the population size that produces the maximum rate of net productivity and the maximum number that can be supported by the ecosystem. For species or populations designated as depleted, the Act authorizes the preparation of conservation plans to restore them to OSP levels. Species designated as depleted also are considered strategic stocks for which take reduction plans are to be prepared if they are taken incidentally in a category I or II fishery (see Appendix A for explanation of fishing categories).

- Taking incidental to commercial fishing: The Act calls for reducing mortality and serious injury of marine mammals incidental to commercial fisheries, first to below a stock's potential biological removal (PBR) level and ultimately to "insignificant levels approaching a zero mortality and serious injury rate." PBR is defined as the number of animals that can be removed from a population, not counting natural mortality, while retaining a high degree of assurance that the population will remain within the OSP range or, if it is depleted, will increase toward its OSP level. As the implementing agency, NMFS must place all U.S. commercial fisheries into one of three categories based on their level of incidental taking. Depending upon the classification, fishermen must undertake actions to meet the standards of the Act. For fisheries that are not meeting those standards, NMFS is required to convene a take reduction team to prepare a plan for that purpose.

THE ENDANGERED SPECIES ACT

In 1973 Congress passed a major revision of two earlier versions of the ESA—the Endangered Species Preservation Act (ESPA) of 1966 and the Endangered Species Conservation Act (ESCA) of 1969. Like the MMPA, the ESA is intended to conserve individual species and the ecosystems upon which they depend. The aim of the Act is "to bring any endangered species or threatened species to the point at which the measures provided pursuant to this [Act] are no longer relevant." As with the MMPA, the Department of Commerce has lead responsibility for cetaceans and pinnipeds (other than walruses) listed as endangered or threatened, and the Department of the Interior has lead responsibility for the recovery of listed manatees, dugongs, and sea and marine otters.

The Act defines an endangered species as one that is in danger of extinction throughout all or a significant portion of its range. A threatened species is one that is likely to become endangered in the foreseeable future. The Act identifies five factors that must be considered in evaluating whether to list a species under either category:

- The present or threatened destruction, modification, or curtailment of the species' habitat or range;
- Overutilization for commercial, recreational, scientific, or education purposes;
- Disease or predation;
- The inadequacy of existing regulatory mechanisms; and
- Other natural or manmade factors affecting the species' survival.

The economic impact of a listing may not be considered in listing determinations.

Specific protection provisions in the ESA include the following:

- Prohibition on taking endangered and threatened species: The ESA makes it unlawful to take an endangered or threatened species. Taking includes intentional and unintentional harm or harassment, including modification of habitat that significantly impairs essential behavioral patterns to the extent that it kills or injures listed species. This prohibition also is generally applied to activities affecting threatened species through regulations issued by the two Services. Exemptions to this prohibition include the following:

  - Taking by certain Alaska Natives and non-native permanent residents of Alaska Native villages primarily for subsistence purposes. Such taking may be regulated if it is found that the taking materially and negatively affects the species;
  - Taking for scientific research or enhancement of a population;
  - Taking incidental to an otherwise lawful activity provided there is an acceptable plan and funding to mitigate takings and that the takings will not "appreciably reduce the likelihood of the survival and recovery of the species in the wild"; and
  - Taking incidental to federal actions that are subject to section 7 consultation for which a "no-jeopardy" biological opinion is issued.

- Designation of critical habitat: The ESA requires designation of critical habitat for listed species, with some exceptions. Critical habitat includes geographical areas "on which are found those physical or biological features essential to the conservation of the species and which may require special management considerations or protection." Unlike listing decisions, a decision to designate critical habitat may consider economic impacts. The Act requires that federal agencies avoid destruction or adverse modification of critical habitat.

- Preparation of recovery plans: The ESA requires the development and implementation of a recovery plan for a listed species unless the Secretary of the Interior or the Secretary of Commerce finds that a recovery plan will not promote the conservation of a listed species. These plans must include objective and measurable criteria for removing the species from the list of endangered and threatened species, measures needed to recover the species, and estimates of the time and costs required to carry out those measures.

- Section 7 consultations: Section 7 of the ESA requires that all federal agencies use their authorities to further the conservation objectives of the Act and that they consult with the Services to ensure that any action they authorize, fund, or carry out is not likely to jeopardize the continued existence of threatened or endangered species or result in the destruction or adverse modification of critical habitat. Consultation may be informal or formal, depending on the likely effect of the activity. A formal consultation results in the preparation of a written biological opinion by the relevant Service on whether the activity is likely to jeopardize the existence of the listed species or modify its habitat. If so, reasonable and prudent alternatives to the proposed action must be identified to avoid jeopardy or adverse modification.

OTHER AUTHORITIES

Listed marine mammals also are protected by other federal statutes and international agreements to which the United States is a party (Appendix A). Among the more important domestic statutes are provisions under the National Environmental Policy Act requiring the preparation of environmental assessments and impact statements; the Magnuson–Stevens Fishery Conservation and Management Act requiring the preparation of fishery management plans; the National Marine Sanctuaries Act, which authorizes the establishment of marine sanctuaries; and the Outer Continental Shelf Lands Act, which authorizes and regulates the leasing of U.S. outer continental shelf areas for purposes of oil, gas, and hard mineral exploration and development. Important international agreements include the International Convention for the Regulation of Whaling and the Convention on International Trade in Endangered Species of Wild Fauna and Flora.

III.   SPECIES-SPECIFIC PROTECTION PROGRAMS

SIRENIANS

Florida Manatee

Status: The Florida manatee (*Trichechus manatus latirostris*) is a subspecies of the West Indian manatee that occurs only in the southeastern United States. The species as a whole occurs from the southeastern United States through the Greater Antilles and Central America to northern Brazil. It was first listed as endangered under the ESPA in 1967 (FWS 2001), and that listing was carried forward under the ESCA and ESA. Florida manatees are not listed separately but are considered endangered by virtue of the species' listing as endangered throughout its range. In April 2005 the Service announced plans to begin a five-year review of the Florida manatee to determine whether information is sufficient to warrant downlisting or delisting the species (FWS 2005c). Florida manatees also are protected under the state of Florida's Manatee Sanctuary Act.

Although the Florida subspecies ranges as far west as Texas and as far north as Rhode Island, its distribution is concentrated in coastal waters and rivers of Florida (Lefebvre et al. 2001). Four subpopulations have been identified for management purposes, including two along Florida's Atlantic coast and two on the Gulf of Mexico coast. Forty-seven percent of the total population is estimated to be in the Atlantic subpopulation, 4 percent in the St. Johns River subpopulation, 12 percent in the northwest subpopulation, and 37 percent in the southwest subpopulation (FWS 2001).

A reliable method for estimating total abundance has not been developed because of shortcomings in survey techniques; however, a minimum population has been estimated based on counts of animals at winter refuges (FWS 2001). In the 1980s the total population was estimated to number at least 1,200 manatees. More comprehensive surveys involving aerial and ground counts were initiated in 1991, and in January 2001 a total of 3,300 manatees were counted. The current population is therefore thought to number at least 3,300 (Haubold et al. 2005). Roughly equal numbers of manatees occur on Florida's east and west coasts. In the absence of a series of reliable total population estimates, trends in abundance have been assessed using survival rates from photo-identification, mortality records, and reproduction rates. The 2001 revision of the Florida manatee recovery plan includes the assessments shown in Table 1 for each of the four subpopulations. (See also Table 3 for recovery criteria.)

The most recent stock assessment report for Florida manatees estimates the potential biological removal (PBR) level to be between 0 and 3 and notes that human-related manatee mortality far exceeds those levels (FWS 2000). The report also concludes that establishing any level for PBR would be inappropriate and inconsistent with the Florida manatee recovery plan.

Table 1. ***Status of four major subpopulations of Florida manatees relative to recovery criteria in the 2001 recovery plan (FWS 2001)***

Northwest	Southwest	Upper St. Johns	Atlantic
Exceeds survival, reproduction, and population growth criteria	Estimates of survival and population growth not yet available; reproduction criterion has been exceeded for group that summers in Sarasota Bay	Meets or exceeds survival, reproduction, and population growth criteria	Meets reproduction criterion; may meet survival and population criteria
Although overall deaths are relatively low, watercraft-related deaths are increasing rapidly	Overall deaths are high; watercraft-related deaths are increasing rapidly	Overall deaths are moderate; watercraft-related deaths increasing slowly	Overall deaths are high; watercraft-related deaths increasing moderately

Major Threats: About one-third of all known Florida manatee deaths are directly related to human activities, principally collisions with vessels, which constitute the most immediate threat to their survival (Rathbun and Wallace 2000, MMC 2005). Overall, the total number of manatee deaths has grown steadily since 1976 when mortality records were first compiled. Between the 1980s and 1990s average annual reported mortality doubled (MMC 2001). Without good estimates of population size, it is unclear whether this change reflects an increased mortality rate, a relatively stable mortality rate accompanying an increased population size, or some combination of the two. In the long term, the major threat to Florida manatees is thought to be the potential loss of warm-water habitat necessary to survive cold winter periods. Other threats include entrapment in floodgates and navigation locks, incidental take in fishing gear, habitat destruction, cold stress, and naturally produced biotoxins associated with red tides (FWS 2001).

Boat Collisions: Boat collisions are the largest source of human-caused manatee deaths and injuries in Florida, accounting for about one-quarter to one-third of all known deaths. Between 1976 and 2005 watercraft-related deaths of manatees ranged from a low of 15 in 1983 to a high of 95 in 2002 with an average of 81 deaths per year between 2001 and 2005 (Laist and Shaw 2006). Although the total number of deaths has been increasing steadily, the proportion of annual mortality caused by boats has remained relatively stable.

Loss of Warm-Water Refuges: Perhaps the major long-term threat to Florida manatees is the loss of warm-water refuges. This is due both to the likely closure of industrial facilities, principally power plants, that produce warm-water discharges now used by most Florida manatees in winter, and potential declines of warm-water flows at natural springs due to groundwater withdrawal for human uses (FWS 2001, Laist and Reynolds 2005a,b). In the past, manatees likely relied on warm-water springs in central Florida and passive thermal basins (i.e., persistent pockets of warm water) in southernmost Florida to survive the lethal effects of cold winter temperatures. Hunting prior to the 1900s apparently drastically reduced manatee use of natural springs and, as Florida developed and warm-water outfalls from power plants became available, manatees expanded their restricted winter range in southernmost Florida using those discharges as refuges. About 60 percent of all Florida manatees currently winter at 10 major power plant outfalls. Along the Atlantic coast, 85 percent depend on five power plant outfalls (Laist and Reynolds 2005b). Of nine warm-water refuges with at least one winter count of more than 200 manatees, six are power plants, one is a natural spring, and two are passive thermal basins in southernmost

Florida. Even at power plants, manatees wintering there can be at risk due to plant malfunction or maintenance shutdowns or because the plants do not heat water to temperatures warm enough for manatees.

Although some power plants have recently been upgraded to operate for another 20 to 30 years, others will likely be shut down, perhaps as soon as the next few years (MMC 2005). Plants built before the early 1970s, including those that have been or may be upgraded after 1972, are allowed to continue discharging warm water from plant cooling systems under a regulatory variance. Power plants built since the early 1970s are not allowed to do so. According to the 2001 Florida manatee recovery plan, "in the absence of stable, long-term sources of warm water and winter habitat, large numbers of manatees may succumb to the cold" (FWS 2001).

Discrete groups of manatees also depend on discharges from warm-water springs (Laist and Reynolds 2005b). Nearly the entire subpopulation of 170 manatees in the upper St. Johns River depends on Blue Spring to survive winter cold periods. In recent years, drought and groundwater withdrawals for domestic and agricultural uses may have contributed to reduced flow rates. In a few other cases, manatee access to warm-water springs is restricted by human modifications. At Homosassa Springs on the gulf coast of Florida, a fence has been placed across the spring run to confine a few captive manatees near the spring discharge where they serve as an attraction for visitors to a state wildlife park. Ironically, this restricts wild manatees to lower portions of the spring run where water temperatures in winter are somewhat cooler than the discharges at the head of the spring run (MMC 2005). In other cases, dams and locks have blocked access to springs once used by manatees. Spring runs made shallow by siltation also limit manatee access to some warm-water spring discharges.

Floodgates and Navigation Locks: The second largest source of human-related manatee mortality is crushing and drowning in floodgates and navigation locks. Between 1976 and 2000 these structures caused between 3 and 16 deaths per year, representing about 4 percent of total manatee mortality (MMC 2005).

Other Anthropogenic Causes: Other anthropogenic causes of manatee death include entanglement and ingestion of marine debris such as monofilament fishing line, incidental take in shrimp nets, vandalism, and entrapment in sewer pipes. Between 1976 and 2000 these sources combined to account for approximately 3 percent of all recorded manatee deaths (FWS 2001).

Other Habitat Degradation: Large portions of habitat upon which manatees rely for food, resting, calving, nurturing young, or as travel corridors have been and are being altered by expanding development (FWS 2001). Some areas once inaccessible for boating are now heavily used navigation routes and open to other human activities. Polluted runoff, boat propellers, and dredging have damaged or destroyed grass beds on which manatees feed (MMC 2001). Hydrilla, an exotic plant that has supplanted native aquatic species, has become a new food source for manatees (FWS 2001). Although eaten by manatees, Hydrilla is managed as a nuisance plant (FWS 2001). Table 2 lists some of the habitat-related concerns for each of the four subpopulations of Florida manatees (FWS 2001).

Table 2.   *Major habitat protection concerns for the four subpopulations of Florida manatees (FWS 2001)*

Northwest	Southwest	Upper St. Johns	Atlantic
• Spring flow rates • Water quality effects on submerged aquatic vegetation (SAV) • Storm-related salinity fluctuation effects on SAV • Storm-related effects on adult survival • Human disturbance at springs • Conflicts between weed control and SAV • Papilloma virus	• Manatee dependence on power plants as thermal refuges • Increasing boat traffic • Red-tide-related deaths • Water control structure deaths • Water quality effects on SAV • Storm-related salinity fluctuation effects on SAV • Storm-related effects on adult survival • Human disturbance	• Spring flow rates • Increasing boat traffic • Water quality effects on SAV • Water control structure deaths • Conflicts between weed control and SAV	• Manatee dependence on power plants as thermal refuges • Increasing boat traffic • Use of Intra-coastal Waterway as a manatee travel corridor • Water control structure deaths • Water quality effects on SAV • Storm-related salinity fluctuation effects on SAV • Human disturbance

Natural and Undetermined Causes: About two-thirds of all known manatee deaths between 1976 and 2000 (FWS 2001, MMC 2005) were caused by natural and undetermined causes. Natural causes include disease, parasitism, and reproductive complications. In some years, exposure to cold has been a major cause of death. The greatest number of cold-related deaths occurred following a winter cold spell in 1989 when at least 46 manatees died. Red tides also cause episodes of high manatee mortality. In the spring of 1996 at least 145 manatees died during a red-tide event in southwestern Florida. In many cases, causes of death cannot be determined because of badly decomposed carcasses or other reasons. Undetermined deaths may be caused by either natural or human-related factors.

Management Framework: At the federal level, FWS has lead responsibility for conservation and recovery of Florida manatees (FWS 2001, MMC 2004). Among other things, FWS oversees development and implementation of the Florida Manatee Recovery Plan (FWS 2001), conducts section 7 consultations on federally authorized projects that may affect manatees, enforces federal and state manatee protection regulations, and oversees efforts to rescue and rehabilitate injured manatees (MMC 2001). The Sirenia Project and the Patuxent Wildlife Research Center in the U.S. Geological Survey's (USGS) Biological Resources Division have the lead in manatee research at the federal level. Among other things, they develop population models, assess life history information from photo-identification records, and conduct research on feeding ecology and habitat needs.

The Florida manatee recovery program is unique among marine mammal recovery programs in that staff and funding levels provided for recovery work by the state agencies exceed those provided by the federal government. At the state level, the Florida Fish and Wildlife Conservation Commission exercises lead responsibility through its Imperiled Species Management Section and the Fish and Wildlife Research Institute. The management section oversees state regulatory, planning, and public education activities related to manatee protection, including the development of boat speed regulations and oversight of manatee protection plans developed by Florida counties with important manatee habitat. The Fish and Wildlife Research Institute oversees the carcass salvage and necropsy program, conducts aerial surveys, assists in the rescue of injured manatees, and maintains a geographic information system of data on manatees and manatee habitats.

Other agencies and organizations play important roles as well. The Army Corps of Engineers and the South Florida Water Management District have been designing and installing devices to prevent manatees from being crushed and drowned in floodgates and navigation locks. The U.S. Coast Guard and the Florida Fish and Wildlife Conservation Commission's Division of Law Enforcement enforce boat speed zones. The non-profit Save the Manatee Club has purchased equipment, funded research, and lobbied state and federal legislatures for funding and actions to support manatee recovery. The Florida Power & Light Company has funded aerial surveys of manatee abundance at power plants and produced public education materials. A number of marine aquaria and zoological parks have provided facilities and medical treatment to rehabilitate injured and distressed manatees for release back into the wild. The Marine Mammal Commission provides support for projects and helps in identifying recovery priorities through periodic reviews of manatee recovery efforts.

FWS first established a recovery team for West Indian manatees in 1976. The recovery team, which has been restructured and expanded several times, was last restructured in 2002. It now includes more than 140 people representing 60 agencies and groups and carries out its work through 12 working groups.

Critical Habitat: Critical habitat for manatees was designated in several areas of Florida in 1976 (40 Fed. Reg. 58308). It was the first of any listed marine mammal species to have such areas designated. The designated areas include most of the species' Florida range as it was known in 1976. Since that time, critical habitat has not been revised to reflect new understanding of manatee distribution and habitat needs.

Recovery Plan: FWS first adopted a recovery plan for West Indian manatees in 1980 (FWS 2001). The initial plan focused principally on the Florida subspecies and, to a lesser extent, on Antillean manatees in Puerto Rico and the U.S. Virgin Islands. When it first revised the plan, the Service developed separate recovery plans for Florida manatees (adopted in 1989) and Puerto Rico manatees (adopted in 1986, see below.) Two subsequent plan revisions were adopted for the Florida manatee in 1996 and 2001. Steps to prepare a fourth revision are currently underway. The goal of the current recovery plan is "to assure the long-term viability of the Florida manatee in the wild," allowing for downlisting to threatened and later to delisting, based in part of criteria shown in Table 3 (FWS 2001).

The recovery plan includes four objectives and dozens of associated tasks. The objectives and some of the major tasks include the following (FWS 2001):

Minimize causes of manatee disturbance, harassment, injury, and mortality

- Continue state and federal review of permitted activities to minimize impacts to manatees and their habitats
- Minimize collisions between manatees and watercraft

Table 3. ***Criteria for downlisting and delisting Florida manatees under the Endangered Species Act of 1973 (FWS 2001)***

Downlist to Threatened	Delist
1. Reduce threats to manatee habitat or range as well as threats from natural and manmade factors by— • Identifying minimum spring flows • Protecting selected warm-water refuge sites • Identifying foraging habitats associated with warm-water refuges for protection • Identifying other important habitat (e.g., migratory corridors, feeding areas, and calving/nursing areas) for protection • Reducing unauthorized human-caused "take"	1. Reduce or remove threats to manatee habitat or range, as well as threats from natural and manmade factors, by enacting and implementing federal, state, or local regulations that— • Adopt and maintain minimum spring flows • Protect a network of warm-water refuge sites • Protect foraging habitats associated with the network of warm-water refuge sites • Protect a network of other important manatee habitats • Reduce or remove unauthorized human-caused "take"
2. Achieve the following population benchmarks in each of the four regions for the most recent 10-year period, with 95 percent level of statistical confidence: • Average annual rate of adult manatee survival is 90 percent or greater • Average annual percentage of adult female manatees with first or second year calves in winter is 40 percent or greater • Average annual rate of population growth is equal to or greater than zero	2. Achieve the following population benchmarks in each of the four regions for an additional 10-year period after downlisting to threatened, with 95 percent level of statistical confidence: • Average annual rate of adult manatee survival is 90 percent or greater • Average annual percentage of adult female manatees with first or second year calves in winter is 40 percent or greater • Average annual rate of population growth is equal to or greater than zero

- Enforce manatee protection regulations
- Assess and minimize mortality caused by large vessels
- Eliminate manatee deaths in water-control structures, navigational locks, and drainage structures
- Rescue and rehabilitate distressed manatees and release back into the wild
- Eliminate or minimize harassment due to other human activities

Determine and monitor the status of manatee populations

- Conduct a five-year status review
- Determine life history parameters, population structure, distribution patterns, and population trends
- Evaluate and monitor causes of mortality and injury
- Define factors that affect health, well-being, physiology, and ecology

Protect, identify, evaluate, and monitor manatee habitats

- Protect, identify, evaluate, and monitor existing natural and industrial warm-water refuges and investigate alternatives
- Establish, acquire, manage, and monitor regional protected area networks and manatee habitat

- Ensure that minimum flows and levels are established for surface waters to protect resources of importance to manatees
- Assess the need for revising critical habitat

<u>Facilitate manatee recovery through public awareness and education</u>

- Develop, evaluate, and update public education and outreach programs and materials
- Coordinate development of manatee awareness programs and materials in order to support recovery
- Develop consistent manatee viewing and approach guidelines

Major Management Actions: Major actions to protect and conserve the Florida manatee include the following:

<u>Boat Collisions</u>: In 1989 the state of Florida initiated major efforts to reduce boat collisions with manatees. In conjunction with steps being taken by FWS, the state's initiative called for a three-pronged approach: regulations to limit boat speed and access in 13 key counties and specific areas where collision risks are greatest; enforcement of those rules; and restrictions on developing boating access facilities in key manatee habitat (MMC 2005).

Reducing speeds of watercraft may reduce manatee injuries and deaths largely by providing manatees more time to detect and avoid oncoming watercraft (Laist and Shaw 2006). It also provides vessel operators more time to detect and avoid manatees and reduces the force of collisions to levels that manatees might survive. By 2000 the state had established speed zones in all 13 key counties, with additional speed zones in parts of 11 other counties. Several types of speed zones are used depending on site-specific assessments of manatee habitat, vessel traffic patterns, and other factors. The two principal types of speeds zones include one that exempts marked channels and another that includes them. Speed limits within zones typically vary from idle or slow in non-channel areas and up to 30 mph in marked channels (MMC 2005). A third type of zone (i.e., shoreline slow speed zones) limits speeds within certain distances of shore and a fourth type (i.e., no entry areas) excludes all watercraft. The Florida Fish and Wildlife Conservation Commission has continued efforts to expand and refine speed zones and to introduce them in other counties. In addition, FWS has restricted boat speeds in several national wildlife refuges and has established 13 manatee refuges in various parts of Florida for purposes of strengthening or complementing state boat speed rules to protect manatees.

Development of boat speed rules is a demanding, iterative effort conducted county-by-county and area-by-area. The process involves the collection and analysis of manatee distribution and vessel traffic data, interagency meetings, public hearings, sign posting, public education, and enforcement operations. Controversy has often surrounded establishment of these zones. In Lee County in southwestern Florida—which often has led all Florida counties in annual watercraft-related manatee deaths—an appellate court invalidated state speed zones in five areas in 2004 after a particularly contentious rule challenge (MMC 2005). In the absence of those county rules, FWS issued emergency rules under the MMPA and the ESA to reinstate measures comparable to the annulled state speed zones (70 Fed. Reg. 17863).

Efforts to enforce boat speed restrictions were limited as new rules were adopted in the 1990s (MMC 2001). In 1997 the Service began dedicated enforcement operations in selected areas. In 2000 the Service received a special congressional appropriation that enabled it to establish a part-time enforcement strike team that increased its enforcement efforts fivefold. In 1998 the Coast Guard also began increasing its enforcement efforts. In 2000 the Florida Division of Law Enforcement, the primary source of enforcement for manatee rules, significantly increased its efforts. Boater compliance studies have been conducted periodically in various areas, principally by the state, to assess boater compliance and help identify enforcement priorities.

There has been little evidence of a decline in watercraft-related manatee deaths since the establishment of speed zones. Indeed, the total annual number of watercraft-related deaths has increased at roughly the same pace as the increase in total mortality. The failure to reduce watercraft-related deaths may be due to low compliance, inadequately designed speed zones, and/or increasing numbers of boats and manatees. A review of manatee deaths in two connected waterways in eastern Florida since 2002 suggested an abrupt decrease in the number of collision-related manatee deaths when channels with speed-limit exemptions were removed and all boaters were required to go slow both inside and outside the marked channels (Laist and Shaw 2006). The removal of speed-exempt channels also may have simplified enforcement and enhanced compliance.

A second approach to reducing watercraft-related deaths has been to limit the development of marinas and other watercraft access facilities. Both the Florida Department of Environmental Protection and the U.S. Army Corps of Engineers require permits for new marinas, boat ramps, private piers, and docks, and the Florida Fish and Wildlife Conservation Commission and FWS have a formal role in reviewing such permit applications. Restrictions and limitations imposed through this process to protect manatees have been controversial.

To facilitate review and approval of boating facilities, the governor of Florida launched an effort in 1989 to encourage the 13 key counties to adopt comprehensive manatee protection plans as part of required growth management plans. The manatee protection plans, which are reviewed by the Commission and FWS, are to include guidance on locating new watercraft access facilities in a manner consistent with the protection of manatees. By the end of 2004, 10 Florida counties had adopted state-approved manatee protection plans.[2]

Floodgates and Navigation Locks: Efforts in the 1980s to reduce manatee deaths in floodgates and navigation locks involved simple modifications in the timing of gate closures. Those measures appeared to reduce such deaths until the early 1990s when they increased sharply to a high of 16 deaths in 1994 (FWS 2001). In response, an interagency task force was established early in the 1990s, including representatives of the South Florida Water Management District, the U.S. Army Corps of Engineers, the Florida Wildlife Commission, FWS, and other agencies. The task force has overseen efforts to design and install pressure-sensing devices on gates and locks implicated in manatee deaths. The sensors trigger mechanisms that reverse closing gates, operating much like elevator doors. By 2006 most of the structures responsible for manatee deaths prior to the early 1990s (approximately 25 structures) had been modified. Manatee deaths

---

[2] James A. Valade, personal communication. 2005. U.S. Fish and Wildlife Service, 6620 Southpoint Drive, Room 310, Jacksonville, FL 32216.

at retrofitted structures subsequently declined substantially; however, some deaths have continued at structures not previously implicated and at retrofitted gates not operating properly. Adjustments have been developed for those not operating properly, and plans for retrofitting the remaining structures are being developed. The cost for modifying lift gates at flood control structures and some navigation lock gates has been about $150,000 per gate, while the cost for modifying navigation locks with swinging barn door-style gates has been about $1 million per lock.

Warm-Water Refuges: In 1999 FWS and Florida Power & Light Company convened a workshop to evaluate the potential impact of the loss of industrial warm-water refuges in the event that power plants are retired. As a result of this workshop, a Warm-Water Task Force was formed within the Florida Manatee Recovery Team. The task force is composed of representatives of state and federal agencies, power companies, environmental organizations, and the scientific community. Its purpose is to develop and implement measures to assure the availability of natural warm-water springs as winter refuges for manatees while minimizing mortality associated with future power plant closures.

Research supported by the Florida Power & Light Company, the Marine Mammal Commission, and Reliant Energy examined ways of mitigating the potential effect of power plant closures by developing solar-heated refuges that could sustain manatees during the winter pending an increase in manatee subpopulations dependent on natural springs (Laist and Reynolds 2005a, MMC 2005). These findings were incorporated into a draft warm-water refuge action plan by the Warm-Water Task Force. Among other things, the plan calls for maintaining a network of warm-water habitats for each of the four Florida manatee subpopulations to maintain their current range.

In 2000 Florida Governor Jeb Bush and the Florida Department of Environmental Protection convened a Springs Task Force (not part of the manatee recovery team) to restore, protect, and enhance Florida springs. Its charge includes establishing and maintaining minimum spring discharge levels for a variety of environmental reasons, including manatee protection. At the behest of representatives from the Florida Manatee Recovery Team, the St. Johns Water Management District, which has management responsibility for Blue Spring, supported a study to identify the minimum spring flow necessary to maintain an optimal population of manatees at the spring during the winter. Based on this study, the district proposed minimum spring flows for the next 25 years.

Other Habitat Degradation: Several approaches have been taken to prevent or mitigate degradation of important manatee habitat. As noted above, FWS and the state of Florida review hundreds of permit applications to the U.S. Army Corps of Engineers and Florida Department of Environmental Regulation for construction projects in areas that include important manatee habitat (FWS 2001). County manatee protection plans also are expected to include provisions incorporated into local growth management plans, including policies on locating boat facilities (FWS 2001).

Both the state of Florida and FWS also have acquired tens of thousands of acres of land, particularly in the Crystal and Homosassa Rivers area intended, in part, to protect manatee habitat (FWS 2001). FWS also has adopted regulations for designating manatee refuges (areas in which human activities may be regulated) and manatee sanctuaries (areas in which all waterborne activity is prohibited) (44 Fed. Reg. 60962). Manatee sanctuaries have been designated primarily to prevent divers from driving animals away from warm-water discharges at the Crystal and Homosassa Rivers. Eight small sanctuaries covering a total of about 60 acres have been established at those locations. With access by swimmers as well as boats prohibited in marked sanctuary boundaries, manatees quickly learned to use those areas to escape unwanted human attention. About a dozen manatee refuges covering many thousands of acres also have been established by FWS to regulate boat speeds in several areas of Florida where state measures were deemed inadequate or have been annulled following legal challenges.

Manatee Rescue and Rehabilitation Efforts: A recovery team working group led by FWS staff coordinates a network of state and local agencies and private organizations that rescues, rehabilitates, and releases dozens of injured and distressed manatees annually (FWS 2001). Such animals typically include animals hit by boats, entangled in fishing line or marine debris, caught in pipes or other structures, or debilitated due to exposure to red tides or cold. Between 1973 and 2005 more than 375 manatees were captured, treated, and returned to the wild, and many others were assisted and released on site (FWS 2001). Although a significant number of animals brought into captivity for special treatment died of their injuries or health problems during transport or treatment, animals released after successfully completing treatment appear to have a high rate of success in readapting to the wild. In 2005, FWS estimated that rehabilitation costs exceeded $5 million, with about two-thirds of that provided by oceanariums.

Staff and Funding Levels: Information on FWS and USGS funding allocations for research and management activities on Florida manatees is provided in annual administrative reports required by the MMPA (FWS 1981–1996, FWS, FWS and National Biological Service 1996, FWS and USGS 1997–2004). Although those reports do not itemize funding for all management activities in detail, they indicate that departmental funding levels between 1980 and 2000 ranged from at least $373,000 in 1986 to $1.4 million in 2000 (Table 4). In most of those years, funding for research accounted for between one-half and two-thirds of all itemized funding for manatees. In 2000 nearly $500,000 was appropriated specifically for enforcing manatee protection rules, principally boat speed rules.

FWS annual reports on endangered species expenditures by all federal and state agencies (FWS 2003b-d, 2005d-f, 2006) provide information on the total level of manatee funding by all federal and state agencies. Those reports indicate that total federal funding for Florida manatee recovery averaged about $3.1 million per year (Table 5, Appendices C.1-7). Unlike all other marine mammal recovery programs, state expenditures for recovery have exceeded those of federal agencies since 2000. State of Florida funding for Florida manatee activities remained relatively steady at nearly $6 million annually between 2000 and 2004. An uncertain amount of additional funding is provided by private organizations, such as oceanaria, which help maintain and treat injured and distressed manatees, and the Save the Manatee Club, which helps provide funding for research and certain equipment needs. Regarding staff, FWS currently estimates that it devotes about 11.3 full-time equivalents (FTEs) per year to manatee recovery activities[3]; the

---

[3] James A. Valade, personal communication. 25 June 2006. U.S. Fish and Wildlife Service, 6620 Southpoint Drive, Room 310, Jacksonville, FL 32216.

Table 4. *Department of the Interior funding allocations (in $ thousands) for West Indian manatee research and management activities under the MMPA and ESA as cited in administrative reports required by the MMPA: 1980–2000 (FWS 1981–1996, FWS and National Biological Service 1996, FWS and USGS 1997–2004)*

Year	Research and Development	Management †	Grants to States ‡	Total
1980	330	N/A	184	514
1981	379	320	396	1,095
1982	333	234	0	567
1983	320	191	0	511
1984	262	117	15	399
1985	379	114	117	610
1986	248	87	38	373
1987	310	31	115	456
1988	310	75	75	460
1989	325	75	105	505
1990	344	350	100	799
1991	625	389	87	1,101
1992	673	145	70	888
1993	670	621	90	1,381
1994	597	N/A	77	674
1995	468	N/A	76	544
1996	483	N/A	26	509
1997	556	N/A	26	582
1998	648	N/A	26	674
1999	810	N/A	26	836
2000	823	551	26	1,400

† Includes only management costs specifically identified for manatees; does not include support for all enforcement, permit, or administrative tasks
‡ Includes grants under section 6 of ESA to Florida and Georgia

USGS also supports about 13.3 FTEs who work on manatee research and monitoring studies as part of its Sirenia Project. It is not known whether or to what extent staff salaries are included in the funding estimates presented here

According to the Marine Mammal Commission survey of federally funded marine mammal research (Waring 2002), expenditures for biological and population assessment studies on manatees and dugongs in FY1991–FY2000 ranged from $544,000 in FY2000 to $1.3 million in FY1995 (see Appendix F). The principal sources of funding were FWS and USGS.

Projected cost estimates for work during the first five years under the Florida manatee recovery plan adopted in 2001 (Table 6) identified annual expenditures of approximately $8.3 million by all involved governmental and non-governmental groups (FWS 2001). Those costs include

Table 5. *Federal and state expenditures (in $ thousands) for recovery of the West Indian manatee, 1998–2004 (Source: FWS 2003b–d; 2005d–f; 2006)*

Fiscal Year	FWS	USGS	NMFS	USCG	Other Federal	Total Federal	State	Total State and Federal
1998	927	526	–	–	99	1,551	13	1,565
1999	1,145	526	–	619	117	2,407	1,945	4,351
2000	2,727	466	–	461	166	3,820	5,923	9,743
2001	2,363	510	–	480	85	3,438	5,936	9,373
2002	1,710	523	–	228	182	2,643	5,929	8,571
2003	2,070	971	–	713	75	3,830	5,969	9,799
2004	2,432	428	–	831	226	3,917	5,945	9,862

activities ranked under three priority categories. However, several significant costs—such as enforcement by the U.S. Coast Guard and state agencies and the installation of gate-reversing mechanisms on floodgates and navigation locks by the Army Corps of Engineers and South Florida Water Management District—were excluded from those cost estimates.

Table 6. *Projected funding needs (in $ thousands) to implement recovery activities for Florida manatees during the first five years after adoption of the 2001 Revised Florida Manatee Recovery Plan (FWS 2001)*

Objective	Year 1	Year 2	Year 3	Year 4	Year 5	Total
Objective 1: Minimize causes of manatee disturbance, harassment, injury, and mortality	4,238	4,238	4,238	4,193	4,193	21,100
Objective 2: Determine and monitor the status of manatee populations	2,488	2,449	2,506	2,496	2,511	12,450
Objective 3: Protect, identify, evaluate, and monitor manatee habitats	1,370	1,333	1,331	1,331	1,343	6,708
Objective 4: Facilitate manatee recovery through public awareness and education	288	258	258	258	258	1,320
TOTAL	8,384	8,278	8,333	8,278	8,305	41,578

Antillean Manatee, Puerto Rico Population

Population Status: The Antillean manatee (*Trichechus manatus manatus*) is a subspecies of the West Indian manatee that inhabits the coastal waters of Central America and northern South America and the larger Caribbean Islands (USGS 2005a). The species as a whole was first listed as endangered under the ESPA in 1967. That listing was carried forward under the ESCA and ESA. The Antillean subspecies is not listed separately but is considered endangered by virtue of the species' overall listing. Other than the Florida manatee, the Puerto Rico population of the Antillean subspecies is the only other group of manatees under U.S. jurisdiction. This subspecies is believed to be a relatively discrete population occurring in rivers and coastal waters of Puerto Rico. The extent to which manatees move between Puerto Rico and other parts of the Greater Antilles is uncertain.

Historical accounts of manatees in Puerto Rico include references to their use as food by aborigines and Spanish explorers, but information is insufficient to estimate former abundance or the extent to which hunting reduced their numbers (Rathbun and Possardt 1986). Aerial surveys since the late 1970s and mid-1980s reveal that most manatees in Puerto Rico occur on the eastern end of the island and along the southern coast in shallow, protected bays, and in sea grass beds along the northwestern shore of Vieques Island, about 10 miles east of Puerto Rico (Rathbun et al. 1985). Based on actual counts of animals during surveys conducted in 2005, the Puerto Rico population of Antillean manatees numbers at least 121 animals. Considering animals possibly not seen during that survey, some researchers suspect there are between 150 and 360 manatees and that the population is not declining. The PBR level has been set at zero (FWS 1994a).

Major Threats: In the 1980s the principal causes of manatee deaths in Puerto Rico were identified as poaching for food and unintentional entanglement in gillnets (Rathbun and Possardt 1986). Over time, poaching has become less frequent although boat collisions have increased. During the late 1980s and early 1990s, 43 percent of all known manatee mortalities in Puerto Rico were due to boat collisions (FWS 1994a). More recently, however, an assessment by USGS suggests that loss of habitat and small population size also are primary threats to this population (FWS 2005b).

Management Framework: The principal agencies involved with research and recovery efforts are the Commonwealth of Puerto Rico's Department of Natural and Environmental Resources, the Fish and Wildlife Service, the Caribbean Fishery Management Council, the U.S. Navy, and the U.S. Coast Guard (Rathbun and Possardt 1986, USGS 2005a). The non-profit Caribbean Stranding Network has conducted manatee carcass salvage and manatee rescue, rehabilitation, and release activities in Puerto Rico over the last 20 years.

Critical Habitat: None designated.

Recovery Plan: FWS adopted a recovery plan for Puerto Rico manatees in 1986 (Rathbun and Possardt 1986). The lack of information on historical and current abundance prevented the development of a quantitative recovery target for this population, and the plan's goal was therefore to establish a population "large enough to maintain sufficient genetic variation to enable it to evolve and respond to natural habitat changes and stochastic and catastrophic events." The plan's objectives were defined as follows:

- Identify, assess, and reduce human-related mortality, especially that related to gillnet entanglement;
- Identify and minimize alteration, degradation, and destruction of habitats important to the survival and recovery of the Puerto Rico manatee population; and
- Develop the criteria and biological information necessary to determine whether to reclassify the Puerto Rico population of manatees and, if so, when.

Among other actions, the plan recommended continuation of aerial surveys, improvements in the carcass salvage program, and public education aimed at reducing entanglement in gillnets.

Major Management Actions: Over the years, aerial surveys have been conducted intermittently, and carcass salvage and necropsy efforts have been maintained and improved to help monitor population status and trends. Past management efforts have stressed public education aimed at preventing poaching and reducing entanglement in gillnets. Boat speed zones have been established in some areas, including an identified manatee feeding area located within a naval base at Roosevelt Roads on the eastern end of the island. As noted earlier, some injured and distressed animals have been rescued, rehabilitated, and released back to the wild. In recent years, USGS has carried out a number of research projects to better identify habitat-use patterns through radio tracking individual animals and mapping their nearshore benthic habitats (USGS 2005a). Some management actions also have been taken to prevent disturbance and to restrict development in specific areas where manatees feed, rest, and obtain fresh water.

Staff and Funding Levels: Because West Indian manatees are listed as a species, FWS administrative reports under the MMPA and expenditure reports under the ESA do not separate funding data for Puerto Rico manatees from Florida manatees. As a result, information on funding is uncertain but is believed to be a very small fraction of total funding reported for all West Indian manatees (see Florida manatee above and Appendices C.1–7). FWS supported at least one FTE to work on manatees in Puerto Rico in 2005 and USGS supported 0.8 FTE.[4]

SEA OTTERS

Southern Sea Otter

Status: The southern sea otter (*Enhydra lutris nereis*) is one of three subspecies of sea otters. Its historical range is thought to have stretched from southern Canada to central Baja California. All three sea otter subspecies were hunted to near-extinction in the 18th and 19th centuries until hunting was prohibited in 1911 under the North Pacific Fur Seal Convention (Wilson et al. 1991). The species as a whole once ranged in coastal waters from Hokkaido, Japan, through the Kuril Islands around the North Pacific rim and south to Baja California. The population is

---

[4] James A. Valade, personal communication. 25 June 2006. U.S. Fish and Wildlife Service, 6620 Southpoint Drive, Room 310, Jacksonville, FL 32216; Cathy Beck, personal communication. 1 November 2006. Sirenia Project, U.S. Geological Survey. 2201 NW 40th Terrace, Gainesville, FL 32605

thought to have numbered between 150,000 and 300,000 animals before commercial exploitation (Rotterman and Simon-Jackson 1988). In 1938 a remnant colony of approximately 50 southern sea otters was discovered in central California. In 1977 the southern sea otter was listed as threatened under the ESA because of its low abundance, limited distribution, and vulnerability to impacts from oil spilled by tankers and offshore oil development. To promote recovery and minimize the risk of a single large oil spill affecting the entire population, an attempt was made in the 1980s to establish a second southern sea otter population by translocating animals from the central California mainland coast to San Nicolas Island off southern California. The San Nicolas Island colony has not increased as expected and now numbers about 25 to 30 animals (FWS 2003b).

Based on annual surveys conducted since the 1970s, the number of southern sea otters has increased slowly, despite two apparent periods of decline. In 1976 the population numbered an estimated 1,789 individuals; it then declined to 1,372 animals in 1984 (FWS 2003b). After 1985 population growth resumed and counts peaked at 2,377 animals in 1995 before beginning a four-year decline to 2,090 animals in 1999. Recent surveys suggest that population growth has resumed. In 2003 and 2004 counts of sea otters during spring surveys rose to 2,505 and 2,825, respectively, for a three-year average of 2,490 animals (USGS 2004). However, the overall rate of growth (less than 5 percent per year) has remained far below recovery rates of 15 percent or more observed in sea otter populations in some areas of Alaska prior to the 1970s and the 20 percent recovery rate reported for expansion into some unoccupied areas (FWS 2003b). Because the legislation authorizing a translocation of southern sea otters included provisions to address interactions with fisheries, California sea otters have been exempted from the fishery management provisions of the MMPA, and no PBR has been calculated for this population (FWS 1995).

Major Threats: At the time of listing in 1977 the primary threat to southern sea otters was thought to be a major oil spill from a tanker (42 Fed. Reg. 2968). Since then, other threats have emerged, including mortality incidental to commercial fishing, disease, chemical contaminants, naturally occurring biotoxins, and increased exploration and development of oil and gas resources off the California coast (FWS 2003b). The slow recovery of sea otters in California appears to be due to relatively high mortality among all age classes rather than low reproduction rates (MMC 2004). Among the likely explanations for the slow rate of recovery is incidental mortality in coastal fishing gear, increases in the rate of infectious disease, and decreases in food abundance (FWS 2003b).

Oil Spills: Sea otters with oiled fur face a high probability of dying due to hypothermia and toxic effects. Although the death of oiled otters depends, in part, on the extent to which they are covered, the recovery plan estimates that the probability of an oiled otter dying from related impacts is likely to be at least 50 percent (FWS 2003b).[5] The plan states, "we do not believe it is possible to avoid a catastrophic loss to the sea otter population in the event of a major spill in the vicinity of the sea otter's current range." The *Exxon Valdez* oil spill in 1989, which spread over an area covering hundreds of miles, underscored the scale of this threat. Spreading more than

---

[5] It is believed that sea otters may survive with oil on less than 10 percent of their body surface but that levels of coverage greater than 25 percent will lead to death (FWS 2002e).

400 miles in 30 days, that spill covered an area equal to the entire central California range of southern sea otters.

Incidental Catch in Commercial Fisheries: Between the late 1960s and early 1980s entanglement and drowning in gillnets and trammel nets are estimated to have caused an average of 80 sea otter deaths a year (Wendell et al. 1985). This mortality was apparently sufficient to cause a decline in the population that was reversed after a series of incremental actions taken by the state of California between 1982 and 1990 to restrict the use of gillnets in and around key sea otter habitats (Estes 1990). Fishing gear used in coastal pot and set net fisheries also may pose an entanglement hazard for southern sea otters; however, the revised recovery plan concludes that there is insufficient information to evaluate its possible impact on sea otters (FWS 2003b).

Disease: Infectious disease is believed to have been an important factor limiting population growth (Lafferty and Gerber 2002). Between 1991 and 1995 disease and infections from parasites, fungi, and bacteria were responsible for roughly 40 percent of all deaths for which causes were determined by the southern sea otter carcass salvage and necropsy program (Thomas and Cole 1996). Other causes of death included emaciation (10 percent), miscellaneous conditions such as gastrointestinal obstructions (13 percent), shark predation (7 percent), gunshot (4 percent), and unknown (18 percent). The most frequent infection was peritonitis induced by parasitic acanthocephalan worms in the digestive tract, followed by bacterial infections, protozoal encephalitis, and coccidioidomycosis (a systemic infection caused by a fungus) (FWS 2003b).

The variety and prevalence of infectious diseases found in necropsied sea otters suggest that southern sea otters are far more vulnerable to death by diseases than are other marine mammals (Thomas and Cole 1996). This, in turn, suggests that the immune function of southern sea otters may be compromised due to congenital, genetic, or environmental factors. The degree to which high exposure to pathogens may contribute to the frequency of infection in sea otters is unknown. There is evidence from live animals that these infectious agents are particularly common near human population centers (O'Shea et al. 1999).

Other Threats: Food availability and emaciation also may threaten southern sea otters. Emaciation, in turn, may compromise immune systems and expose sea otters to infectious diseases (Thomas and Creekmore 2005). The movement of male otters south of Point Conception may indicate limitations in food availability in the core of their current range. Examination of carcasses also suggests that the rate of pre-weaning mortality is higher in central California than it is in the large Alaska sea otter populations (FWS 2003b).

Management Framework: FWS is the lead federal agency for recovery of the southern sea otter. The California Department of Fish and Game is the principal state agency involved in recovery efforts. Annual fall and spring surveys of sea otters in California began in 1982 and are conducted cooperatively by scientists from USGS, the California Department of Fish and Game, FWS, and the Monterey Bay Aquarium, and with experienced volunteers. These organizations, together with the California Academy of Sciences, the Santa Barbara Museum of Natural History, beach clean-up crews for coastal cities, and others, are the principal members of the California Sea Otter Stranding Network. The network is responsible for recovering and examining carcasses. Since southern sea otters were first listed, FWS has established a sea otter recovery team and reconstituted it twice. The team's principal task has been to develop and revise recovery plans. For much of the 1980s recovery efforts focused on developing a translocation plan to move otters from the mainland colony to San Nicolas Island, and the recovery team did not meet. Instead FWS convened an Interagency (Translocation) Project Review Team to help guide and oversee recovery work during that period.

Critical Habitat: None designated.

Recovery Plan: A recovery plan for the southern sea otter was first adopted in February 1982 (FWS 1982). Its goals included the following:

- Establishing new sea otter colonies outside the existing sea otter range;
- Reducing vandalism, harassment, and incidental take;
- Incorporating recovery measures into local coastal development plans;
- Setting the recovery target as the OSP size; and
- Establishing a research program to assess and monitor the status of sea otters and their habitat.

In 1989 FWS reconstituted the recovery team to update the 1982 plan. FWS subsequently prepared revised draft plans in 1991 and 1996, but neither was adopted. In January 2000 a third draft revised recovery plan was circulated for public and agency review and, based on comments from the public and the recovery team, FWS adopted a final revised recovery plan in February 2003 (FWS 2003b). Its goal is "to establish the long-term viability of the southern sea otter population sufficiently to allow delisting the species." The revised plan concludes that a genetically viable population would be one with a minimum three-year average count of 1,850 animals. It therefore identifies that population size as the threshold for reclassifying the southern sea otter population as endangered under the ESA. The plan also establishes a three-year average count of 3,090 animals as the threshold for evaluating whether to remove southern sea otters from the list of threatened and endangered species. If delisted, the population could still be considered depleted under the MMPA because the lower limit of the OSP level for southern sea otters currently is estimated to be approximately 8,400 animals.

To develop a recovery strategy for the new plan, FWS reviewed the results of past management actions and concluded, in part, that the San Nicolas Island translocation had not been successful either in significantly reducing the chances of a large loss of otters due to a single major oil spill or other catastrophic event or in creating a separate population that could be used to restock the mainland population. The revised recovery plan therefore set forth the following elements for its recovery strategy (FWS 2003b):

- Restriction of range due to management provisions related to the translocation program: Evaluate the translocation program in light of changed circumstances and determine whether one or more criteria for declaring the translocation a failure have been met.
- Disease: Collect and analyze tissues for evidence of stress or disease; determine sources of disease agents and stress; minimize factors causing stress and disease.

- Incidental take in fishing gear: Evaluate the causes of mortality; monitor incidental take in commercial fisheries; evaluate the effectiveness of fishing regulations for preventing bycatch; evaluate incidental take in trap/pot fisheries; determine and take possible steps to reduce or eliminate mortality incidental to fisheries.
- Oil spills: Implement and monitor Coast Guard vessel management plans; assess the current risk of tanker accidents and other sources of oil spills, including offshore platforms, pipelines, and marine terminals; implement an oil spill contingency plan that includes a sea otter response plan.
- Contaminants: Evaluate causes of mortality; analyze tissues for environmental contaminants and archive tissues for future analysis; determine sources of environmental contaminants; determine contaminant levels in sea otter prey and habitat.
- Intentional take: Evaluate causes of mortality; minimize intentional take.

Major Management Actions: Efforts to protect and recover southern sea otters have focused on (1) establishing a new sea otter colony by translocating some otters to San Nicolas Island, (2) establishing a vessel traffic management system to reduce the chance of an oil tanker spill that could affect the sea otter range, and (3) reducing the incidental take of sea otters in commercial fisheries.

Translocation: To mitigate the possible impact of a major oil spill, the 1982 recovery plan recommended a translocation of sea otters to establish a new colony far enough removed from the mainland colony that it would be unlikely that a single spill would affect both areas (FWS 2003b). San Nicolas Island off southern California was selected as the appropriate translocation site, and in 1986 Congress passed legislation authorizing the creation of an experimental sea otter colony at that location by translocating otters from the mainland population (PL 99-625). To address concerns about subsequent range expansion into areas where sea otter foraging could affect commercial and recreational shellfish fisheries, the legislation also created a management zone south of the sea otter's mainland range. Any sea otters that moved into that management area were to be removed by non-lethal means and transported back to their range farther north (52 Fed. Reg. 29754). It was expected that the translocated population would stabilize at roughly 70 sea otters within one or more years and would reach carrying capacity in 10 or more years.

Between August 1987 and July 1993 more than 180 sea otters were moved from their mainland range to San Nicolas Island (FWS 2003b). Most translocated otters quickly disappeared or returned to their mainland range, leaving a small number of animals at the island. Since then, counts at San Nicolas Island have increased very slowly, and the population numbered about 27 animals in 2002. At the same time, increasing numbers of animals from the mainland population moved into the management zone where the Service had limited success in capturing and removing them. In light of these developments, FWS is considering steps to formally declare the translocation a failure, discontinue the otter-free management zone in southern California, and allow the otters at San Nicolas Island to remain there (FWS 2005a).

Vessel Traffic Management: Under auspices of the Monterey Bay National Marine Sanctuary, the National Oceanic and Atmospheric Administration (NOAA) and the Coast Guard worked with stakeholders to develop a plan for managing large vessel traffic in and near the sanctuary area to reduce the risk of oil spills, groundings, and collisions (FWS 2003b). The plan called for transiting vessels to remain minimum distances from shore, instituting an offshore vessel traffic separation scheme, monitoring vessel traffic, establishing a response network to assist vessels in distress, and implementing a mariner education program. To date, several of these recommendations have been implemented. In May 2000 the International Maritime Organization approved a U.S. proposal to establish offshore vessel traffic lanes for ships entering and leaving ports north and south of the sea otter range. In addition, the California Department of Fish and Game's Office of Spill Prevention and Response has developed contingency plans to protect wildlife, including sea otters, from the impacts of oil spills (FWS 2003b). This program also sponsors a network of professionally trained volunteers, paid staff, and veterinarians who can retrieve and attempt to rehabilitate oiled animals.

Fisheries Interactions: To reduce the bycatch of sea otters, as well as other marine mammals and seabirds in trammel nets and gillnets, the California legislature adopted a series of area closures between 1982 and 1990. The first closure adopted in 1982 closed a portion of Monterey Bay out to 10 fathoms from shore, but the measure simply displaced fishermen to other parts of the sea otter's range. In 1985 the measure was expanded to include the entire sea otter range out to the 15-fathom contour. Although this level reduced the incidental take of sea otters, animals continued to be taken in deeper waters, and in 1986 and 1990 the state legislature extended the closed area to 20 and 30 fathoms, respectively. The 1986 action reduced observed takes to low levels and in the late 1980s sea otter counts began to increase. The 1990 action essentially eliminated all sea otter bycatch. Since 1990 the closed area has been extended out to the 60-fathom contour to reduce bycatch of marine mammals other than sea otters and seabirds (FWS 2003b). In addition, the state has required that traps used to catch nearshore finfish be outfitted with a 5-inch ring in the entry funnel to prevent sea otters from getting caught in trap openings.

Staff and Funding Levels: Funding allocations by FWS and USGS for southern sea otter research and management work are identified in annual administrative reports prepared by those agencies pursuant to requirements of the MMPA (FWS 1981–1996, FWS and National Biological Service 1996, FWS and USGS 1997–2004). Although those reports do not itemize funding for all management activities (e.g., funding for enforcement and permit management is combined for all marine mammals under the jurisdiction of the Department of the Interior), they indicate that departmental funding for southern sea otter recovery work increased during the 1980s to a high of $1.3 million in 1990 when steps were being taken to implement the sea otter translocation (Table 7, Appendices C.1–7). During the 1990s funding levels declined substantially.

According to FWS reports on expenditures for endangered species by all federal and state agencies since 1998 (FWS 2003 b–e, 2005 d–f, 2006), annual federal funding of sea otter recovery again increased from $495,000 in 1998 to $1.37 million in 2003 (Table 8, Appendices C.1–7). FWS funding during that period ranged between $95,200 in 1999 and $184,100 in 2001. Most funding for southern sea otter activities was provided by USGS for research. In 2003, for example, USGS reported expenditures of $1,152,986 for southern sea otter activities. State of California funding for southern sea otter activities between 1998 and 2004 ranged between $35,100 and $156,000 (FWS 2005d)

Table 7. *Department of the Interior funding allocations (in $ thousands) for southern sea otter research and management activities under the MMPA and ESA as cited in administrative reports required by the MMPA: 1980–2000 (FWS 1981–1996, FWS and National Biological Service 1996, FWS and USGS 1997–2004)*

Year	Research/ Development	Management *	Grants to States ^	Total
1980	405	Not provided	162	567
1981	353	120	160	553
1982	318	144	0	462
1983	320	64	141	525
1984	244	171	93	508
1985	289	421	92	802
1986	362	377	88	827
1987	362	449	102	913
1988	310	448	106	864
1989	756	350	100	1,206
1990	821	386	100	1,307
1991	756	399	0	1,155
1992	605	366	0	971
1993	498	244	0	742
1994	403	Not provided	0	403
1995	429	Not provided	10	439
1996	398	Not provided	0	398
1997	389	Not provided	0	389
1998	389	Not provided	60	389
1999	233	Not provided	0	456
2000	290	Not provided	0	290

* Includes only management costs specifically identified for southern sea otters; does not include support for all enforcement, permit, or administrative tasks
^ Includes grants under section 6 of ESA to California

According to the Marine Mammal Commission's survey of federally funded marine mammal research (Waring 2002), federal expenditures for biological and population assessment research on sea otters between FY1991 and FY2000 ranged from $463,000 in FY1997 to $1.4 million in FY2000 (see Appendix F). The principal sources of funding were FWS and USGS. The Commission's survey also reported funding to investigate fisheries/sea otter interactions. That work ranged between $132,000 in FY1996 and FY1997 to $1.3 million in FY2000 with most of the funds provided by FWS.

Table 8. *Federal and state expenditures (in $ thousands) for the recovery of southern sea otters, 1998–2004 (Source: FWS 2003b–d; 2005d–f; 2006)*

Fiscal Year	FWS	USGS	NMFS	USCG	Other Federal	Total Federal	State	Total State and Federal
1998	97	389	–	–	9	495	–	495
1999	95	317	–	–	47	459	156	615
2000	174	403	–	–	13	589	35	624
2001	184	868	–	–	7	1,059	35	1,094
2002	170	856	–	–	5	1,031	35	1,066
2003	156	1,154	–	–	26	1,336	40	1,376
2004	134	578	–	–	3	714	20	734

Northern Sea Otter, Southwest Alaska Population

Status: Sea otters once ranged from the Hokkaido, Japan, through the Kuril Islands around the North Pacific rim south to Baja California and numbered between 150,000 and 300,000 animals (Rotterman and Simon-Jackson 1988, FWS 2002e). The range of the northern sea otter (*Enhydra lutris kenyoni*), one of three subspecies of sea otters, extends along the coast from the Aleutian Islands to the state of Washington (Jameson et al. 1982). FWS considers sea otters west of the entrance to Cook Inlet and Kodiak Island and along the Aleutian Islands to be a distinct population segment of northern sea otters, referred to as the southwest Alaska population (FWS 2002e).

Commercial hunting between the late 1700s and early 1900s reduced all northern sea otter populations to a combined total of perhaps 1,000 to 2,000 animals scattered among 13 remnant populations. Six of those remnant populations were within the range of the southwest Alaska sea otter population. In 1911 commercial hunting of sea otters was banned under the Convention on Conservation of North Pacific Fur Seals (Rotterman and Simon-Jackson 1988). After cessation of hunting, sea otter numbers grew rapidly. By 1976 the southwest Alaska population had increased to an estimated 94,050 to 128,650 animals and was thought to be at or above its pre-exploitation population size (Calkins and Schneider 1985). Since the mid-1980s, however, the population has declined precipitously (Doroff et al. 2003). Periodic surveys suggest their number has decreased by at least 55 to 67 percent with declines of more than 90 percent in some areas. Surveys since 2000 indicate annual rates of decline of 12 percent on the south side of the Alaska Peninsula and 29 percent in the western and central Aleutians (70 Fed. Reg. 46366). With the exception of the Kodiak area, there is no evidence that the decline has abated. Based on aerial surveys in 2000–2004, FWS estimates that the southwest Alaska sea otter population numbers 41,865 animals (70 Fed. Reg. 46366). Although the Service was petitioned in 2001 to list all sea otters in Alaska as depleted, the petition was rejected on grounds that substantial declines were limited largely to southwest Alaska and that sea otters in that area constituted a separate population. In 2005 FWS designated the southwest Alaska sea otter population of the northern sea otter as threatened under the ESA (70 Fed. Reg. 46366).

Major Threats: Despite the sharpness and geographic extent of the southwest Alaska sea otter population decline, its cause remains uncertain. In listing the population as threatened, FWS evaluated the following possible factors (70 Fed. Reg. 46366):

Oil Spills: Like the southern sea otter, the northern sea otter is extremely vulnerable to oil spills. At this time, oil and gas development occurs only in Cook Inlet, and tanker transport is relatively infrequent in the range of the southwest Alaska sea otter population. Although there is no evidence to suggest that oil spills caused the decline, the threat of a major oil spill remains a matter of concern, given experience with the *Exxon Valdez* spill, which demonstrated that a large oil spill could affect coastlines hundreds of miles from a spill site.

Hunting: Subsistence hunting of sea otters does not appear to have been a factor in the decline of the southwest Alaska sea otter population. In Kodiak, where most sea otter hunting occurs, the harvest has ranged between 0.4 and 1.3 percent of the estimated population size. Little or no subsistence hunting occurs in areas with the steepest declines in sea otter numbers.

Habitat Loss: FWS has found no evidence that the loss of habitat has contributed to the sea otter decline although it may be an important factor in recovery.

Competition for Prey: FWS has found no evidence that commercial catch of prey species has been a factor in the decline, that sea otters are nutritionally stressed, or that their foraging success has declined.

Predation: Perhaps the most plausible explanation for the decline in southwest Alaska sea otters is increased mortality caused by killer whale (*Orcinus orca*) predation (Estes et al. 1998). FWS cites the following evidence in support this hypothesis:

- An increase in the number of observed attacks by killer whales on sea otters during the 1990s;
- A correspondence between the decrease in sea otter numbers and expectations from computer models of killer whale energetics;
- The scarcity of beachcast otter carcasses, which would be expected if disease or starvation were the cause of the decline; and
- Markedly lower mortality rates between sea otters in sheltered lagoons compared to those in exposed bays more accessible to killer whales.

Management Framework: FWS has lead federal responsibility for the management and recovery of southwest Alaska sea otters. Some aspects of management are implemented though a cooperative agreement with an Alaska Native organization called the Alaska Sea Otter and Steller Sea Lion Commission. Collaboration between the United States and Russia also is carried out under the auspices of the U.S.-Russia Agreement on Cooperation in the Field of Protection of the Environment and Natural Resources. Other agencies that support or participate in recovery work include USGS and the Alaska SeaLife Center, both of which conduct research. Since designating the population as threatened, FWS has convened a recovery team to help develop a southwest Alaska sea otter recovery plan (70 Fed. Reg. 46377).

Critical Habitat: When designating southwest Alaska sea otters as threatened, FWS concluded that designation of critical habitat for the population segment would be prudent (70 Fed. Reg. 46377). However, the Service stated that it was unable to identify the physical and biological features essential to the conservation of the population. Given that finding and the lack of understanding about the cause for the population's decline, it therefore deferred critical habitat designation.

Recovery Plan: In 1994 the Service released a conservation plan for all Alaska sea otters in response to amendments to the MMPA authorizing such plans (FWS 1994b). The plan proposed three goals: (1) maintain the Alaska sea otter population level within its OSP range; (2) maintain healthy habitats for sea otters; and (3) allow for a variety of human uses.

The plan then identified the following objectives to achieve those goals:

- Identify the OSP range for sea otters, including factors that may influence how such a range is defined;
- Monitor the size, status, and trends of sea otter populations and collect life history data for developing population models and establishing removal guidelines;
- Establish cooperative working relationships with Alaska Natives to help support their conservation and management efforts related to Native sea otter harvest and use;
- Characterize and monitor sea otter habitat, status, and trends;
- Identify, avoid, and minimize human threats to sea otters and their habitat and, if possible, resolve resource conflicts; and
- Establish cooperative programs to further the conservation and management of sea otters in Alaska.

Accompanying each of the objectives was a list of specific activities with projected funding needs for the first five years of implementation. As of the date of this report, initial efforts were being taken by the recovery team to develop a draft southwest Alaska sea otter recovery plan.

Major Management Actions: Since the mid-1990s FWS has entered into an annual cooperative agreement with the Alaska Sea Otter and Steller Sea Lion Commission. The commission represents a consortium of 60 Alaska tribes and tribal organizations. With FWS, the Commission co-manages subsistence uses of sea otters throughout Alaska and facilitates sea otter research by tribes and local residents. Through the cooperative agreement, support is provided for skiff surveys to determine local sea otter population trends, for collecting samples from harvested animals, and for documenting traditional Alaska Native knowledge of sea otters. Other actions taken in support of recovery have focused on population monitoring and research planning.

Staff and Funding Levels: Because southwest Alaska sea otters were not added to the list of endangered and threatened species until 2005, funding data does not appear in past FWS expenditure surveys and past estimates of funding for research and management are not available. FWS estimates that it devoted 2.5 FTEs to southwest Alaska sea otter research and management in 2005.[6] In 2005 the FWS Alaska Regional Office allocated approximately

---

[6] Rosa Meehan, personal communication. 23 August 2005. Chief, Marine Mammal Management, U.S. Fish and Wildlife Service, 1011 Tudor Road, Anchorage, AK 99503.

$120,000 to charter a research vessel and administered a $663,000 congressional add-on for studies of southwest Alaska sea otters by the Alaska SeaLife Center. Information was not available on expenditures by other agencies, such as USGS.

Funding needs projected for the first five years of conservation work under the Alaska sea otter conservation plan (FWS 1994b) suggested that annual expenditures should have ranged from $700,000 to $1.04 million per year for a five-year total of $4.36 million. Actual expenditures during that period are uncertain.

PINNEPEDS

Caribbean Monk Seal

Caribbean monk seals (*Monachus tropicalis*) once inhabited the Caribbean Sea and parts of the Gulf of Mexico from the the Bahamas west to the Yucatan Peninsula and south along the east coast of Central America (44 Fed. Reg. 1979). They were listed as endangered throughout their range under the ESPA in 1967. That listing was carried forward under the ESCA, but for uncertain reasons was omitted from the initial list of endangered and threatened species under ESA. By the time the ESA was passed in 1976, some scientists already considered the species to be extinct; however, in 1979, it was again listed as endangered at the recommendation of the Marine Mammal Commission to afford protection in the event of its rediscovery. Presently, no Caribbean monk seals exist in captivity and no populations are known to occur in the wild. The last reliable record of the species was at a small colony at Seranilla Bank west of Jamaica in 1952. The species is now widely considered to be extinct (Kenyon 1977) and in 1994 the IUCN listed the species as such on its Red List of Threatened Species (Groombridge 1994).

Major Threats: Like the Hawaiian monk seal, the Caribbean monk seal appears to have been quite approachable and vulnerable to hunting and human disturbance. Organized and opportunistic hunts reduced the number of monk seals in the 17th and 18th centuries.

Management Framework: NMFS has lead responsibility for the species. As no Caribbean monk seals have been sighted since passage of the ESA and MMPA, no species-specific management teams have been established. In November 2006 the Service announced plans to carry out a five-year status review of the Caribbean monk seal under the provisions of the ESA to determine whether the species should be removed from the list of endangered and threatened species or reclassified (71 FR 69100).

Critical Habitat: None designated.

Recovery Plan: None drafted or adopted.

Staff and Funding Levels: NMFS has devoted no staff or funding to Caribbean monk seal recovery work. In 1985 the Marine Mammal Commission provided about $1,000 to help determine the validity of rumored Caribbean monk seal sightings and to survey remote Caribbean fishing villages for evidence of surviving animals. The survey produced no firm evidence of the species' continued existence. Based on FWS surveys of funding for listed endangered and threatened species between 1998 and 2004 (FWS 2003b–d, 2005d–f, 2006), a combined total of $18,000 was spent on this species over that seven-year period (Appendix C).

Hawaiian Monk Seal

Status: The Hawaiian monk seal *(Monachus schauinslandi)* occurs only in the Hawaiian archipelago. It is the most endangered seal in U.S. waters and one of the most endangered seals in the world. It was listed as endangered under the ESA in 1976. The population consists of six main breeding colonies in the Northwestern Hawaiian Islands (NWHI) and a dispersed, but growing population in the main Hawaiian Islands (NMFS 2006a). Monk seals apparently did not occur in the main Hawaiian Islands when Captain James Cook discovered the islands in the late 1700s, and it seems likely that earlier Polynesian settlers had eliminated them from that portion of their range (Baker and Johanos 2004, MMC 2001).

The breeding colonies in the NWHI are relatively isolated. Movement of seals between colonies is limited, and the individual colonies therefore constitute relatively discrete subpopulations with independent trends and recovery issues. For example, between the 1950s and the 1980s the colony at French Frigate Shoals grew rapidly to become the species' largest group, producing nearly half of all monk seal pups. During the same period, other colonies declined or remained relatively stable. These trends were reversed in the late 1980s when juvenile survival, and perhaps reproduction, at the French Frigate Shoals colony began declining sharply, and the western colonies began increasing slowly. In 2001 a total of 1,224 seals were observed in the NWHI, and 52 were counted in the main Hawaiian Islands, with the total abundance estimate about 60 percent less than estimates based on counts in 1958 (NMFS 2006a). It appears that their overall numbers declined by 4.2 percent per year until 1993. Since then, the rate of decline has been 1.1 percent per year. The current best estimate of abundance is 1,252 animals (NMFS 2006a). Because of the species' low abundance and declining trend, a PBR level for the Hawaiian monk seal is undetermined.

Major Threats: Intensive hunting in the 19th century is thought to have significantly reduced Hawaiian monk seal abundance in the NWHI (Ragen and Lavigne 1999). After recovering somewhat in the early 20th century, most subpopulations declined again in the last half of the 20th century. The suspected cause of declines between the 1950s and early 1980s was human disturbance on pupping and resting beaches as a result of military and Coast Guard activity (Kenyon 1972, Ragen and Lavigne 1999, MMC 2002). Perhaps the greatest current threat to monk seals in the NWHI is reduction in prey availability due to commercial fishing and/or natural environmental change. The small, isolated nature of NWHI atolls makes their populations especially vulnerable to human and natural perturbations. Most of the species' decline since the 1980s has occurred at French Frigate Shoals where reduced juvenile survival rates characterized the decrease. Based on observations of weaned pups in emaciated or underweight condition, limited prey availability is believed to have precipitated the decline at that atoll. Similar signs of poor juvenile survival have been observed more recently at other atolls.

Fishery Interactions: Monk seals are known to feed on lobsters as well as other species caught incidentally in lobster traps. Intensive fishing for spiny lobsters began in the NWHI in the late 1970s shortly before the monk seal decline began at French Frigate Shoals. At the peak of the NWHI lobster fishery between 1985 and 1990, fishing effort exceeded one million trap nights per year, most of which focused on the banks and atolls nearest to French Frigate Shoals. In 1999 the fishery was closed after spiny lobster abundance declined dramatically. Spiny lobsters have shown little sign of recovery since 1999, and parts of their range are now dominated by slipper lobsters, suggesting a major shift in the ecology of lobster populations in the NWHI. Decadal climate cycles also are a possible factor affecting lobster populations and other monk seal prey (Polovina 2005), but information is not sufficient to distinguish between the effects of climate and fishing operations (MMC 2001).

Direct interactions between monk seals and the lobster, pelagic longline, and bottomfish fisheries also have been documented. At least one monk seal was entangled and drowned in lobster gear, and several others are known to have been injured by hooks from longline, bottomfish gear, and recreational fishing. Information on monk seal deaths and injuries in fisheries is limited, partly because efforts to monitor fishing operations have been inadequate (Ragen and Lavigne 1999, NMFS 2006a).

Entanglement in Marine Debris: Entanglement of monk seals in marine debris, particularly derelict fishing nets, also is a significant threat in the NWHI. Seven entanglement deaths and 238 cases of live entangled seals have been recorded through 2003 (NMFS 2006a). Almost all of these entanglements were seen on beaches. In most instances, either the animals were disentangled or the entanglements were considered minor ones from which the seals would be able to free themselves. Of greater concern is the unknown number of seals that become entangled and die unobserved at sea because they are unable to swim to shore. With rare exceptions, derelict fishing gear found attached to seals or fouling atoll reefs and beaches are from remote fisheries operating outside Hawaiian waters.

Other Sources of Mortality: Other sources of mortality for NWHI seals include aggressive behavior by adult male seals towards pups, juveniles, and females; shark predation; and naturally occurring biotoxins. Adult male aggression has caused the death and serious injury of numerous pups and females at Laysan and Lisianski Islands. It has been identified as a major impediment to the recovery of colonies at both atolls and also has been observed at French Frigate Shoals where at least eight pups were killed by aggressive males in 1997 (NMFS 2006a). Shark predation has recently become a significant source of mortality at French Frigate Shoals. Approximately 25 percent of all pups born at that colony in 1999 were killed by sharks.

In 1978 ciguatera, a naturally occurring biotoxin, is thought to have killed a few tens of seals although no similar die-offs have been recorded since. Disease and contaminants do not appear to have been a major source of past mortality for monk seals in the NWHI (Ragen and Lavigne 1999). However, disease risks are a growing concern due to the possibility of seals becoming exposed to new diseases in the main Hawaiian Islands (Hawaiian Monk Seal Recovery Team 2005, Braun and Yochem 2006). Contaminant risks exist in the NWHI from occasional vessel groundings and fuel spills and from discarded equipment and pollution left from earlier Navy and Coast Guard activities (Hawaiian Monk Seal Recovery Team 2005).

Threats in the main Hawaiian Islands. Monk seal pups and adults in the main Hawaiian Islands tend to be larger than those in the NWHI, suggesting that prey availability is not a limiting factor in the main Hawaiian Islands at this time. Rather, the major threats in this area are disturbance at haul-out and pupping sites by beachgoers and dogs, hooking on fishing gear (particularly with recreational fishing), collisions with boats, exposure to oil spills, and diseases transmitted from other animals. To date, two seals are known to have been killed by fishing gear in the main

Hawaiian Islands, and a number of seals have been found with embedded hooks or entangled in gillnets. One seal is thought to have been killed by a boat collision. There is limited evidence that disease has been a cause of deaths for monk seals in the past, but currently it is a significant concern (Hawaiian Monk Seal Recovery Team 2005). Recent information suggests that since 2003 one seal may have died as a result of leptospirosis and another from toxoplasmosis, representing the first reported cases of each (NMFS 2006a).

Management Framework: Although NMFS has lead responsibility for recovery of Hawaiian monk seals, other agencies play important roles. FWS manages wildlife habitat and human activities on lands and waters of the Hawaiian Islands National Wildlife Refuge and the Midway Atoll National Wildlife Refuge (MMC 2002). The Coast Guard assists with enforcement and control of pollution. NOAA and FWS, in coordination with the state of Hawaii manage the Papahānaumokuākea Marine National Monument, which extends out 50 nautical miles (nmi) from atolls and submerged banks in the NWHI. The Western Pacific Fishery Management Council is responsible for developing fishery management plans for federal waters in the region. The Marine Mammal Commission holds periodic reviews of the monk seal recovery program, makes recommendations for recovery needs, and provides funding for research and management projects on an opportunistic basis.

The state of Hawaii, which owns Kure Atoll, also has jurisdiction over waters from the refuge boundaries out to 3 nmi around all emergent lands in the NWHI with the exception of Midway Atoll (MMC 2002). In 2005 the state of Hawaii adopted rules designating all NWHI state waters as a marine refuge within which all commercial activity, including almost all fishing, is banned. The state government also is an important partner in management efforts in the main Hawaiian Islands.

Critical Habitat: In 1986 NMFS designated all beaches and nearshore waters shallower than 10 fathoms around all of the NWHI (except Sand Island on the Midway Atoll, which was then used as a naval air station) as critical habitat for Hawaiian monk seals. In 1988 the seaward boundary was extended to the 20-fathom isobath around the NWHI (again excluding Sand Island), partly at the recommendation of the Marine Mammal Commission (OPR 2005).

Recovery Plan: In 1980 NMFS established a Hawaiian Monk Seal Recovery Team composed of scientists and agency resource managers (MMC 2002). The team developed a draft plan adopted by NMFS in March 1983 (Gilmartin 1983). In 1989 NMFS appointed a new recovery team that met annually to review monk seal recovery efforts and provide advice on research and management. In 2001 NMFS again reconstituted the recovery team and charged it with updating the 1983 recovery plan. A draft revised plan was submitted to NMFS in 2005 and circulated for public comment in late 2006 (NMFS 2006e). The goal of the draft plan is "…to assure the long term viability of the Hawaiian monk seal in the wild, allowing initially for reclassification to threatened status and, ultimately, removal from the List of Endangered and Threatened Wildlife" (NMFS 2006e). To accomplish this goal, four major actions are identified:

- Improving the survival of females, particularly juvenile females, in subpopulations of the NWHI by maintaining and enhancing the species' habitat and prey base, targeting research to better understand factors affecting juvenile survival, intervening when possible to improve rates of juvenile and adult female survival, protecting females from aggressive groups of male seals and shark predation, and continuing to remove marine debris and disentangle seals;

- Maintaining field teams in the NWHI to carry out research and management actions;
- Ensuring continued natural growth of the monk seal population in the main Hawaiian Islands; and
- Reducing the possibility of inadvertent introduction of infectious diseases.

The draft plan also describes specific actions to conserve monk seal habitat, reduce interactions with commercial fisheries, investigate factors affecting prey limitation, conduct population monitoring and research, prevent the spread of infectious diseases, minimize the impact of natural biotoxins, reduce aggression by groups of male seals toward females, prevent entanglement in marine debris, reduce sources of human disturbance, reduce the impact of vessel groundings, minimize risks of shark predation, reduce the impact of contaminants, prepare a main Hawaiian Island monk seal management plan, and carry out a public education and outreach program.

The draft plan recommends that reclassification as threatened be considered when the following criteria are met: (1) the total number of monk seals in the NWHI exceeds 2,900 seals, (2) at least five of the six major breeding colonies have 100 individuals or more and the subpopulation in the main Hawaiian Islands exceeds 500 animals, and (3) female survivorship and birth rates in the major NWHI and main Hawaiian Islands colonies are high enough to assure that population growth rates are not declining

Major Management Actions: Since publication of the initial monk seal recovery plan in 1983, much has been done to address the most direct and obvious causes of the monk seal decline. Some of those actions are summarized below.

Improve survival rates of juvenile females: To address problems related to poor juvenile survival and limited prey availability, NMFS has undertaken two types of interventions: (1) a "head start" program at Kure Atoll and (2) a capture, rehabilitation, and release program for undersized pups from French Frigate Shoals. Both efforts sought to enhance survival of female pups to save their reproductive potential. Under the head start program, newly weaned female pups at Kure Atoll were captured, placed in pens at the atoll, and fed for several months to improve their chances of survival during the first year of life. Under the pup rehabilitation program, female pups at French Frigate Shoals judged unlikely to survive because of their small size (girth) at weaning were captured, transported to facilities in the main Hawaiian Islands for rehabilitation, and later released at Kure Atoll where prey availability did not appear to be limiting survival. These programs were successfully carried out between 1981 and 1992 but were suspended in 1993 when a group of 12 female pups taken into captivity for rehabilitation developed an undiagnosed eye disease that blinded most of them. An attempt was made to reinitiate the program with releases at Midway Atoll in the mid-1990s, but it was discontinued because of poor survival of the released animals. More recently, NMFS developed plans for a "second chance" program at French Frigate Shoals. Under that program, juvenile seals (rather than newly weaned pups) showing signs of poor nutrition a few months after weaning are to be caught, placed in pens at the atoll for feeding, and released on site after fattening. Although steps were taken to implement the new program in the summer of 2004, no seals deemed eligible for the program were observed at that time. The program may be resumed in the future, depending on funding.

Interactions with Commercial Fisheries: The potential effects of NWHI fisheries on monk seal prey resources, as well as direct interactions between monk seals and fishing gear, are considered within the context of four fishery management plans developed by the Western Pacific Fishery Management Council and implemented by NMFS. These include fishery plans for crustaceans (i.e., lobster), bottomfish (e.g., snapper and grouper), pelagic species (e.g., tuna and swordfish), and precious corals.

Crustacean Fishery—In the late 1970s and early 1980s a fishery targeting spiny lobsters in the NWHI grew rapidly. As the fishery expanded, the Western Pacific Fishery Management Council recommended a fishery management plan adopted by NMFS in 1983. To protect monk seal foraging habitat, the plan established no-fishing zones within 20 nmi of Laysan Island and within the 10-fathom contour around all other atolls. To prevent monk seals from wedging their heads in trap openings, the plan also specified a maximum trap opening size. Initially, the plan allowed the take of all the lobsters that could be caught above a minimum size limit. As lobster abundance quickly declined, the plan was modified to allow catch levels that were expected to maintain lobster population abundances at or above 20 percent of the size thought to occur in the absence of fishing. As this and other major amendments to the plan were proposed, NMFS conducted formal section 7 consultations pursuant to the ESA. Despite concern expressed by the Marine Mammal Commission and others throughout the 1990s that the fishery was reducing available monk seal prey, NMFS concluded that lobster fishing had no effect on monk seal prey availability (MMC 2004). In early 2000, shortly after a lawsuit challenged the basis for this conclusion, NMFS suspended the fishery on grounds that it was uncertain about the status of NWHI lobster populations (MMC 2004). Since then, NMFS has kept the NWHI lobster fishing quota at zero.

Bottomfish fishery—The bottomfish fishery is a hook-and-line fishery that targets sizes and species of fish not normally eaten by monk seals. Occasionally, monk seals become hooked while taking bait or caught fish off of hooks. Monk seals also sometimes remain near fishing vessels and feed on discarded bycatch. After passage of the Magnuson-Stevens Fishery Conservation and Management Act in 1976, the number of fishing vessels and landings of bottomfish grew until 1987 when they began to decline to a much lower level, around which they now fluctuate. Requirements relative to monk seals have been limited primarily to observer and reporting requirements. In the NWHI bottomfish fishery, vessels must carry observers when requested to do so and must report interactions with monk seals. Most interactions reported by fishermen and observers involve seal sightings near fishing vessels and, very rarely, hookings. In 2002 NMFS prepared a section 7 biological opinion on the bottomfish fishery management plan and concluded that the fishery would not jeopardize monk seals or their critical habitat. The state of Hawaii also requires logbooks for state waters around the main Hawaiian Islands; however, information on interactions with protected species is not required, and the logbooks therefore provide no information on interactions with monk seals (NMFS 2006a).

Pelagic longline fishery—In the early 1990s as a pelagic longline fishery developed for swordfish and tunas near the NWHI, several seals were found with embedded longline hooks and other injuries thought to be associated with this fishery. In response the fishery management council recommended, and NMFS adopted, a 50-nmi no-fishing zone for this fishery around the NWHI and in corridors between the islands. The measure appears to have nearly eliminated hookings in this fishery (NMFS 2006a).

Precious corals—Although no commercial harvests of precious corals used in the jewelry industry have occurred in the NWHI, the Western Pacific Fishery Management Council drafted a fishery management plan to allow some coral harvesting in the area. The council, however, has recommended against harvesting of gold corals because some seals forage in beds of this species at depths of 500 meters or greater (NMFS 2006a). NMFS has not adopted the draft plan.

New fishery restrictions in federal waters around the NWHI—In late 2000 and early 2001 fishery management in the NWHI became subject to new management restrictions when President Clinton signed two Executive Orders designating the NWHI Coral Reef Ecosystem Reserve (MMC 2002). The reliance of Hawaiian monks seals on this regional coral reef ecosystem was cited as an important consideration leading to the designation. The Presidential orders directed that all landings and fishing permits for commercial fishing within reserve waters be capped at levels that existed in the year prior to the 4 December 2000 designation date. As bottomfish were the only landings taken from reserve waters during that period, the designation precluded fishing for other species. The directive also required the use of precautionary management principles and the establishment of 15 "reserve preservation areas" within which no fishing of any kind is allowed. The orders also directed that the National Marine Sanctuary Program consider designation of the area as a national marine sanctuary. The sanctuary designation process, however, was superceded on 15 June 2006 when President Bush signed an Executive Order designating the reserve as the Papahānaumokuākea Marine National Monument. In doing so, he instituted a ban on all commercial fishing except bottomfish fishing, which is to be phased out within five years.

Fishery restrictions in state waters of the NWHI—In 2001 the state of Hawaii proposed designating all state waters in the NWHI as a state fishery management area to establish access permit requirements that would allow the state to control commercial fishing. Following receipt of comments urging the adoption of more restrictive measures, the state modified its proposal and, late in 2005, adopted rules designating the area as a state marine refuge within which all commercial and recreational fishing is prohibited.

Entanglement in Marine Debris: For more than 15 years, field teams responsible for monk seal research have routinely disentangled seals found entangled in marine debris and removed hazardous debris from beaches. Since the late 1990s divers also have removed derelict nets and lines from submerged reefs in the NWHI. Between 1996 and 2003 NMFS and cooperating organizations removed 470 metric tons of nets and other debris from NWHI coral reefs (NMFS 2006a).

Aggression by Groups of Male Seals: To minimize seal deaths and injuries caused by aggressive male seals, NMFS has captured adult male seals known or suspected to have displayed aggressive behavior and relocated them in other areas. In 1994, 22 adult males were captured at Laysan Island for relocation to the main Hawaiian Islands (Ragen and Lavigne 1999, NMFS

2006a). Since then, the number of seals killed by aggressive males at Laysan Island has declined dramatically (NMFS 2006a). Similarly, in 1998 two aggressive males responsible for killing pups at French Frigate Shoals were relocated to Johnston Atoll, after which injuries to pups at French Frigate Shoals declined.

Shark Predation: NMFS also has taken steps to reduce shark predation on monk seals at French Frigate Shoals. Research field teams have attempted to catch and kill those sharks that patrol pupping beaches and prey on pups when they enter the water. In 2001 NMFS field teams killed five sharks exhibiting predatory behavior at Trig Island. Also in 2001 field teams moved 18 weaned pups to other islands at the atoll where no sharks exhibited patrolling behavior (MMC 2002).

Human Disturbance: To help minimize seal disturbance by people and pets at pupping and haul-out sites in the main Hawaiian Islands, NMFS and the State of Hawaii Division of Aquatic Resources have launched cooperative efforts with volunteers and local officials to educate the public about seal protection needs and to mark off temporary seal safety zones around hauled-out animals (MMC 2002). On Kauai, where seals haul out most frequently, a fulltime coordinator was hired by the state to work with local authorities and the volunteer Monk Seal Watch Program. NMFS also has hired a similar coordinator for the other main islands. To mitigate the injury to seals hooked on fishing gear or entangled, procedures have been put in place to expedite a response by trained experts and to provide veterinary assistance as needed. In some cases where interactions with people pose particular risks for seals or people, seals have been captured and relocated.

Disease and Contaminants: To address disease and contaminant risks, monk seals are occasionally captured and moved away from hazardous areas, and efforts are made to monitor for the presence of pathogens. Efforts also have been taken to improve monitoring of seals for the presence of disease and contaminants. Steps also are currently being taken to investigate the feasibility and safety of vaccinating Hawaiian monks seals against phocine morbillivirus, a distemper virus that has caused significant mortality in other seal species and may be spread to monk seals from other pinnipeds that occasionally visit the Hawaiian Islands (Braun and Yochem 2006).

Staff and Funding Levels: According to the Marine Mammal Commission survey of federally funded marine mammal research (Waring 2002), expenditures for biological and population assessment research on Hawaiian monk seals between FY1991 and FY2000 ranged from less than $500,000 in FY1991 to nearly $1.9 million in FY2000 (see Appendix F). NMFS was the principal source of funding.

Efforts to recover Hawaiian monk seals have received regular appropriations from Congress for many years. According to FWS annual reports on endangered species expenditures (FWS 2003b–d, 2005d–f, 2006), NMFS allocated an average of about $2.1 million per year to monk seal recovery work between 1998 and 2004 (Table 9, Appendices C.1–7). Although not reported in endangered species expenditure reports, FWS also has allocated funding annually for monk seal-related activities in its Hawaiian Islands National Wildlife Refuge since the 1970s. Recent funding levels have been approximately $75,000 per year (FWS and USGS 1997–2004). The

Table 9. *Federal and state expenditures (in $ thousands) for the recovery of Hawaiian monk seals, 1998–2004 (Source: FWS 2003b–d; 2005d–f; 2006)*

Fiscal Year	FWS	USGS	NMFS	USCG	Other Federal	Total Federal	State	Total State and Federal
1998	–	–	1,504	–	12	1,516	–	1,516
1999	–	–	1,052	48	4	1,104	0.4	1,105
2000	–	–	1,210	–	43	1,253	14	1,267
2001	–	–	2,100	2	5	2,108	14	2,121
2002	–	–	2,100	46	38	2,184	14	2,197
2003	–	–	2,100	–	30	2,130	15	2,145
2004	–	1	2,164	105	51	2,321	–	2,321

state of Hawaii, the Marine Mammal Commission, and NOAA's Hawaii Humpback Whale National Marine Sanctuary also have contributed modest amounts of funding not reflected in the FWS annual expenditure surveys. NMFS budget documents specify budget allocations for Hawaiian monk seal activities below those levels reported to FWS for the annual expenditures reports. Line items specifically related to monk seals in those documents rose from $798,000 in 2001 to $816,000 in 2004 (see Appendix E).

Table 10. *Projected funding needs (in $ thousands) to implement recovery activities for Hawaiian monk seals during the first five years after adoption of the 2005 draft revised recovery plan (NMFS 2006e)*

Action Objective	Year 1	Year 2	Year 3	Year 4	Year 5	Total
Conserve monk seal habitat	11,362	312	312	112	112	12,210
Reduce interactions with fisheries	1,625	1,625	1,625	1,625	1,625	8,125
Investigate food limitation	940	970	1,020	970	870	4,770
Population research, monitoring	1,550	1,500	1,450	1,450	1,450	7,400
Prevent infectious disease	610	567	567	567	567	2,898
Minimize impacts of biotoxins	425	200	125	75	75	900
Reduce aggression by male seals	*	*	*	*	*	*
Prevent entanglements	1,335	1,325	1,310	1,285	1,270	6,525
Reduce human disturbance	1,249	1,249	1,249	1,249	1,249	6,245
Reduce effects of vessel groundings	487	75	62	62	132	818
Reduce shark predation	350	250	250	250	250	1,350
Reduce impacts of contaminants	65	-	-	-	-	65
Main Hawaiian Islands mgmt. plan	40	10	-	-	-	50
Public education and outreach	310	150	150	150	150	910
TOTAL	20,368	8,233	8,120	7,795	7,750	52,226

* The cost for this task is included in costs for other tasks.

NMFS estimates that its headquarters and regional offices devoted 1.2 FTEs to monk seal management activities in 2005, while its fishery science centers devoted at least 21 FTEs to Hawaiian monk seal research activities.[7] Most of those positions are devoted to research and conservation efforts (e.g., disentangling seals, capturing and moving aggressive male seals, removing sharks, etc.) by field teams visiting the NWHI annually to monitor major breeding colonies. As shown in Table 10, the revised draft monk seal recovery plan (NMFS 2006e) projects total implementation costs for the first five fiscal years after adoption at $52.3 million (including activities ranked from priority 1 through 3).

Guadalupe Fur Seal

Population Status: The range of the Guadalupe fur seal (*Arctocephalus townsendi*) once extended south from Monterey, California, to the Revillagigedo Islands off southern Baja California, Mexico. The species' initial population size has been estimated to have been at least 20,000 animals and perhaps as many as 100,000 (Fleischer 1987, NMFS 2006a). Commercial hunting in the 19th century nearly drove the species to extinction. In 1911, commercial harvesting was prohibited under terms of the North Pacific Fur Seal Treaty.

Following the capture of two adult males at Guadalupe Island off Mexico in 1928, this species was not reported again until 1949 (Bartholomew 1950). Since then, its abundance has increased at an estimated annual growth rate of 13.7 percent. The current best estimate of abundance, which is based on extrapolations from counts of animals on rookeries in 1993, is 7,408 seals. Based on that estimate, a PBR of 91 animals was calculated (NMFS 2006a). The species also has been expanding into its former range. Guadalupe fur seals are regularly sighted in low numbers on San Miguel and San Nicolas Islands off southern California, and in 1997 a pup was born at San Miguel Island.

The species was listed as threatened under the ESCA in 1970, but for unknown reasons it was omitted from the list of threatened species carried forward under the ESA. In November 1983 the Center for Environmental Education (now The Ocean Conservancy) petitioned NMFS to list the species as endangered. In December 1985 NMFS listed the species as threatened. It also is listed as threatened under California state law.

Major Threats: The cessation of commercial hunting in the early 1900s removed the major cause of the species' decline. Other possible threats include incidental mortality and injury in commercial fisheries and entanglement in debris. Incidental mortality of Guadalupe fur seals has not been documented in any U.S. or Mexican fisheries (NMFS 2006a). However, in the 1990s incidental mortalities of unidentified marine mammals that may have included Guadalupe fur seals were documented in drift and set gillnet fisheries off southern California and off the Pacific coast of Baja California, Mexico. Some fur seals also may be killed as a result of entanglement in derelict fishing gear and marine debris. As indicated above, however, such mortality has not prevented the species' abundance from increasing steadily.

---

[7] P. Michael Payne, personal communication. 17 August 2005. Chief, Marine Mammals Division, Office of Protected Species, National Marine Fisheries Service, Silver Spring, MD 20910; John Bengtson, personal communication. 8 December 2006. National Marine Mammal Laboratory, National Marine Fisheries Service, Seattle, WA 98115

Management Framework: NMFS is the lead agency for implementation of the ESA and the MMPA regarding Guadalupe fur seals. No recovery teams have been established specifically to promote the recovery of this species.

Critical Habitat: In listing Guadalupe fur seals as threatened under the ESA, NMFS rejected a request by the petitioner to designate waters in the Channel Islands off southern California as critical habitat (50 Fed. Reg. 51254). NMFS concluded that other management measures would provide sufficient protection and noted that the species' primary breeding grounds are under the jurisdiction of Mexico.

Recovery Plan: No recovery plan has been prepared. When the species was listed as threatened in 1985, NMFS identified criteria for initiating a status review to determine whether Guadalupe fur seals should be delisted (50 Fed. Reg. 51256):

- Growth of the population to 30,000 animals (the lower end of estimates of the initial population size);
- Establishment of one or more additional rookeries within the species' historical range; and
- Growth in abundance to the level at which maximum net productivity level occurs.

Major Management Actions: NMFS does not actively manage the conservation of Guadalupe fur seals although it has provided some funding for research.

Staff and Funding Levels: According to FWS annual reports on endangered species expenditures for 1998–2004 (FWS 2003b–d, 2005d–f, 2006), federal agencies reported expenditures for Guadalupe fur seal activities that ranged between zero in most years to $2,200 in 2000 (Appendices C.1–7). NMFS budget documents for the period FY2001–FY2005 did not identify any funding specifically for Guadalupe fur seals. NMFS estimates that its fishery science centers devoted at least 0.2 FTE on Guadalupe fur seal research activities in 2005, but that its headquarters and regional offices spent no time on this species that year.[8]

Northern Fur Seal, Eastern Pacific (Pribilof Islands) Population

Population Status: Northern fur seals (*Callorhinus ursinus*) range from southern California north to the Bering Sea and west as far as Honshu Island in Japan (Angliss and Lodge 2003d). There are five populations on at least six island groups: the Commander Islands (Russia), the Kuril Islands (Russia), Robbin Island (Russia), the Pribilof Islands and Bogoslof Island in the eastern Bering Sea (United States), and San Miguel Island off southern California (United States) (NMFS 1993). In the past, about 75 percent of all northern fur seals worldwide occurred on the Pribilof Islands during the breeding season (Angliss and Lodge 2003d). From 1918 until 1984 fur seals from this population were harvested commercially for their pelts under terms of the Convention on Conservation of North Pacific Fur Seals. The Convention was established to stop pelagic sealing practices that had nearly eliminated all populations by the late 1800s. Under its

---

[8] P. Michael Payne, personal communication. 17 August 2005. Chief, Marine Mammals Division, Office of Protected Species, National Marine Fisheries Service, Silver Spring, MD 20910.

terms, harvests were limited to juvenile male seals that haul out at rookeries in the spring. Pelts from the land-based harvest were allocated among the four signatory nations (i.e., the United States, the Soviet Union, Japan, and Canada). This harvest practice resulted in a steady increase in abundance through the first half of the 1900s. By the 1950s the Pribilof Islands' fur seal herd may have exceeded two million animals—a level thought to be near their pre-exploitation population size (NMFS 1993).

In the late 1950s harvest practices were changed to include a take of adult females. At the time, it was thought this would result in a brief decline in population size, followed by an increase in pup production, which would increase the number of juveniles available for harvest. The population size soon began to decline as expected, but after a take of about 300,000 females over several years, pup production failed to increase. As a result, harvests were again limited to juvenile males in the late 1960s. It was expected that the decline would reverse within a few years; however, the decline continued through the early 1980s, by which time the Pribilof Islands fur seal population was less than half its size in the early 1950s. As a result of the decline, harvests were steadily reduced, and in 1984 the United States declined to ratify an extension of the Convention. Management authority therefore reverted to domestic legislation under the MMPA and the Fur Seal Act. Under this authority, commercial harvests are prohibited, and taking is limited to subsistence harvests by Alaska Natives at a much-reduced level.

The reason for the continued decline long after the harvest of females was suspended has not been determined. Entanglement of juvenile seals in marine debris was postulated a possible cause. Based on a status review done by NMFS in response to a petition to list North Pacific fur seals as threatened under the ESA, NMFS designated the Pribilof Island fur seal population as depleted under the MMPA in 1988. The action was taken because the population was less than 50 percent of its size in the 1950s and below 60 percent of its carrying capacity (53 Fed. Reg. 17888). In the late 1980s and early 1990s the population stabilized at its reduced level, but in the mid-1990s it again began to decline for uncertain reasons. Based on a count made in 2004, the current best estimate of abundance for the Pribilof Islands fur seal population is 688,028. The calculated PBR level is 14,546 animals (NMFS 2005a).

Major Threats: The following have been identified as known or potential threats to the Pribilof Islands fur seal population:

Prey Availability: In its analysis of population trends at the time fur seals were designated as depleted in 1988, NMFS concluded that expansion of groundfish fisheries in the North Pacific (i.e., trawl fisheries for pollock, flatfishes, and other demersal finfish) had not reduced the carrying capacity for northern fur seals (53 Fed. Reg. 17891). However, in a conservation plan for the fur seal population adopted in 1993 (NMFS 1993), NMFS noted that the biomass of Pacific herring and walleye pollock in the Bering Sea and Aleutian Islands area had changed significantly since the 1960s. Given the importance of pollock as prey for northern fur seals, NMFS suggested that expansion of fisheries for those species may have altered the northern fur seal's food supply, but that the causes for the shifts in prey abundance and their impact on northern fur seals were largely unknown. In the conservation plan NMFS also drew parallels with the decline of the Steller sea lion.

<u>Incidental Catch in Fisheries</u>: In designating Pribilof Islands fur seals as depleted in 1988, NMFS evaluated information on the number of fur seals caught incidentally in commercial fisheries. It concluded that although some animals were taken in foreign and domestic fisheries, the number was insignificant (53 Fed. Reg. 17893). More recently, NMFS estimated that minimum annual mortality in commercial fisheries is 15 fur seals per year based on observer data and self-reporting by fishermen (NMFS 2005a). This level of mortality is well below the PBR level for this population and is considered insignificant and approaching a zero mortality and serious injury rate.

<u>Entanglement in Marine Debris</u>: Mortality of juvenile seals due to entanglement in marine debris, particularly packing bands and derelict trawl nets, has been suggested as a significant factor in the decline of the population in the 1970s and early 1980s (Fowler 1982, 1985). Those analyses suggested that as many as 50,000 fur seals per year may have been entangled and drowned at sea in derelict fishing nets and other marine debris adrift in the North Pacific Ocean. Juvenile fur seals, which spend their first two years of life entirely at sea after leaving the rookeries, are thought to be particularly susceptible to entanglement because of their smaller head size relative to trawl net mesh sizes and their tendency to interact with floating objects. Documentation of this hypothesis, however, has proved elusive because of the vast pelagic habitat used by fur seals. Entanglement rates observed on rookeries have been on the order of three to four per thousand animals observed but may not accurately reflect pelagic entanglement rates because they are limited to animals that survive long enough to swim ashore. The rate of entanglement among subadult males observed on rookeries, however, appears to have declined somewhat since the early 1980s (NMFS 1993, 2005a).

<u>Habitat Concerns</u>: Recent industrial and other development on the Pribilof Islands may affect fur seal rookeries through the discharge of seafood processing waste, oil and contaminant spills, increased direct human disturbance, and increased levels of noise and olfactory pollution (NMFS 2005a). Pup production at two of three rookeries nearest to human settlements and sewer outfalls has declined.

Management Framework: As noted previously, fur seals were managed under the Fur Seal Convention until 1984. While the Convention was in force, it was implemented in the United States under the Fur Seal Act, which superseded the authority of the MMPA. When the Convention expired in October 1984, management authority reverted to the MMPA. NMFS is responsible for management actions, some of which are implemented in cooperation with the Aleut communities of St. Paul and St. George Islands (Pribilof Islands), which continue to take some fur seals for subsistence purposes. There currently is no conservation or recovery team specifically for northern fur seals.

Critical Habitat: Not applicable

Recovery Plan: Because northern fur seals are not listed as endangered or threatened, no recovery plan has been prepared. However, in June 1993 NMFS approved a final conservation plan for northern fur seals under authority added to the MMPA in 1988 (NMFS 1993). The plan is presently under revision. Its goal is to restore the population of northern fur seals to the point where it is no longer considered depleted. The 1993 plan used a population estimate for the

1940s and 1950s of 2.1 million animals as the basis for estimating the population's OSP level. The plan also used the peak production of pups in the same period as a benchmark. The point at which the population could be considered not depleted is described as follows:

> The population level at which maximum productivity would occur, and the level at which NMFS would reconsider the depleted classification, would occur at a sustained population level (total abundance estimate) and/or a sustained level of annual pup production which are 60 percent of the peak historical estimates.

The plan identifies the following two objectives to achieve its goal:

- Continue and, as necessary, expand research or management programs to monitor population trends and detect natural or human-related causes of change in the population and habitats essential to its survival and recovery; and
- Assess and avoid or mitigate possible adverse effects of human-related activities on or near the Pribilof Islands and other essential habitat throughout the population's range.

Specific recovery actions described in the plan include monitoring the status and trend of the population; monitoring health, condition, and vital parameters; assessing causes of mortality; minimizing effects of disturbance; investigating feeding ecology and factors affecting energetic requirements; investigating relationships between fur seals and fishery resources; assessing effects of natural ecosystem changes; and coordinating conservation efforts with other agencies and countries.

Major Management Actions: Upon expiration of the Fur Seal Convention in 1984, management authority reverted to the MMPA and the Fur Seal Act. With that shift, the commercial harvest was prohibited, and the Service issued regulations to manage subsistence taking by residents of the Pribilof Islands. Prior to that time, the Aleut community relied on fur seals killed in the commercial harvest for meat. In June 1986 NMFS issued a final rule regulating the subsistence take of fur seals (51 Fed. Reg. 24828). Like the past commercial harvest, the subsistence harvest is limited to juvenile male seals. Under the harvest regulations, annual projections of harvest needs are developed by NMFS based on household surveys of Pribilof Island Native hunters. Those projections are used to develop annual harvest level guidelines. Since the late 1980s harvest levels have declined gradually. Between 1999 and 2003 they declined from 1,193 to 654 (NMFS 2005a). NMFS officials have observed the hunt annually. NMFS, in cooperation with Native hunters, also has supported various research projects, including efforts to monitor entanglement rates among seals on the rookeries. As noted above, NMFS also adopted a conservation plan in 1993. Designation of the northern fur seal as depleted in 1988 imposed additional restrictions on taking of the species, as presented in the description of the MMPA discussed previously.

Staff and Funding Levels: NMFS budget documents for the period FY2001–FY2005 do not identify specific funding for research or management activities involving Pribilof Island fur seals. NMFS estimates that its headquarters and regional offices devoted at least 1.7 FTEs on northern fur seal management activities and that its fishery science centers currently devote at least 8.4 FTEs on research activities for this population during 2005.[9] The Marine Mammal Commission's survey of federally funded marine mammal research (Waring 2002) reports that expenditures for biological research and population assessment for northern fur seals in FY1991–FY2000 ranged from $6,000 in FY1991 to $1.9 million in 2000 (see Appendix F). NMFS was the principal source of funding.

Cost estimates for the first five years of recovery work, developed when the northern fur seal conservation plan was adopted in 1991, projected annual funding needs ranging from $1.27 to $1.67 million per year for a five-year total of $7.2 million (NMFS 1991). Actual expenditures during that period are uncertain but are believed to have been much lower. NMFS administrative reports required by the MMPA do not provide information on expenditures for this population, and FWS annual reports on expenditures for threatened and endangered species do not include data on this species because it is not listed as endangered or threatened.

Steller Sea Lion, Eastern Population

Status: The eastern population of Steller sea lions (*Eumetopias jubatus*), one of two recognized Steller sea lion populations, is distributed east and south of Cape Suckling, Alaska (i.e., a point at 144° W longitude west of Prince William Sound in the northern Gulf of Alaska) along the west coast of North America to southern California (NMFS 2005a). The population was initially listed as threatened under the ESA in 1990 when the entire species was listed as such. In 1997 the listing was modified to recognize the western population as endangered while retaining the threatened status for the eastern population.

Based on aerial surveys from southeast Alaska, British Columbia, Washington, Oregon, and California in 2002, the eastern population numbers an estimated 44,996 animals and is increasing (NMFS 2005a). However, between 1980 and 2001 Steller sea lion abundance in central and southern California at the southern extreme of the population's range declined by half to 1,500 to 2,000 animals older than pups. Elsewhere in California and Oregon, counts of non-pups at trend sites have remained relatively stable since the 1980s. Counts of non-pups in southeast Alaska increased at about 2 percent annually between 1979 and 2002 to 9,951 while non-pup counts in British Columbia increased at an average annual rate of 2.8 percent between 1971 and 1998 (NMFS 2005a). The status of the population relative to its OSP size is unknown. The PBR level was calculated as 1,967 (NMFS 2005a).

Major Threats: From 1999 to 2003 observers monitored several commercial fisheries believed to take Steller sea lions incidentally (NMFS 2005a). The observed fisheries included longline, trawl, gillnet, and troll fisheries in Alaska, Oregon, Washington, and California. Combining data from observers and reports by fishermen, the average incidental take in U.S. fisheries between 1999 and 2004 has been estimated to average 3.8 eastern Steller sea lions per year. Incidental take in both U.S. and Canadian fisheries is estimated to number at least 4.2 sea lions per year.

---

[9] P. Michael Payne, personal communication. 17 August 2005. Chief, Marine Mammals Division, Office of Protected Species, National Marine Fisheries Service, Silver Spring, MD 20910; John Bengtson, personal communication. 8 December 2006. National Marine Mammal Laboratory, National Marine Fisheries Service, Seattle, WA 98115

Because this total is less than 10 percent of the PBR level, it is considered insignificant and approaching a zero mortality and serious injury rate. Between 1999 and 2002 an average of about 45 animals were shot annually because they were preying on salmon in aquaculture pens in British Columbia. Such shooting is no longer allowed (NMFS 2005a).

Mortality from other known human-related sources is also relatively low. Between 2000 and 2003 subsistence takes by Alaska Natives averaged just four animals per year (NMFS 2005a). Before Steller sea lions were listed as threatened in 1990, indiscriminate shootings were thought to be a potentially significant source of mortality (NMFS 2005a) despite the fact that it was illegal under the MMPA after 1972. Since 1999 two illegal shootings of Steller sea lions were documented from stranded animals and were successfully prosecuted.

Management Framework: The management framework for the eastern population of Steller sea lions is described in the recovery plan adopted in 1992. The framework is the same as for the western Steller sea lion population and is discussed later.

Critical Habitat: In 1993 the Service designated waters and lands within 3,000 ft of rookeries and major haul-out sites east of 144° W longitude as critical habitat.

Recovery Plan: A recovery plan for Steller sea lions throughout their U.S. range was approved in 1992 (see the western Steller sea lion section). A plan specific to the eastern population has not been developed. However, a new plan addressing both the western and eastern populations was developed and made available for public review in 2006 (71 Fed. Reg. 29919).

Major Management Actions: Other than steps taken to designate critical habitat, population-specific management actions to promote recovery of eastern Steller sea lions have been limited largely to section 7 consultations concerning activities that could potentially affect the population.

Staff and Funding Levels: Until recently, the cost of recovery activities for eastern Steller sea lions has not been reported separately from that of the western population. Before 2003 FWS annual expenditure reports for endangered species (FWS 2003b–d, 2005d–e) combined funding for both eastern and western Steller sea lion populations. In 2003 and 2004 those surveys indicate that NMFS spent $4.1 and $9.6 million, respectively, on the eastern population's recovery, while the state of Alaska spent $1.2 million each year (FWS 2005f, 2006) (Table 11, Appendix C.6–7, Appendix D). For the most part, those efforts included measuring parameters in the relatively healthy eastern population for purposes of comparison with the endangered western population to help elucidate causes of the latter's decline. NMFS estimates that it devoted at least 6.4 FTEs in staff effort on eastern Steller sea lion recovery work (1.3 FTEs by its regional offices and headquarters and 5.1 FTEs by its science centers) during 2005.[10]

---

[10] P. Michael Payne, personal communication. 17 August 2005. Chief, Marine Mammals Division, Office of Protected Species, National Marine Fisheries Service, Silver Spring, MD 20910; John Bengtson, personal communication. 8 December 2006. National Marine Mammal Laboratory, National Marine Fisheries Service, Seattle, WA 98115

Table 11. *Federal and state expenditures (in $ thousands) for the recovery of the eastern population of Steller sea lions, 1998–2004 (Source: FWS 2003b–d; 2005d–f; 2006) (Dash means no data were provided.)*

Fiscal Year	FWS	USGS	NMFS	USCG	Other Federal	Total Federal	State	Total State and Federal
1998 [a]	–	–	3,040	–	20	3,060	19	3,079
1999 [a]	–	–	4,879	2,291	56	7,226	8	7,234
2000 [a]	–	–	5,243	7,810	54	13,107	6	13,113
2001 [a]	–	–	33,312	11,067	66	44,445	2,338	46,783
2002 [a]	–	–	29,295	24,172	35	53,502	2,496	55,998
2003 [b]	–	–	4,090	N/A	4	4,094	1,203	5,297 [c]
2004 [b]	–	–	9,605	N/A	3	9,608	1,203	10,811 [c]

[a] Includes funding for both eastern and western populations
[b] Includes funding only for eastern population
[c] Excludes Coast Guard support for enforcement

Steller Sea Lion, Western Population

Status: The western population of Steller sea lions, one of two currently recognized populations, occurs along the North Pacific Ocean rim from the Kuril Islands and Okhotsk Sea to Cape Suckling, Alaska. Between the 1970s and late 1990s western Steller sea lions declined by 80 percent in the Gulf of Alaska and the Bering Sea/Aleutian Islands (NOAA Fisheries 2000). In 1990 the entire species was listed as threatened throughout its range (NMFS 1992). Subsequent research revealed that the species was comprised of two separate populations, and in 1997 NMFS designated the western population as endangered while continuing to recognize the eastern population as threatened.

The number of Steller sea lions in the western population was estimated to be at least 140,000 animals in the 1950s and 1960s (NMFS 2005a). Counts in the late 1970s indicated a decline to roughly 110,000 animals, and between 1975 and 1985 the population continued to decline at an average annual rate of 5.9 percent (National Research Council 2003). The rate of annual decline increased dramatically to 15.9 percent between 1985 and 1990 before returning to about 5 percent through the 1990s. Since 2000 counts of the population have increased slightly. Between 2002 and 2004 counts at trend sites increased about 5.2 percent per year. The best estimate of total population size based on surveys in 2004 is 38,513 sea lions, which is is 32 percent less than the count in 1990 and more than 70 percent below counts estimates from the 1950s and 1960s. The current PBR level is 231 animals (NMFS 2005a).

Major Threats: The cause of the decline of Steller sea lions has been the subject of great controversy and scientific debate because of the potential effect of conservation measures on major groundfish fisheries in Alaska (NRC 2003, MMC 2002, NOAA Fisheries 2000). Possible causes of the decline include disease, pollution, entanglement in marine debris, commercial and subsistence harvest of sea lions, illegal killing, predation by killer whales and sharks, natural environmental changes in carrying capacity, and interactions with commercial fisheries, including both incidental catch and depletion of available prey resources. Most of these factors are not thought to have been likely causes of the population decline.

- Disease, pollution, and entanglement in marine debris are not considered significant sources of mortality (MMC 2002).
- Steller sea lions have not been harvested commercially since the passage of the MMPA in 1972 (National Research Council 2003). Between 1963 and 1972, 45,178 pups were harvested in the eastern Aleutian Islands and the Gulf of Alaska (NMFS 1992). Although half of the pups on some islands were killed in some years, the effect of this take does not explain the long-term decline since the early 1970s.
- The mean annual subsistence take by hunters in Alaska coastal communities—principally in the Pribilof Islands—was 187 sea lions between 2000 and 2003 (NMFS 2005a), a level not considered a likely cause of the decline.
- After the initial listing of Steller sea lions as threatened in 1990, shootings of sea lions by fishermen are thought to have become less frequent. In 1998 two such violators were successfully prosecuted, but no successful cases were brought between 2000 and 2003 (NMFS 2005a).
- The role of predation by killer whales is controversial. Evidence suggests that such predation had limited effects during the major part of the decline in the 1970s and 1980s but may now be more significant given the species' much-reduced population size (NMFS 2005a).
- Analyses of fishery observer data between 1990 and 2003 suggest an average annual take of 25 sea lions incidental to groundfish trawl, longline, and trap, and salmon gillnet fisheries in the Bering Sea/Aleutian Islands and in the Gulf of Alaska (NMFS 2005a). When self-reporting by fishermen and stranding data are added, the minimum mean annual mortality rate increases to 31 sea lions per year. Because this level exceeds 10 percent of the PBR level for western Steller sea lions, current levels of incidental take in fisheries are not considered insignificant and approaching a zero mortality and serious injury rate (NMFS 2005a).[11] Although incidental taking in fisheries exceeds this target level for fishery-related mortality, the current minimum estimate of all sources of human-caused mortality (218 animals) is below the calculated PBR level.

Much of the debate about causes of the decline of Steller sea lions has centered upon the degree to which climate change and fishing have reduced prey and, by extension, the nutritional fitness of Steller sea lions (National Research Council 2003, MMC 2002, NMFS 1992). The oceanographic regime of the North Pacific undergoes periodic shifts that can have profound effects on fisheries and wildlife populations, including sea lion prey species. A significant regime shift occurred in the late 1970s, and one hypothesis is that the shift led to a decrease in available prey of high nutritional quality, thereby compromising growth and survival of juvenile sea lions and reproduction of adult females. Alternatively, intensive fishing by foreign fleets off Alaska between the late 1950s and early 1970s may have been a major factor in changing the abundance levels of prey populations.

---

[11] In calculating the PBR level for the western population of Steller sea lions, NMFS applied the recovery factor for an endangered species of 0.1 (NMFS 2005a). At the same time, NMFS noted that this recovery factor and the entire regime of PBR were based on the assumption that direct human-related mortalities would be the primary reason for declines in marine mammal abundance—an assumption that may not be warranted for Steller sea lions.

Currently operating fisheries also may affect Steller sea lion populations by reducing prey. Both fisheries (including those for pollock, Atka mackerel, and Pacific cod) and sea lions exploit the same species in the same geographic regions during the same seasons (MMC 2002). During the course of the sea lion decline, harvests were managed to reduce the biomass of some prey species by as much as 65 percent or more. Recent management strategies are attempting to limit reductions to 60 percent of their estimated unfished biomass. The extent to which prey species can be removed without significant ecological effects on marine predators such as the Steller sea lion is not clear and is a subject being addressed in section 7 consultations. The effects of removing such a large percentage of available biomass are further confounded by the manner in which they are removed. Much of the controversy regarding fishery effects on Steller sea lions has focused on where and when the prey are removed because the concentration of fishing effort in time and space can exacerbate effects by causing excessive localized depletions. In addition, fishing concentrated in areas close to rookeries and haul-out sites can exacerbate general reductions in biomass because sea lions must then extend their foraging range and use more energy to find the prey needed. All of these effects are considered to be most significant for young animals making the transition to independent foraging and for females that must support their own nutritional needs plus those of dependent pups and developing fetuses. Evidence collected in the 1970s and 1980s indicated that growth, survival, and reproduction all may have been compromised during that period, suggesting the animals were subject to nutritional limitations. Unfortunately, the effects of oceanic regime shifts and fishing may become expressed more or less identically, making discrimination between these potential causes difficult.

A National Academy of Sciences panel reviewed the principal hypotheses for the decline of the western population of Steller sea lions and divided them into two trophically based categories: bottom-up and top-down categories (National Research Council 2003). The former includes effects that alter the carrying capacity of the ecosystem and that could affect the physical condition of sea lions (e.g., large-scale fisheries, climate change, pollutants, and disease). The latter includes effects that are independent of the system's carrying capacity but could still cause sea lion mortality (e.g., increased predation by killer whales or sharks, incidental taking in fishing gear). The panel concluded that there is no definitive evidence to support any particular hypothesis for the decline of the western population of Steller sea lions.

Management Framework: NMFS is the lead federal agency responsible for managing Steller sea lions. Implications that fisheries off Alaska have been a major factor in the decline of Steller sea lions have received great attention. Fishery management plans for walleye pollock, Pacific cod, and Atka mackerel in the Bering Sea/Aleutian Islands region and the Gulf of Alaska have been the subject of numerous formal consultations under section 7 of the ESA and numerous directives by the courts and Congress. Between 1998 and 2003 NMFS conducted six different section 7 consultations related to Steller sea lions, all but one of which examined groundfish fisheries.

The initial forum within which these fishery management plans are discussed and developed is the North Pacific Fishery Management Council. Like other regional fishery management councils, the North Pacific council has the lead in drafting and recommending measures under which the fisheries operate. Those measures must be reviewed by NMFS and meet standards of the Magnuson–Stevens Fishery Conservation and Management Act, the ESA, the MMPA, and the National Environmental Policy Act.

Congress also has played an active role in managing interactions between Alaska groundfish trawl fisheries and Steller sea lions. For instance, in its appropriations bill for FY2001, Congress modified the reasonable and prudent alternatives in a biological opinion. Congress also required that measures aimed at compliance with the ESA be developed consistent with the procedures and requirements of the Magnuson–Stevens Fishery Conservation and Management Act.

NMFS administers a coordinated Steller sea lion research program that includes participants from the Alaska Department of Fish and Game, the North Pacific Universities Marine Mammal Research Consortium, the Alaska SeaLife Center, and other agencies and organizations. The program includes extensive studies to monitor population trends and elucidate possible causes of the Steller sea lion decline (NOAA Fisheries 2000). Since Steller sea lions were listed in 1990, NMFS has conducted annual subadult/adult and biennial pup counts. Other studies have examined sea lion feeding ecology and prey biomass. The University of Alaska Fairbanks and a consortium of fishing companies have undertaken research under the aegis of the Pollock Conservation Cooperative Research Center.

NMFS also has taken steps to manage subsistence harvests of Steller sea lions in cooperation with Alaska Native hunters. From 1995 to 1997 NMFS sponsored efforts to increase Native awareness of the status of Steller sea lions and to encourage local management of the subsistence harvest. In 1997 representatives from Alaska Native communities in the Aleutian and Pribilof Islands formed a regional marine mammal commission to help manage certain marine mammals, including Steller sea lions, taken for subsistence purposes (NOAA Fisheries 2000). In 1999 an Alaska Native organization known then as the Alaska Sea Otter Commission added Steller sea lions to its responsibilities. Since then NMFS has worked with both the Native commission and the tribal government of St. Paul to develop a range-wide conservation program for Steller sea lions.

Critical Habitat: In 1993 NMFS designated critical habitat in three types of areas (58 Fed. Reg. 45269):

- Waters within 20 nmi of all rookeries and major haul-out sites west of 144° W longitude;
- Foraging areas in Shelikof Strait, the southeastern Bering Sea, and Seguam Pass in the central Aleutian Island chain; and
- Waters and lands within 3,000 ft of all rookeries and major haul-out sites east of 144° W longitude (i.e., for the eastern Steller sea lion population).

Recovery Plan: Soon after the 1990 listing of Steller sea lions as threatened throughout their range, NMFS convened a Steller Sea Lion Recovery Team, which prepared the first recovery plan for the species (NMFS 1992). The plan's goal was to promote the recovery of Steller sea lions "…to a level appropriate to justify removal from the ESA listings." It also identified criteria for reclassifying and delisting the species based on an initial benchmark of 90,000 animals older than pups counted at selected trend sites located between the Kenai Peninsula to Kiska Island in the Aleutians. The recovery team recommended the following:

- If the counts at designated trend sites in the area fall below 17 percent of the benchmark value, the species should be listed as endangered;
- If the counts are greater than 17 percent but less than 40 percent of the benchmark, the species should remain threatened, with the following exception; if the count is greater than 17 percent but less than 25 percent of the benchmark, the population should be listed as endangered if any of the following conditions apply:
  - The count at designated trend sites declines by at least 10 percent over three or more consecutive survey years;
  - The overall pup production index at trend sites declines by 10 percent over the count in the previous two-year period; or
  - The number of animals declines by at least 10 percent over a three-year period in three or more of the six other regions from Russia to California.

The recovery plan included the following criteria for delisting the Steller sea lion (NMFS 1992): (1) the trend count in the area is greater than 40 percent of the benchmark value of 90,000 animals older than pups, and (2) the number of animals is stable or increasing in at least three of the six other regions. NMFS decided not to adopt these criteria, pending further analysis.

The recovery plan also identifies recovery actions to accomplish the following:

- Identify habitat requirements and protect areas of special biological significance;
- Identify management stocks;
- Monitor status and trends of sea lions;
- Monitor health, condition, and vital parameters;
- Assess and minimize causes of mortality;
- Investigate feeding ecology and factors affecting energetic status; and
- Implement a recovery plan and coordinate recovery activities.

In 2001 NMFS convened a new 20-member recovery team to draft a revised recovery plan for both the western and eastern Steller sea lions. A revised recovery plan has been developed by the team and was made available for public review in 2006 (71 Fed. Reg. 29919).

Major Management Actions: Management actions put into place with the initial listing of Steller sea lions in 1990 include the following (MMC 2001):

- Prohibiting the discharge of firearms within 100 yards of a sea lion;
- Prohibiting most vessels from transiting within 3 nmi of major rookeries in the Aleutian Islands and Gulf of Alaska; and
- Monitoring incidental mortality and reducing the allowable annual take quota from 1,350 to 675 sea lions.

Between 1991 and 1998 NMFS established no-trawl zones within 10 nmi of 37 sea lion rookeries in Alaska, with seasonal extensions to 20 nmi around six major rookeries in the eastern Aleutian Islands and the Bering Sea, and prepared several biological opinions on the effects of trawl fisheries on sea lions. Among other things, the opinions led the North Pacific Fishery Management Council and NMFS to adjust time and area catch allocations to prevent concentrated fishing effort in foraging areas beyond the no-trawl zones around major haul-out sites (MMC 2001).

1998 Fishery Actions: NMFS issued several biological opinions finding that the pollock fisheries in the Bering Sea /Aleutian Islands areas and Gulf of Alaska could jeopardize Steller sea lions and their critical habitat. The opinions included reasonable and prudent measures that further dispersed fishing effort and limited catches in sea lion foraging areas. The agency also recommended studies on the efficacy of no-trawl zones, the foraging range of young-of-the-year Steller sea lions, and site-by-site relationships between fishing effort and trends in juvenile survival. Partially in response to litigation, NMFS issued additional biological opinions late in December 1998 on management plans for all three fisheries. Although one opinion for the proposed Atka mackerel fishery concluded that the fishery was not likely to jeopardize Steller sea lions or their designated critical habitat, a separate opinion concluded that the proposed plan for the Gulf of Alaska and the Bering Sea/Aleutian Islands groundfish fishery would do so. Upon reaching this conclusion, the opinion proposed a management framework to avoid jeopardy by dispersing fisheries adjacent to rookeries and haul-out sites, both temporally and spatially. NMFS later incorporated measures developed by the North Pacific Fishery Management Council into the biological opinion as reasonable and prudent alternatives, allowing the fishery to proceed.

1999 Fishery Actions: Measures developed in the December 1998 biological opinions were implemented by regulation in January 1999. In December 1999 NMFS issued a biological opinion on the total allowable catch of groundfish recommended by the North Pacific Fishery Management Council for 2000 (NOAA Fisheries 2000). The opinion concluded no jeopardy or adverse modification of critical habitat.

2000 Fishery Actions: In November 2000 NMFS issued a biological opinion on new measures for Gulf of Alaska and the Bering Sea/Aleutian Islands groundfish fisheries (NOAA Fisheries 2000). The opinion found that the fisheries, as implemented under the fishery management plans, would jeopardize the continued existence of Steller sea lions and adversely modify their critical habitat. The biological opinion set out the following reasonable and prudent alternatives to be phased in, beginning in 2001:

- Adopting a more precautionary rule for setting overall catch limits;
- Extending 3-nmi no-fishing zones around rookeries and haul-out areas to sites not already protected;
- Closing areas around some rookeries and haul-out sites out to 20 nmi;
- Establishing catch limits on a seasonal basis inside critical habitat and two seasonal releases of quotas outside of critical habitat; and
- Establishing a procedure for setting limits on catch levels in critical habitat based on the biomass of target species in critical habitat.

To help address uncertainties about interactions between fisheries and Steller sea lions, Congress authorized a significant increase in funding for Steller sea lion research late in 2000. The legislation also directed that certain modifications be made in the reasonable and prudent alternatives and that the North Pacific Fishery Management Council and the National Academy of Sciences undertake an independent review to assess underlying hypotheses regarding interactions between Steller sea lions and fisheries and recommend reasonable and prudent management measures.

2001 Fishery Actions: NMFS began phasing in reasonable and prudent alternatives reflective of its 2000 biological opinion and congressional directives. A new biological opinion was released recommending additional measures to avoid interactions between sea lions and fisheries. A National Research Council report concluded that fishing might have negative effects on Steller sea lions, but that data are limited and circumstantial (National Research Council 2003). The report recommended studies to monitor population trends and investigate temporal and spatial scales of sea lion foraging and hypotheses concerning local prey depletion. The report also concluded that, on a single-species basis, the fish stocks in the Alaska region were generally well managed although long-lived species with low recruitment may require more protective management. The review also concluded that there is not a sufficient basis to conclude that the existing management strategy is safe on an ecological basis and therefore protective of the ecosystem as a whole.

2002 Fishery Actions: NMFS issued rules making previous measures adopted in 2001 permanent (60 Fed. Reg. 956). Ongoing litigation resulted in a court decision recommending that NMFS further modify its reasonable and prudent alternatives.

2004 Fishery Actions: In December 2004 NMFS issued a final rule revising Steller sea lion protection measures in the pollock and Pacific cod fisheries in the Gulf of Alaska (69 Fed. Reg. 75865). The regulations changed fishing closures near four Steller sea lion haul-out sites and revised the seasonal quotas for pollock. In doing so, NMFS concluded that the measures would be unlikely to affect Steller sea lion populations beyond levels identified in the 2000 biological opinion.

Staff and Funding Levels: Cost projections developed for the first five years of recovery work when the Steller sea lion recovery plan was adopted (NMFS 1992) suggested funding needs ranging from between $1.18 to $2.83 million per year for a five-year total of $11.4 million. Actual expenditures during that period are uncertain; however, according to the Marine Mammal Commission's survey of federally funded marine mammal research (Waring 2002), annual expenditures for biological and population assessment research on Steller sea lions (including both eastern and western populations) during the 1990s ranged from $4,000 in FY1991 to $1.9 million in FY1997 (Appendix F). The principal sources of funding were NMFS and the National Ocean Service, which funded studies on foraging patterns and competition for prey.

Prior to 2003 FWS annual reports on endangered species expenditures also combined funding data for eastern and western Steller sea lions consistent with their listing as a single species under the ESA. According to those reports, federal expenditures for recovery of both populations in 1998 were about $3.1 million, and state expenditures were $19,000 (FWS 2003d). Federal expenditures grew quickly in succeeding years to $7.2 million in 1999, $13.1 million in 2000, and $44.4 million in 2001 (Table 12, Appendices C.1–7) (FWS 2003b–d, 2005d–f, 2006). In 2003 overall federal funding for western Steller sea lions alone reached $48.3 million. Of that total, $8.2 million was spent on research by NMFS (largely on contracts with other institutions) and $39.9 million was spent on enforcement by the U.S. Coast Guard (FWS 2005d).[12] NMFS estimates that it devoted at least 14.4 FTEs in staff effort on eastern Steller sea lion recovery work (1.1 by its regional offices and headquarters staff and 13.3 by its science centers) during 2005.[13]

NMFS budget documents indicate that budget allocations for Steller sea lions (including both eastern and western populations) declined from $35 million in 2001 to $17.7 million in 2004 (see Appendix E).

Table 12. Federal and state expenditures (in $ thousands) for the recovery of western population of Steller sea lions, 1998–2004 (Source: FWS 2003b–d; 2005d–f; 2006) (Dash means no data were provided.)

Fiscal Year	FWS	USGS	NMFS	USCG	Other Federal	Total Federal	State	Total State and Federal
1998[a]	–	–	3,040	–	20	3,060	19	3,079
1999[a]	–	–	4,879	2,291	56	7,226	8	7,234
2000[a]	–	–	5,243	7,810	54	13,107	6	13,113
2001[a]	–	–	33,312	11,067	66	44,445	2,338	46,783
2002[a]	–	–	29,295	24,172	35	53,502	2,496	55,998
2003[b]	–	–	8,180	39,940	194	48,314	1,200	49,514
2004[b]	–	–	9,605	20,856	85	30,546	1,200	31,746

[a] Includes funding for both eastern and western populations
[b] Includes funding for western population only

CETACEANS

Blue Whale

Population Status: Blue whales (*Balaenoptera musculus*), the largest animals ever to live on earth, are found in all the world oceans. They have been divided into three subspecies: *B. m. intermedia* in Antarctic waters, *B. m. musculus* in the Northern Hemisphere, and *B. m. brevicauda* in the southern Indian Ocean and southwestern Pacific Ocean. For purposes of preparing stock assessment reports required under the MMPA, blue whales in U.S. waters have been divided into three populations: western North Atlantic, eastern North Pacific, and western North Pacific (NMFS 2006a). Blue whales were listed as endangered as a species throughout their range under the ESCA in 1970. That designation was carried forward under the ESA. The International Whaling Commission (IWC), the international organization responsible for

---

[12] Coast Guard cost estimates include the cost of vessel operations, including all crew and prorated maintenance costs, during periods when the vessel's primary mission is identified as enforcement of fishery regulations to protect Steller sea lions.
[13] P. Michael Payne, personal communication, 17 August 2005. Chief, Marine Mammals Division, Office of Protected Species, National Marine Fisheries Service, Silver Spring, MD 20910; John Bengtson, personal communication. 8 December 2006. National Marine Mammal Laboratory, National Marine Fisheries Service, Seattle, WA 98115.

regulating commercial and subsistence whaling, classifies all populations of blue whales worldwide as "protection stocks" (i.e., stocks at less than 10 percent of their maximum sustainable yield level and for which no commercial whaling is allowed).

Western North Atlantic Population: In the western North Atlantic, blue whales are most common off the east coast of Canada and only occasionally enter U.S. waters (NMFS 2002c). The only basis for an estimate of abundance for this population is a count of 308 blue whales made in the Gulf of St. Lawrence in 1987.

Eastern North Pacific Population: Although the IWC considers blue whales throughout the North Pacific as a single population, it is now thought that as many as five separate populations occur in the North Pacific (NMFS 2005a, Reeves et al. 1998). One of these feeds principally along the coasts of California, Oregon, and Washington in summer and winters in calving grounds off Mexico and Central America. Based on surveys off California between 1996 and 2002, NMFS (2005a) concluded that the best estimate of abundance for this population is 1,744 whales. Based on a different analysis of those data by Calambokidis and Barlow (2004), however, the size of the population was estimated to be 2,994 whales. In general, their abundance appears to be increasing although it is possible that increases in blue whale counts since the mid-1990s simply reflect an increasing use of the California feeding grounds. The PBR level calculated for this population is 1.4 whales, which is greater than the documented mortality from ship strikes or fisheries (NMFS 2006a).

Western North Pacific Population: The western North Pacific population of blue whales is thought to winter in the central North Pacific and summer along the Aleutian Islands. However, based on rare sightings and acoustic recordings, blue whales enter the U.S. Exclusive Economic Zone off Hawaii at least occasionally (NMFS 2006a). No data are available to estimate population size or PBR level.

Major Threats: All populations of blue whales worldwide, including those in U.S. waters, were nearly eliminated by commercial whaling. A prohibition on hunting for blue whales was adopted by the IWC in 1966 (NMFS 2006a), but by that time whalers had taken at least 9,500 blue whales in the North Pacific and 11,000 in the North Atlantic, leaving populations in each ocean estimated to be fewer than 1,000 animals at that time. Current threats include the following: Fishery Interactions: Although blue whales may have been incidentally taken in offshore drift gillnet fisheries and longline fisheries, there are no confirmed records of such takings off Hawaii, California, or the U.S. Atlantic coast (NMFS 2006a,b).

Vessel Collisions: Blue whales are occasionally injured or killed by collisions with ships (Laist 2001, NMFS 2006a). In March 1998 a 66-ft male blue whale, likely killed when struck, was carried into Rhode Island waters on the bow of a tanker. In the eastern North Pacific, ship strikes were implicated in the deaths of at least four blue whales between 1980 and 1993 (Jensen and Silber 2003).

Noise: Rising levels of anthropogenic noise in all the world's oceans may disrupt long-distance communication of blue whales as well as other species of great whales. Whether such effects could alter their population abundance and trend is unknown.

Management Framework: NMFS is the lead federal agency responsible for managing blue whales. In cooperation with the Department of State, NMFS develops and coordinates scientific advice and U.S. positions on related management issues considered at meetings of the IWC. No interagency management teams currently exist to assist or oversee management activities specifically related to blue whales.

Critical Habitat: None designated.

Recovery Plan: In July 1998 the Service adopted a recovery plan for blue whales (Reeves et al. 1998). Its primary purpose is "…to identify a set of actions that will minimize or eliminate effects of human activities that are detrimental to the recovery of blue whale populations." Its immediate objectives "are to identify factors that may be limiting the populations and actions necessary to allow the populations to increase." Key actions highlighted in the plan focus on research to improve understanding of blue whale populations. The identified actions involve (1) determining population structure, (2) estimating population sizes and trends, (3) identifying and protecting essential habitats, (4) minimizing sources of human-caused injury and mortality, (5) coordinating federal, state, and international recovery efforts, (6) assessing detrimental effects of interactions with vessels, and (7) improving the collection of information from stranded and entangled animals.

Major Management Actions: To address the impact of commercial whaling, the IWC imposed a ban on hunting blue whales in the North Atlantic in 1955 and in the North Pacific in 1966 (Reeves et al. 1998). In 1986–1987 the ban was extended globally when the IWC, with the support of the U.S. delegation, adopted a moratorium on all commercial whaling. Other than preparing a blue whale recovery plan and blue whale stock assessment reports, NMFS has undertaken no management measures designed specifically to protect blue whales in U.S. waters. Most management actions related to blue whales involve actions focused on endangered whales in general. Although a few directed studies have been undertaken to assess the occurrence and movements of blue whales in the population off California, Oregon, and Washington, most information on blue whales in U.S. waters has been collected opportunistically (e.g., through stranding programs or incidental to studies on other species) or through studies to assess the regional composition of fauna.

Staff and Funding Levels: According to available budget data, NMFS allocated $994,000 in FY2003 for the recovery of endangered large whales (e.g., bowhead, blue, fin, sei, and sperm whales). The amount devoted specifically to blue whales is uncertain (see Appendix E). NMFS estimates that its headquarters, regional offices, and fishery science centers devoted at least 1.6 FTEs to blue whale recovery activities (0.4 by its headquarters and regional office staff and 1.2 by its regional science centers) in 2005.[14] According to FWS annual expenditure reports on endangered species (FWS 2003b–d, 2005d–f, 2006), very little or no funding has been devoted explicitly to blue whales by NMFS in recent years (Table 13, Appendices C1–7). Most recent funding has involved Coast Guard enforcement activities.

---

[14] P. Michael Payne, personal communication. 17 August 2005. Chief, Marine Mammals Division, Office of Protected Species, National Marine Fisheries Service, Silver Spring, MD 20910; John Bengtson, personal communication. 8 December 2006. National Marine Mammal Laboratory, National Marine Fisheries Service, Seattle, WA 98115

Table 13. *Federal and state expenditures (in $ thousands) for the recovery of blue whales, 1998–2004 (Source: FWS 2003b–d; 2005d–f; 2006)*

Fiscal Year	FWS	USGS	NMFS	USCG	Other Federal	Total Federal	State	Total State and Federal
1998	–	–	–	–	3	3	1	4
1999	120	–	–	–	5	125	–	125
2000	–	–	–	–	6	6	–	6
2001	–	–	–	–	1	1	–	1
2002	–	–	–	7	1	8	–	8
2003	–	–	–	199	4	203	–	203
2004	–	–	–	60	4	65	2	67

Cost projections developed for the first five years of recovery work when the blue whale recovery plan was adopted in 1998 (Reeves et al. 1998) suggested funding needs ranging from between $138,000 and $673,000 per year between 1999 and 2003 with a five-year total of $1.95 million. Actual expenditures during that period are uncertain but were clearly below those levels.

Bowhead Whale, Western Arctic Population

Population Status: The only population of bowhead whales (*Balaena mysticetus*) occurring in U.S. waters is the western Arctic population. This is the largest of five bowhead whale populations found worldwide (NMFS 2005a). The western Arctic population migrates annually from winter areas in the northern Bering Sea through the Chukchi Sea to summer grounds in the Beaufort Sea. Arctic Native communities have hunted bowhead whales for more than 1,000 years at levels that are not thought to have had a significant effect on overall abundance. From the late 1800s to the early 1900s, however, commercial whaling reduced the western Arctic population to fewer than 3,000 bowhead whales, and in 1970 the species was listed as endangered throughout its range under the ESCA. That designation was carried forward under the ESA. The IWC has classified all populations of bowhead whales as protection stocks for which no commercial whaling is allowed.

Based on a count in 2001, the best abundance estimate for the western Arctic population is 10,545 whales (NMFS 2005a). Past counts suggest that the population has been increasing steadily at an average annual rate of 3.1 percent since 1978. The PBR level is 95 whales. Based on an estimated pre-exploitation population size of 12,599 whales, the lower limit of its OSP size has been estimated at between 6,500 and 10,500 whales (Shelden et al. 2003a).

Major Threats: With the cessation of commercial whaling, the principal management issues concerning western Arctic bowhead whales have been the subsistence harvest by Alaska Natives, the effects of noise and possible oil spills associated with offshore oil and gas development, and, more recently, the effects of climate change. Vessel collisions and entanglement in fishing gear also pose potential threats.

Subsistence whaling: Under subsistence whaling quotas established by the IWC, the number of bowhead whales taken annually by Alaska Natives has been below calculated PBR levels for the western Arctic bowhead whale population since such calculations were first made in the mid-1990s. The number of whales landed annually between 1999 and 2003 ranged from 35 whales in 2000 and 2003 to 49 whales in 2001 (NMFS 2006a). As indicated previously, the western Arctic bowhead whale population has continued to increase in size steadily over the past 20 years under the existing harvest management measures.

Oil and Gas Development: Because much of the habitat of the western Arctic bowhead whale population is within active or potential lease sale areas, oil and gas exploration and development off Alaska have increased the species' risk of exposure to pollutants and noise (Shelden and Rugh 1995, NMFS 2005a). Although bowhead whales are sensitive to noise and appear to avoid seismic operations, there is little evidence that increased levels of noise associated with activities to date have impeded their recovery (NMFS 2005a). Oil spills also pose a potential threat; however, to date no major spills are known to have affected bowhead whales within their range.

Entanglement: Incidents of entanglement by bowhead whales in commercial fishing gear appear to be infrequent. Available information on such interactions comes principally from whales found entangled in fishing gear by Alaska Natives during the subsistence harvest. It suggests that such interactions occur principally in crab pot gear. From 1999 to 2003 the estimated average annual rate of entanglement was 0.2 whale per year (NMFS 2005a).

Climate Change: Although there are insufficient data to make reliable predictions, changes in Arctic weather, sea-surface temperatures, ice extent, and prey availability may affect ice-associated animals such as bowhead whales (NMFS 2005a). Both positive and negative effects are possible (Shelden et al. 2003a).

Vessel Collisions: Injury and mortality caused by collision with vessels appear to be infrequent although this is probably due largely to the low levels of commercial vessel traffic within the species' Arctic habitat (Laist et al 2001). Three of 236 bowhead whales taken during the aboriginal subsistence hunt in the Beaufort Sea showed evidence of vessel injuries, and no known mortalities have been recorded (67 Fed. Reg. 55768). Collision risks could increase substantially in the future if seasonal pack ice coverage continues to retreat and northern sea routes are developed for shipping.

Management Framework: NMFS and the Alaska Eskimo Whaling Commission have primary responsibility for conservation and management of bowhead whales. However, as a member of the IWC, the United States follows management recommendations for subsistence whaling developed by the IWC (Shelden and Rugh 1995). Subsistence harvests are managed and monitored by the Alaska Eskimo Whaling Commission under a cooperative agreement with the National Oceanic and Atmospheric Administration (NOAA), NMFS's parent agency. The Commission is composed of whaling captains and crewmembers and is directed by a board of 10 commissioners, one from each whaling village. Besides allocating quotas among its member villages and providing funds to the North Slope Borough for periodic censuses of the bowhead whale population, the Commission has funded research to improve harpoons used in the hunt and to reduce the number of whales struck but lost.

Together with the Department of State and the Alaska Eskimo Whaling Commission, NMFS and other NOAA offices develop policies and quota requests and coordinate scientific advice for IWC meetings.

Critical Habitat: No critical habitat has been designated for western Arctic bowhead whales. In February 2000 the Center for Biological Diversity and the Marine Biodiversity Protection Center petitioned NMFS for such action, but the petition was rejected (67 Fed. Reg. 55767) for the following reasons:

- The decline in bowhead whale abundance and reason for listing the species was overexploitation by commercial whaling; habitat issues were not a factor in the decline;
- There is no indication that habitat degradation is impeding population growth;
- The population is abundant and increasing; and
- Existing laws and practices adequately protect the species and its habitat.

Recovery Plan: In June 1998 NMFS determined that a recovery plan for bowhead whales was not needed due to the population's abundance and trend and the effectiveness of the agreement between NOAA and the Alaska Eskimo Whaling Commission in managing the subsistence hunt (67 Fed. Reg. 55769).

Major Management Actions: Since 1977 the IWC has recommended quotas for the subsistence hunt of bowhead whales by Alaska Natives. Those quotas, which have ranged between 14 and 67 whales per year (not including unused strikes that can be carried forward), have represented 0.1 to 0.5 percent of the estimated total population size. In recent years, Russian Natives also have taken a few whales under these quotas. The most recent IWC quota is a block quota of 280 whales for the period 2003–2007 with a limit of 67 strikes in any single year. The average annual take by Natives in Alaska and Russia has been 52 whales. Since 1996, when NMFS began calculating PBR levels, the IWC has set annual strike quotas of 65 to 67 whales, which have been below the PBR level.

NMFS manages potential impacts of noise from oil and gas operations through incidental harassment authorizations issued under the MMPA exemption for the small take of marine mammals incidental to activities other than fishing. Such authorizations can be issued only if the actions they permit are believed to have no more than a negligible impact on the population and no immitigable adverse effect on the availability of bowhead whales to subsistence users. NMFS also consults with the Minerals Management Service, the Army Corps of Engineers, and the Environmental Protection Agency on the effects of oil and gas exploration and development on the outer continental shelf under section 7 of the ESA and the Fish and Wildlife Coordination Act. Recent opinions have concluded that effects of proposed offshore oil and gas exploration on bowhead whales do not jeopardize the population.

Staff and Funding Levels: According to NMFS budget documents (Appendix E), the agency allocated $994,000 in FY2003 for the recovery of endangered large whales (e.g., bowhead, blue, fin, sei, and sperm whales). The amount devoted specifically to bowhead whales is uncertain. NMFS also has transferred funds appropriated by Congress to the Alaska Eskimo Whaling Commission ranging from $399,000 in FY2001 to $492,000 in FY2003. According to FWS annual expenditure reports for endangered species (FWS 2003b–d, 2005d–f, 2006), total federal funding for work on bowhead whales ranged from zero to $203,000 between 1998 and 2004 (14, Appendices C1–7); however, all federal funding for this species (e.g., funding passed to the Alaska Eskimo Whaling Commission) is not reflected in those numbers. NMFS estimates that it devoted at least 4.1 FTEs in staff effort on bowhead whale recovery work (0.6 by its regional offices and headquarters and 3.5 by its science centers) during 2005.[15] Funding for those salaries clearly has not been included in funding levels reported in the FWS annual expenditure reports.

Table 14. *Federal and state expenditures (in $ thousands) for the recovery of western Arctic bowhead whales, 1998–2004 (Source: FWS 2003b–d; 2005d–f; 2006)*

Fiscal Year	FWS	USGS	NMFS	USCG	Other Federal	Total Federal	State	Total State and Federal
1998	–	–	–	–	–	–	1	1
1999	–	–	–	–	–	–	3	3
2000	–	–	–	–	–	–	3	3
2001	–	–	–	–	–	–	25	25
2002	–	–	–	7	–	7	–	7
2003	–	–	–	199	5	204	–	204
2004	–	–	–	60	130	190	–	190

The Marine Mammal Commission survey of federally funded marine mammal research (Waring 2002) reports that funding for biological and population assessment research on bowhead whales between FY1991 and FY2000 ranged from $280,000 in FY2000 to $1.5 million in 1999 (see Appendix F). The principal sources of funding were NMFS and the Minerals Management Service. Recent funding levels have been increased to more than $1 million to address research questions raised by the IWC Scientific Committee and to help prepare a request to the IWC for a new subsistence quota.

Fin Whale

Population Status: Fin whales (*Balaenoptera physalus*) were listed as endangered throughout their range under the ESCA in 1970, and that designation was carried forward under the ESA. For purposes of preparing stock assessment reports required by the MMPA, NMFS recognizes four fin whale populations in U.S. waters: a western North Atlantic population, a California/Oregon/Washington population, a northeast Pacific population, and a Hawaii population. The stock structure of fin whale populations, however, is not well known (NMFS 2006b). It is thought that populations in different oceans may be divided into subpopulations that use different feeding grounds. Under the IWC management system, the Nova Scotia stock of fin whales (i.e., the western North Atlantic population) and all populations in the North Pacific are classified as protection stocks for which no commercial whaling is allowed.

---

[15] P. Michael Payne, personal communication. 17 August 2005. Chief, Marine Mammals Division, Office of Protected Species, National Marine Fisheries Service, Silver Spring, MD 20910; John Bengtson, personal communication. 8 December 2006. National Marine Mammal Laboratory, National Marine Fisheries Service, Seattle, WA 98115.

Western North Atlantic Population: Fin whales are one of the most common large whales observed along the northeastern U.S. coast. The IWC currently recognizes fin whales off the eastern U.S. coast, Nova Scotia, and Newfoundland to be a separate stock. Roughly half of all individually identified whales observed feeding in Massachusetts Bay have been observed there in multiple years, suggesting a degree of site fidelity. The best available abundance estimate for fin whales between Georges Bank and the Gulf of St. Lawrence is 2,814 (NMFS 2006b). Available information is not sufficient to determine trends in abundance, and the PBR level is 4.7 whales per year. Because documented human-caused deaths have averaged more than one whale per year in recent years, which is greater than 10 percent of the PBR level, the rate of human-caused mortality and injury is not considered insignificant and approaching zero.

California/Oregon/Washington Population: The IWC recognizes two populations of fin whales in the North Pacific Ocean: one in the East China Sea and one elsewhere in the North Pacific (NMFS 2006a). Although there is little information to determine population structure, some genetic studies suggest that fin whales in the Gulf of California are isolated from those elsewhere in the North Pacific and represent an "evolutionary unique population" (NMFS 2006a). By 1973 commercial whaling had reduced North Pacific fin whale abundance from an estimated 42,000 to 45,000 animals to between 13,620 and 18,680 animals (Ohsumi and Wada 1974). Surveys in 1996 and 2001 produced an estimate of 3,279 fin whales off California, Oregon, and Washington. NMFS calculates the PBR level to be 15 fin whales in this area. Recently documented fishery-caused deaths have averaged about 1.0 whale per year, while confirmed vessel related-deaths have averaged 0.4 fin whale per year (NMFS 2006a).

Northeast Pacific Population: This population occurs across the northern North Pacific Ocean from British Columbia to Japan and north to the Bering Strait (NMFS 2005a). A combination of estimates from surveys between 1999 and 2003 in the central and eastern Bering Sea and along the Alaska Peninsula and Aleutian Islands suggests the number of fin whales west of the Kenai Peninsula is at least 5,703 whales (NMFS 2005a). Information to assess the population's trend is insufficient and PBR for the population is calculated to be 11.4 whales per year. About 0.6 fin whale a year is known to have been killed recently in this area, which is less than 10 percent of PBR. Thus, the estimated mortality and serious injury rate for the area west of the Kenai is considered insignificant and approaching zero.

Hawaii Population: Fin whales sightings off Hawaii are rare; however, recordings of fin whale vocalizations indicate their presence (NMFS 2006a). Based on a ship survey in 2002, an abundance of 174 fin whales was estimated for waters within 200 nmi of Hawaii. The calculated PBR level for this stock is 0.2. Fishing-related mortality of fin whales in Hawaiian waters has not been reported, and incidental take levels, if any take occurs, are considered to be insignificant and approaching zero.

Major Threats: A draft recovery plan for fin and sei whales (Reeves et al. 1998) identified the following threats for both species:

Vessel Interactions: Fin whales are the species of whale most commonly injured or killed by ship strikes off both the Atlantic and Pacific coasts of the United States. Based on recent but limited data, NMFS estimates known mortality due to vessel collisions to be at least 1.4 fin whales per year in the North Atlantic. Limited evidence also suggests that fin whales may alter their behavior in response to whale-watching vessels off Atlantic Canada and the northeastern United States. Off the U.S. Pacific coast, the most likely sources of vessel disturbance may be industrial, military, and fishing vessel traffic.

Entrapment and Entanglement in Fishing Gear: Fin whales are killed or injured annually by inshore fishing gear off Atlantic Canada and the eastern United States, as well as off the Pacific coast of the United States and Mexico. During the 1980s the southern California offshore drift gillnet fishery killed an estimated 73 rorqual whales per year. Some of those whales may have been fin whales, but it is unclear how many. Shark and swordfish driftnet fisheries off Baja California, Mexico, also have likely killed fin whales. The frequency of entanglements is difficult to estimate because of limited observer coverage for relevant fisheries and because the offshore distribution of fin whales makes it unlikely that whale carcasses will strand on land.

Habitat Degradation: The principal concern regarding habitat degradation is the possible depletion of fin whale prey (small schooling fish) by commercial fishing. In addition, high-energy, low-frequency underwater sound transmissions for research and military purposes may disturb fin whales or interfere with their vocal communications.

Hunting: Until the mid-1970s fin whales were hunted intensively in the North Atlantic and North Pacific Oceans. Currently, populations occurring in U.S. waters are legally hunted only in Greenland for aboriginal subsistence use. Although commercial hunting is currently banned under the IWC moratorium on commercial whaling, that measure was adopted as a temporary measure that could be removed, thereby opening the possibility for a resumption of commercial harvesting by other nations at some point in the future. The government of Iceland, which withdrew from the IWC several years ago, has recently announced plans to take a small number of fin whales commercially despite IWC provisions against such takes.

Management Framework: NMFS is the lead federal agency responsible for managing activities affecting fin whales. Together with the Department of State, NMFS and other parts of NOAA develop scientific advice and U.S. positions for meetings of the IWC. No recovery team or other interagency management team has been established to oversee or undertake management activities specifically for fin whales. However, take reduction teams have been established to address the take of multiple large whale species, including fin whales, in the offshore drift gillnet fishery off California and in trap and gillnet fisheries along the Atlantic coast (NMFS 2006a,b).

Critical Habitat: None designated.

Recovery Plan: In 1998 NMFS contracted for the preparation of a draft recovery plan addressing both fin and sei whales. Although completed in 1998, the draft plan (Reeves et al. 1998) was never adopted formally by NMFS. In 2006 NMFS released a new draft fin whale recovery plan for public review and comment (NMFS 2006c). The immediate and ultimate goals of the new draft plan are to recover fin whale populations to the point where they can be downlisted to threatened and delisted from the list of endangered species. A two-tier system of criteria is proposed in the draft plan for making reclassification and delisting decisions. The first tier considers population status and trends and identifies the following standards:

- For reclassifying as threatened, the overall population in each ocean basin (1) must have remained stable or increased for at least 1.5 generations (26 years) or (2) must have satisfied a risk analysis standard of no more than a 1 percent chance of quasi-extinction in 100 years.
- For removing the species from the list, the overall population in each ocean basin (1) must have remained stable or increased for at least three generations (51 years) or (2) have less than a 10 percent probability of becoming endangered in 20 years.

The second tier describes standards relative to the five listing factors established by the ESA.

- *Destruction, modification, or curtailment of the species' habitat or range*: For downlisting, fishing interactions, vessel interactions, prey reduction, and effects of anthropogenic noise must have been assessed and needed management actions must have been initiated. For removal from the list, management actions must have been proven effective.
- *Overutilization for commercial, recreational, or educational purposes*: For downlisting, direct human kills must be managed on a sustainable basis by the IWC, and for removal from the list, those management actions must have been proven effective and consistent with MMPA standards for maintaining populations at OSP levels.
- *Disease or predation*: For both downlisting and removal from the list, assessments must have been undertaken showing that these factors are not appreciably affecting recovery.
- *Inadequacy of existing regulatory mechanisms*: For both downlisting and removal from the list, the IWC must be regulating directed take on a sustainable basis, and applicable authorities must be adequately regulating takes due to vessel collisions and fishery interactions.
- *Other natural or manmade factors*: For both downlisting and removal from the list, anthropogenic factors must have been investigated and determined not to be limiting recovery.

To meet these goals and criteria, the draft plan identifies eight actions. These involve tasks to (1) maintain an effective program of international whaling regulation, (2) determine population discreteness and structure, (3) develop and apply methods to estimate population size and monitor trends in abundance, (4) conduct risk analyses for whales in each ocean basin, (5) identify and protect habitat essential to recovery, (6) minimize human sources of injury and mortality, (7) determine and minimize detrimental effects of anthropogenic noise, and (8) develop a plan for monitoring the population after the species is removed from the list. Because the whales move across international borders, the draft plan stresses the importance of a multinational research and management approach.

Major Management Actions: With regard to fin whales, management by NMFS over the last several decades has focused principally on participation in the IWC. The IWC began managing commercial whaling for fin whales in 1969 in the North Pacific and in 1976 in the North Atlantic (Reeves et al. 1998). In 1976 it adopted a ban on hunting fin whales in the North Pacific, and in 1987 it did so for the North Atlantic. Since then, the only authorized take of fin whales likely to belong to a population that occurs in U.S. waters has been an annual quota of 10 whales for aboriginal subsistence hunters in Greenland. In recent years, however, the IWC has received proposals from some members to lift the commercial whaling moratorium. Although these have been rejected to date, regulated harvests of fin whales could resume at some point in the future.

Since the late 1990s the incidental take of fin whales in commercial fisheries (principally trap and gillnet fisheries) has been addressed through take reduction plans developed for multiple species of endangered large whales and through periodic section 7 consultations on fishery management plans. Take reduction plans covering fin whales and other large whales have been developed for trap and gillnet fisheries along the Atlantic coast and for drift gillnet fisheries along the U.S. Pacific coast. Because estimated take levels for fin whales have been below the calculated PBR levels, entanglement risks for fin whales generally have not been a central focus of protection measures. However, because fin whale habitats overlap those of other large whales and because fin whales can be entangled in the same gear types, fin whales are thought to benefit from mitigation measures designed largely with other whale species in mind.

Staff and Funding Levels: NMFS reported no funding specifically for fin whales between 2000 and 2004 in FWS surveys of expenditures for ESA listed species (FWS 2005d-f). According to NMFS budget documents, NMFS allocated $994,000 in FY2004 funding to the recovery of endangered large whales (Appendix E), an uncertain portion of which may have included research relative to fin whales. NMFS estimates that it devoted at least 0.9 FTE in staff effort on fin recovery work (0.6 by its regional offices and headquarters and 0.3 by its science centers) during 2005.[16]

Funding for fin whales reported by other federal agencies and states in FWS annual expenditure surveys (FWS 2003b–d, 2005d–f, 2006) ranged between $4,870 in 2000 to $205,900 in 2004 (Table 15, Appendices C.1–7). Most of this funding was reported by the U.S. Coast Guard for enforcement. For example, in 2003, the Coast Guard reported expenditures totaling $198,897.

Table 15. *Federal and state expenditures (in $ thousands) for the recovery of fin whales, 1998– 2004 (Source: FWS 2003b–d; 2005d–f; 2006)*

Fiscal Year	FWS	USGS	NMFS	USCG	Other Federal	Total Federal	State	Total State and Federal
1998	–	–	–	–	4	4	1	5
1999	–	–	–	9	4	13	0.3	13
2000	–	–	–	–	4	4	1	5
2001	–	–	–	–	22	22	2	24
2002	–	–	–	7	5	13	1	13
2003	–	–	–	199	6	205	1	206
2004	0.2	–	–	63	6	69	3	72

---

[16] P. Michael Payne, personal communication. 17 August 2005. Chief, Marine Mammals Division, Office of Protected Species, National Marine Fisheries Service, Silver Spring, MD 20910; John Bengtson, personal communication. 8 December 2006. National Marine Mammal Laboratory, National Marine Fisheries Service, Seattle, WA 98115.

The draft fin whale recovery plan (NMFS 2006d) projects future funding needs for implementing each of the eight major recovery actions identified above, but the plan does not break down those costs annually. As shown in Table 16, those funding needs were developed for each of the three ocean basins in which fin whales occur and totaled approximately $30.2 million over the next 20 years for all areas.

Table 16. *Projected funding needs ($ thousands) to implement the draft 2006 fin whale recovery plan (NMFS 2006d)*

Ocean Basin*	Action 1	Action 2	Action 3	Action 4	Action 5	Action 6	Action 7	Action 8	Total
N. Atlantic (2012)	301	267	2,150	100	225	1,625	787	75	5,530
N. Pacific (2012)	101	366	1,500	100	225	1,625	788	75	4,780
S. Ocean (2026)	523	667	18,000	200	500	–	–	–	23,140

* Years in parentheses are the earliest expected date for meeting recovery criteria.

Humpback Whale

Population Status: Humpback whales (*Megaptera novaeangliae*) occur in all the world oceans except the Arctic Ocean. All populations were severely depleted by commercial whaling in the 20th century (NMFS 1991b). Humpback whales were listed as endangered throughout their worldwide range under the ESCA in 1970, and that designation was carried forward under the ESA. In the North Pacific, an estimated 28,000 humpbacks were killed during the period of modern commercial whaling, including 2,000 off Oregon and Washington, 3,400 off California, and 2,800 off Baja California. By 1966 their numbers throughout the North Pacific were thought to have been reduced to as few as 1,000 to 1,200 whales. In the North Atlantic, between 14,000 and 18,000 humpback whales were killed. The IWC has classified all populations of humpback whales worldwide as protection stocks for which no commercial hunting is permitted.

Since the 1960s populations in both oceans have been recovering. The total number of humpback whales in the North Atlantic Ocean is currently estimated at 11,570 whales (NMFS 2006b) and more than 6,000 whales are estimated to occur in the North Pacific Ocean (NMFS 2006a). For purposes of preparing stock assessment reports under the MMPA (NMFS 2005a, 2006a,b), NMFS currently recognizes four populations that occur at least seasonally in U.S. waters: one in the North Atlantic (the Gulf of Maine population) and three in the North Pacific (the eastern North Pacific population, the central North Pacific population, and the western North Pacific population).

Gulf of Maine Population: Although almost all humpback whales in the North Atlantic share winter breeding grounds in the Caribbean, they appear to use at least six summer feeding grounds around the rim of the North Atlantic Ocean (NMFS 2006b). A high degree of site fidelity to individual feeding grounds apparently is ingrained in newborn calves as they follow their mothers to the feeding grounds. As a result, discrete groups or subpopulations of whales tend to use different feeding grounds. Humpback whales also occur seasonally in the spring in coastal waters between the Chesapeake Bay and Cape Hatteras. It is not clear if those individuals are part of the subpopulation that uses summer feeding grounds in the Gulf of Maine. The best abundance estimate for the Gulf of Maine subpopulation is 902 animals (NMFS 2006b). Gulf of Maine humpback whales are thought to be increasing at a rate consistent with the overall 3.2 percent annual rate of increase observed for humpback whales throughout the North Atlantic basin (Stevick et al. 2003).

The PBR level for the Gulf of Maine subpopulation is 1.3 (NMFS 2006b). Between 1999 and 2003 recorded fishery-related deaths and serious injures for humpback whales in the Gulf of Maine averaged at least 2.8 per year, exceeding the PBR level. About one-half of all humpback whales in the Gulf of Maine bear scars caused by entanglement in fishing gear, suggesting that the incidence of entanglement is far greater than mortality records indicate. In addition, six other human-related deaths and injuries were recorded between 1999 and 2003 off mid- and south Atlantic states although it is unclear whether those whales were part of the Gulf of Maine subpopulation. Among the documented humpback whale carcasses available for examination, human factors, principally collisions with ships, contributed to or caused death in nearly 60 percent of the cases (Wiley et al. 1995).

Eastern North Pacific Population: The eastern North Pacific population of humpback whales winters in calving grounds off Central America and Mexico and migrates to summer feeding grounds along the coast between California and southern British Columbia. The best estimate of abundance for the eastern North Pacific population is 1,391 animals (NMFS 2006a). The population appears to have been growing steadily, with the exception of a brief period in the late 1990s when it may have declined. The PBR level for this population is 4.6, but because the whales spend half their time outside U.S. waters, the PBR for U.S. waters is estimated at 2.3 whales per year. The total known mortality in recent years, including 1.2 whales per year from entanglement and 0.2 from ship strikes, is less than the PBR level (NMFS 2006a). Because the fishery-related takes off California exceed 10 percent of the PBR level, the fishery mortality and serious injury rate is not considered to be insignificant and approaching zero.

Central North Pacific Population: The central North Pacific population spends winter and spring off the Hawaiian Islands and migrates to feeding areas off northern British Columbia, southeast Alaska, and Prince William Sound west to the Bering Sea (NMFS 2005a). The best estimate of abundance is 4,005 whales based on surveys in Hawaii. As in the North Atlantic, humpback whales in the central North Pacific population appear to maintain a high degree of site fidelity to feeding areas. Minimum estimates of abundance for feeding stocks identified to date include 651 around Kodiak Island, 410 around the Shumagin Islands, 315 in Prince William Sound, 961 in southeast Alaska, and 850 to 1,000 in British Columbia (which may include some animals from southeast Alaska) (NMFS 2005a). The PBR level for the entire central North Pacific population is 12.9, including 3.0 for southeast Alaska and 9.9 for areas north of southeast Alaska (NMFS 2006a). Commercial fisheries are thought to cause at least 3.4 humpback whale deaths per year. Because this rate is more than 10 percent of the calculated PBR level, the incidental mortality and serious injury rate due to fishing is not considered insignificant or approaching zero. Although the population as a whole appears to be increasing, its rate of increase is uncertain.

<u>Western North Pacific Population</u>: Humpback whales in the western North Pacific population spend winter and spring off Japan and probably migrate to the Bering Sea and the Aleutian Islands to feed in summer (NMFS 2005a). Photo-identification studies from winter breeding areas have resulted in an abundance estimate of 394 whales. Because of limited study and overlap with feeding grounds of humpback whales from the central North Pacific population, there are no reliable estimates of abundance on feeding grounds. The PBR level is calculated to be 1.3, and the minimum annual mortality due to U.S. commercial fisheries is estimated as 0.5 whale (NMFS 2005a). Available information suggests that incidental mortality caused by fisheries off Japan and Korea averages at least 1.1 to 2.4 whales per year, which would make the total human-caused mortality exceed the PBR level.

Major Threats: Humpback whales are exposed to human activities more than most other great whales because they spend much of their time in coastal waters near human population centers (NMFS 1991b). Threats to humpback whales include entanglement and entrapment in fishing gear, collisions with vessels, competition for prey with commercial fishing, disturbance by whale-watching vessels, pollution from coastal development, and displacement and disturbance caused by noise and vessel traffic. Although the level of human-caused mortality and serious injury is unknown, current information indicates that these threats may be impeding, but not preventing, recovery of most populations in U.S. waters.

<u>Entanglement and Entrapment</u>: As described above, deaths and serious injuries as a result of fisheries currently exceed the calculated PBR level for humpback whales in the Gulf of Maine subpopulation, and possibly for the western North Pacific population. Data show that whales from the central North Pacific population frequently interact with fishing gear, but the level of serious injury and mortality appears to be below PBR. Entanglement of eastern North Pacific humpback whales in a drift gillnet fishery appears to have been significantly reduced by measures adopted under a take reduction plan requiring the use of pingers and buoy line extenders to increase the depth at which nets are set (NMFS 2006a). However, some entanglements also occur in unidentified fisheries.

<u>Prey Reduction</u>: Although humpback whales feed on small schooling fish such as herring and sardines that are targets for commercial fisheries in some areas, prey removal by fisheries does not appear to be limiting the recovery of humpback whale populations in U.S. waters.

<u>Vessel Collisions</u>: Injuries and deaths due to vessel strikes may be as or more common than those from entanglement. Between 1999 and 2003, 15 vessel-related deaths or injuries were documented for humpback whales along the Atlantic coast; six involved whales that were killed, eight involved cases with insufficient information to determine severity, and one was known to have caused a minor, non-lethal injury (NMFS 2006b). For the eastern North Pacific population, vessel-related deaths and injuries appear to be less frequent, averaging at least 0.2 per year between 1999 and 2003 (NMFS 2006a). At least seven vessel-related deaths and injuries were reported for the central North Pacific population between 1999 and 2001, resulting in a minimum estimate of 0.8 deaths and serious injuries per year in Alaska (NMFS 2006a). There has been a substantial increase in reports of vessel collisions in Hawaii since 2001, and such injuries and deaths will likely increase for this population in coming years. No information is available on collision records for the western North Pacific population.

<u>Whale-Watching</u>: In New England, southeast Alaska, California, and Hawaii, whale-watching activity has increased, raising concerns that disturbance from whale-watching vessels may cause humpback whales to abandon or reduce their use of preferred habitats, particularly preferred calving grounds in Hawaii (NMFS 2005e, NMFS 1991b). In southeast Alaska, noise and disturbance by increased numbers of large tour ships may have caused whales to reduce their use of feeding grounds in Glacier Bay during the 1980s (Baker and Herman 1989).

Management Framework: NMFS is the lead federal agency responsible for managing activities affecting humpback whales. Together with the Department of State, NMFS and other NOAA offices develop policies and coordinate scientific advice for meetings of the IWC. Humpback whales also receive focused attention from managers of several national marine sanctuaries, including designated sanctuaries off Massachusetts, California, and Hawaii, and from the National Park Service at Glacier Bay National Park and Monument in southeastern Alaska. Although a recovery plan was adopted for humpback whales in 1991, no recovery or implementation teams have been established for this species. Interactions with fishing gear are addressed by take reduction teams established by NMFS to recommend take reduction plans for large whale species, including humpback whales.

Critical Habitat: None designated.

Recovery Plan: NMFS adopted a recovery plan for humpback whales in 1991. The plan identifies three goals:

- A biological goal for building and maintaining populations to levels large enough to be resilient to chance events such as episodic changes in oceanographic conditions, epizootics, anthropogenic environmental catastrophes, or inbreeding;
- A numerical goal for achieving a population size consonant both with the biological goal and with continuing human use of the oceans. The long-term goal is to achieve population sizes equal to the historical environmental carrying capacity in U.S. waters; and
- A management goal for changing the classification of particular populations from endangered to threatened and removing them from the list of protected species.

As an interim goal, the plan sought to double the size of humpback whale populations in 20 years. Major identified objectives included (1) maintaining and enhancing habitat, (2) identifying and reducing direct human-related injury and mortality, (3) monitoring population parameters, and (4) improving coordination of recovery activities.

Major Management Actions: The IWC has prohibited commercial exploitation of humpback whales worldwide since 1966. However, an aboriginal subsistence quota of two humpback whales per year has been authorized by the IWC to the government of St. Vincent and The Grenadines in the Caribbean.

Since adopting a recovery plan for humpback whales, NMFS has supported the maintenance of whale photo-identification catalogues to assist in monitoring reproductive rates and other life history parameters. NMFS also has undertaken studies to estimate abundance and determine genetic relationships. Coordinated international research on humpback whales in the North Atlantic was conducted during 1992 and 1993 in an effort known as the Years of the North

Atlantic Humpback (Project YoNAH). A similar effort called Structure of Populations, Levels of Abundance and Status of Humpbacks (SPLASH) was initiated for the North Pacific in 2004; data collection is expected to be completed in 2006. The SPLASH program involves cooperative efforts by NMFS, the National Marine Sanctuaries Program, and various national and foreign research organizations to determine the population status, structure, and trends of humpback whales throughout the North Pacific Ocean basin.

Since 1986 NMFS has monitored fishery interactions through fishery reporting requirements, observer programs in several large pelagic fisheries off the Atlantic coast, and opportunistic sighting reports of entangled animals by aerial survey teams, Coast Guard patrols, and the public (NMFS 2006b). Based on information from these sources as well as stranding records, 11 serious injuries or deaths related to fisheries were identified in trap fisheries in the 1990s, and in 1997 the Service elevated the Gulf of Maine and mid-Atlantic lobster pot fishery from a category III fishery to a category I. Since 1998 entanglement of humpback whales in this fishery and East Coast gillnet fisheries has been addressed by the Atlantic Large Whale Take Reduction Team and the take reduction plan developed to reduce interactions in both types of fishing gear. Major features of that plan have included efforts to disentangle whales, require modification of fishing gear to reduce entanglement risks, and restrict fishing in key whale habitats. Although these efforts have focused primarily on reducing entanglement risks for North Atlantic right whales, the actions, particularly disentanglement efforts, also benefit humpback whales. Experience in disentangling humpback whales in the northeastern United States has led to similar efforts in Alaska, Hawaii, and California.

To address disturbance by whale-watching vessels, NMFS has developed recommended guidelines for whale-watching activities for several regions and promulgated regulations limiting the distances at which vessels can approach whales in waters off both Hawaii in 1995 (50 Fed. Reg. 3775) and Alaska in 2001 (66 Fed. Reg. 29502), and the National Park Service also has restricted vessel speeds and access to Glacier Bay in southeast Alaska to protect feeding humpback whales. The National Ocean Service also has implemented education and outreach efforts to protect humpback whales using national marine sanctuaries at Stellwagen Bank off eastern Massachusetts, the Channel Islands and Farallon Islands off California, and coastal waters around the main Hawaiian Islands. In response to increasing reports of collisions between humpback whales and vessels off Hawaii, managers of the Hawaiian Islands Humpback Whale National Marine Sanctuary have focused particular attention on advising vessel operators as to actions they can take to avoid hitting whales.

Staff and Funding Levels: Cost projections for recovery work during the first five years after the Humpback Whale Recovery Plan was adopted in 1991 were estimated to range from $2.69 to $8.14 million per year with a five-year total of $20.62 million (NMFS 1991b). Actual expenditures during that period are uncertain but are believed to have been much lower. Funding for work on humpback whales reported in annual FWS expenditure surveys (FWS 2003b–d, 2005d–f, 2006) indicate that NMFS funding levels between 2001 and 2004 ranged from $53,000 in Fiscal Year 2001 to $1.15 million in Fiscal Year 2003 (Table 17, Appendices C.1–7). Most funding in 2003 supported the SPLASH program. Recent NMFS budget documents indicate that NMFS received $994,000 in FY 2003 funding for the recovery of endangered large whales. The amount devoted specifically to humpback whales from this source is uncertain (Appendix E).

Table 17. Federal and state expenditures (in $ thousands) for the recovery of humpback whales, 1998–2004 (Source: FWS 2003b–d; 2005d–f; 2006)

Fiscal Year	FWS	USGS	NMFS	USCG	Other Federal	Total Federal	State	Total State and Federal
1998	–	–	240	–	80	320	41	361
1999	–	–	131	277	76	484	8	492
2000	–	–	53	349	154	556	11	567
2001	–	–	53	324	352	729	11	740
2002	–	–	150	280	449	879	11	890
2003	–	–	1,150	199	248	1,597	18	1,615
2004	–	–	–	416	243	659	7	666

NMFS estimates that it devoted at least 7.1 FTEs in staff effort on humpback whale recovery work (1.8 by its regional offices and headquarters and 5.3 by its science centers) during 2005.[17]

The Marine Mammal Commission's survey of federally funded marine mammal research (Waring 2002) reports that between FY1991 and FY2000 funding for research on humpback whales ranged from $107,000 in FY1991 to $673,000 in FY1994 (see Appendix F). In 2000, the most recent year reported, federal research funding was $342,000. The principal sources of funding were NMFS and the Department of Defense's Strategic Environmental Research and Development Program. Recently funding has increased above those levels as a result of support from various agencies for the SPLASH program.

North Atlantic Right Whale

Population Status: All species and populations of right whales worldwide were severely depleted by centuries of commercial whaling that continued into the early 1900s. The IWC has classified all right whale populations as protection stocks. In 1970, when right whales were initially listed as endangered under the ESCA, right whales in the North Atlantic and North Pacific Oceans were considered to be separate populations of a single species called the northern right whale. That designation was carried forward under the ESA. Recent genetic analyses, however, indicate that North Atlantic and North Pacific right whales are separate species (*Eubalaena glacialis* and *E. japonica*, respectively). Based on that information, NMFS is taking steps to reclassify them separately under the ESA. In the North Atlantic, the only remaining population considered viable inhabits the western North Atlantic Ocean off the coasts of the United States and Canada. A population that occurred off Europe has been all but eliminated by commercial whaling. The North Atlantic species currently is estimated to number at least 299 animals; its PBR level is set at zero (NMFS 2006b).

The western North Atlantic population has shown little evidence of increasing since research efforts began in the early 1980s. Modeling studies suggest that the population began to decline at

---

[17] P. Michael Payne, personal communication. 17 August 2005. Chief, Marine Mammals Division, Office of Protected Species, National Marine Fisheries Service, Silver Spring, MD 20910; John Bengtson, personal communication. 8 December 2006. National Marine Mammal Laboratory, National Marine Fisheries Service, Seattle, WA 98115.

about 2 percent per year in the early to mid-1990s (Caswell et al. 1999). The current recovery plan, adopted in 2005, concludes that the possibility of biological extinction within the next century "is very real" (NMFS 2005b). A series of five consecutive years (2001–2005) in which documented calf counts have averaged more than 20 per year, however, has been an encouraging prospect for future recovery.

Major Threats: Deaths due to collisions with ships and entanglement in fishing gear are the principal reasons for the species' failure to recover since the cessation of commercial hunting (MMC 1990, Kraus et al. 2005, NMFS 2005b). Most deaths due to ship collisions are caused by large vessels (Laist et al. 2001). Most entanglements appear to involve lines from actively fished lobster traps and gillnets (NMFS 2005b). Between 1990 and 2005 more than 50 percent of all documented right whale deaths were caused by ship collisions (18 deaths) or entanglements (5 deaths) (MMC 2006). Additional deaths undoubtedly occurred but were not recorded. A recent study concluded that only 17 percent of all deaths are observed (Kraus et al. 2005). Between 2000 and the end of 2005, 25 live right whales were observed entangled in fishing gear, 2 of which were later found dead and 7 of which were in poor condition when last sighted (MMC 2006). For the period 1999–2003 NMFS estimates that human-caused mortality averaged 2.6 deaths per year in U.S. and Canadian waters (NMFS 2006b), including one vessel-related death per year and 1.6 entanglement-related deaths per year.

Other threats to North Atlantic right whales identified in the revised recovery plan include habitat degradation, noise, contaminants, underwater explosives, climate and ecosystem change, and commercial exploitation (NMFS 2005b).

Management Framework: Before the 1980s management of right whales worldwide was principally through the IWC, the international organization responsible for the regulation of whaling. Under the International Convention for the Regulation of Whaling, the management authority that eventually led to the formation of the IWC in 1946, commercial hunting for right whales has been banned worldwide since the 1930s. A dedicated research program on western North Atlantic right whales was not begun until the early 1980s when a small remnant population was discovered off the U.S. East Coast. Dedicated management efforts were not initiated until 1987 when, at the recommendation of the Marine Mammal Commission, NMFS convened a recovery team to develop a draft recovery plan. A final plan was adopted in 1991. The team was then disbanded, and NMFS established two regional recovery plan implementation teams: one for summer feeding areas off the northeastern United States and the other off the southeastern United States where whales calve in winter. The teams, composed of federal, state, and non-governmental representatives, are charged with helping the Service implement recovery actions. The southeastern team continues to meet, but the northeastern team does not.

In 1997 NMFS established the Atlantic Large Whale Take Reduction Team to provide advice on measures to reduce entanglement risks in fishing gear. NMFS also is assisted by the Right Whale Consortium, an organization of non-governmental marine mammal scientists working at various universities and research institutes. The consortium and its members conduct much of the right whale research and monitoring work, manage a right whale photo-identification catalogue and associated data, convene annual reviews of research findings, participate on various management teams, and carry out most disentanglement work with funding from NMFS. Several state agencies also assist in recovery work with supplemental funding provided by appropriations under the ESA. The U.S. Coast Guard carries out fisheries enforcement, vessel management, and other recovery activities in cooperation with NMFS. NMFS also cooperates with Canada's Department of Fisheries and Oceans on related recovery activities.

Critical Habitat: Early studies of right whales identified five seasonal high-use right whale habitats, three of which are in U.S. waters (Kraus and Kenny 1991). These are—

- coastal Florida and Georgia used as a calving ground in winter;
- Cape Cod Bay used as a feeding ground in late winter and early spring;
- the Great South Channel east of Cape Cod, Massachusetts, used as a feeding ground in spring and early summer;
- the Bay of Fundy between New Brunswick and Nova Scotia, Canada, used as a feeding ground in summer and early fall; and
- the Scotian Shelf, including Browns and Baccaro Banks, Roseway Basin, southeast of Nova Scotia, used as a feeding ground principally in the fall.

In 1994 NMFS designated the three areas in U.S. waters as critical habitat for northern right whales. In July 2002 the Ocean Conservancy petitioned NMFS to expand the designated critical habitats based on regular sightings of right whales in adjacent waters. NMFS found that the petition included information warranting consideration, but in August 2003 it concluded that the petition did not provide all the information necessary to justify such an action. It therefore deferred action to revise the boundaries, pending analyses of sighting data. No further action has been taken. Canada's Department of Fisheries and Oceans has designated the two areas in Canada as whale conservation areas.

Recovery Plan: The Service adopted an initial recovery plan for right whales in both the North Atlantic and North Pacific in 1991. In 2005 a revised recovery plan for North Atlantic right whales was adopted (NMFS 2005b). The ultimate goal of the revised plan is to promote recovery of North Atlantic right whales to a level sufficient to warrant their removal from the list of endangered and threatened species. Its interim goal is to achieve a population level that would allow the species to be reclassified as threatened. The plan identifies the following criteria for reclassifying the western Atlantic population as threatened:

- The population ecology (range, distribution, age structure, and gender ratios, etc.) and vital rates (age-specific survival, age-specific reproduction, and lifetime reproductive success) of right whales are indicative of an increasing population;
- The population has increased for a period of 35 years at an average rate of increase equal to or greater than 2 percent per year;
- None of the known threats to northern right whales (summarized in the five listing factors) is known to limit the population's growth rate; and
- Given current and projected threats and environmental conditions, the right whale population has no more than a 1 percent chance of quasi-extinction in 100 years.

The recovery plan does not include criteria for delisting because of the very low abundance and the need for decades of population growth to reach abundance levels at which the species could be considered for delisting.

To achieve its goals, the revised recovery plan identifies five objectives: (1) significantly reduce human-caused mortality, injury, and disturbance; (2) develop demographically based recovery criteria; (3) identify, characterize, protect, and monitor important habitats; (4) monitor the status and trends of the population; and (5) coordinate federal, state, international, and non-governmental recovery actions.

Highest priority under the plan is placed on actions to reduce entanglement in fishing gear and ship collisions.

Major Management Actions: To reduce entanglement, NMFS has relied principally on efforts to (1) develop and require the use of fishing gear thought to be less likely to ensnare whales and (2) disentangle whales that are observed entangled. To develop fishery management strategies, NMFS relies on advice from the Atlantic Large Whale Take Reduction Team. The team, composed of representatives from involved fisheries, state and regional fishery management agencies, conservation groups, federal agencies, and academic organizations, considers entanglement risks for several endangered whale species but focuses almost entirely on North Atlantic right whales. In 1997 NMFS adopted an Atlantic Large Whale Take Reduction Plan. Its goal was to reduce the mortality and serious injury of right whales to below its PBR level, which, because of the species' depleted status, has been set at zero. Measures adopted to meet this goal include (1) actions to disentangle whales found entangled, (2) requirements for modifying gear thought by the Service to reduce whale entanglement risks throughout certain fisheries, (3) seasonal management areas where additional gear modifications are required, and (4) seasonal time/area closures in areas where right whales aggregate seasonally.

Reducing right whale entanglements has proven to be one of the most difficult and controversial challenges of any endangered marine mammal recovery program. Since 1997 the take reduction plan has undergone a series of major and minor modifications, none of which has resulted in meeting required goals. Measures implemented in 1997 resulted in no observable reductions in right whale entanglements, and in 2001 NMFS initiated formal consultations pursuant to section 7 of the ESA on its own fishery management plans for four lobster and gillnet fisheries along the U.S. East Coast. The consultations concluded that the plans were jeopardizing the continued existence of North Atlantic right whales and identified reasonable and prudent alternatives. Those alternatives included new gear modification requirements, development of a dynamic area management process to temporarily close or manage fishing in areas where right whales aggregate to feed, and development of new seasonal management areas. In consultation with the Atlantic Large Whale Take Reduction Team, such measures were implemented late in 2001. They, too, yielded no observable reduction in right whale entanglement. After the take of a whale in gear previously considered safe, NMFS reconvened the take reduction team in 2003 to develop another major revision of the take reduction plan. Reinitiation of consultations on relevant fishery management plans has not been undertaken as of this writing, and implementation of new measures is not expected until 2007.

Efforts to reduce ship collisions have relied on voluntary actions by vessel operators to avoid hitting whales. Major actions identified in the recovery plan include developing educational materials to advise mariners as to how to identify and avoid hitting right whales, implementing mandatory ship reporting systems in key habitats to advise mariners of collision risks and encourage voluntary efforts, conducting aerial surveys in key habitats to locate whales and advise mariners of their location, and developing a ship strike reduction strategy with speed and routing requirements (NMFS 2005). Efforts to develop the latter have been ongoing since the late 1990s but have not yet been completed. NMFS requested comments on its strategy in 2004 (70 Fed. Reg. 36121), and in 2006 it completed a draft environmental impact statement evaluating alternative speed and routing restrictions. Accompanying that statement, NMFS proposed regulations (71 Fed Reg. 36299) to seasonally limit vessel speeds to 10 knots within 30 nmi of major East Coast ports and to impose temporary speed restrictions around large aggregations of right whales wherever they are detected. Final rules are expected in 2007. NMFS also has conducted formal consultations with the Navy and the Coast Guard under section 7 of the ESA on the operation of their vessels in areas where right whales are likely to occur. The consultations recommended that crews of Coast Guard and Navy vessels watch out for right whales and reduce speeds to levels they determine appropriate in key right whale habitats.

Staff and Funding Levels: The Marine Mammal Commission survey of federally funded marine mammal research (Waring 2002) reports that funding for northern right whale biological and population assessment by all federal agencies increased from $641,000 in FY1991 to $3.1 million in FY2000 (Appendix F). Research funding by NMFS grew from $194,000 to $1.8 million during that period. The next largest source of funding was the Navy whose funding declined from $970,000 in FY1997 to $611,000 in FY2000.

Between 1998 and 2004 funding for North Atlantic right whale conservation increased steadily. Since then it has declined substantially. According to annual FWS expenditure reports for work on endangered species (FWS 2003b–d, 2005d–f, 2006), appropriated funding for NMFS right whale conservation activities increased from $1.5 million in 1998 to $5.2 million in 2001 and $11.2 million in 2004 (Table 18, Appendices C.1–7). Although most federal funding appropriated specifically for right whales has been allocated to NMFS, Coast Guard expenditures for enforcement and assistance in disentanglement efforts grew to $4.4 million in 2004. NMFS budget documents indicate that allocations for right whale research and recovery activities declined in 2005 (Appendix E). NMFS estimates that it devoted 29.2 FTEs to North Atlantic right whale conservation working during 2005, including 20.5 in New England, 5.5 in the southeastern United States, and 2.25 at headquarters.[18]

In 2002 the National Fish and Wildlife Foundation established a National Whale Conservation Fund recommended by the Marine Mammal Commission and subsequently mandated by Congress. The foundation is a not-for-profit organization established by Congress in 1984 to help secure non-governmental donations for wildlife conservation work. Since 2002 NMFS has partnered with the foundation to coordinate various grant programs through the fund. The foundation has funded more than 20 gear research projects related to right whale conservation at levels ranging from about $4,000 to $20,000. It also supported related state agency conservation initiatives in Massachusetts, New York, New Jersey, Maryland, North Carolina, South Carolina, Georgia, and Florida at levels ranging from about $50,000 to $500,000 per year.

---

[18] P. Michael Payne, personal communication. 17 August 2005. Chief, Marine Mammals Division, Office of Protected Species, National Marine Fisheries Service, Silver Spring, MD 20910.

Table 18. *Federal and state expenditures (in $ thousands) for the recovery of northern right whales, 1998–2004 (Source: FWS 2003b–d; 2005d–f; 2006)*

Fiscal Year	FWS	USGS	NMFS	USCG	Other Federal	Total Federal	State	Total State and Federal
1998	2	–	1,100	–	357	1,458	1	1,460
1999	–	–	1,542	892	549	2,983	290	3,273
2000	–	–	4,168	433	143	4,744	127	4,872
2001	–	–	5,270	474	147	5,891	145	6,036
2002	–	–	7,120	857	136	8,113	280	8,393
2003	–	–	10,270	1,098	312	11,679	123	11,802
2004	0.2	–	11,225	444	197	11,866	504	12,370

As shown in Table 19, the 2005 revision of the North Atlantic right whale recovery plan projects estimated annual recovery program costs for the first five years of recovery work under the plan (including activities ranked from priority 1 through 3) to be between $7.69 and $9.96 million (NMFS 2005b).

Table 19. *Projected funding needs (in $ thousands) to implement recovery activities for North Atlantic right whales during the first five years after adoption of the 2005 North Atlantic Right Whale Recovery Plan (* = staff time only)*

Action	Year 1	Year 2	Year 3	Year 4	Year 5	Total
1. Significantly reduce sources of human-caused death, injury, and disturbance	6,060	6,250	5,505	4,675	4,565	27,045
2. Develop demographically based recovery criteria	*	*	0	0	0	0
3. Identify, characterize, protect, and monitor important right whale habitats	735	865	880	770	585	3,845
4. Monitor the status and trends of abundance and distribution of the western North Atlantic right whale	2,365	2,645	2,630	2,360	2,235	12,235
5. Coordinate federal, state, international, and private efforts to implement the recovery plan	180	200	250	250	300	1,180
TOTAL	9,330	9,960	9,265	8,055	7,695	44,305

North Pacific Right Whale

The northern right whale was listed as endangered throughout its range under the ESCA in 1970. That designation was carried forward under the ESA. At the time of those listing actions, right whales in both the North Pacific and North Atlantic Oceans were considered to be part of same species. Recent genetic analyses, however, indicate that North Pacific right whales are a separate species (*Eubalaena japonica*), and NMFS is taking steps to reclassify them as such under the ESA. Historical whaling records suggest there are two North Pacific populations—one in the eastern North Pacific Ocean in U.S. waters and one in the western North Pacific Ocean off Russia. Commercial whaling in the late 1800s and early 1900s drastically reduced both populations, and the IWC has classified North Pacific right whales as a protection stock. In its 1991 recovery plan for northern right whales, NMFS suggested that the pre-exploitation abundance of right whales throughout the North Pacific might have exceeded 11,000 animals, and that its abundance in 1991 probably ranged from 100 to 500 (NMFS 1991).

Between the 1960s and mid-1990s the eastern North Pacific population was known only from a few sightings of individuals and pairs scattered between Mexico, Hawaii, and Alaska. In the summer of 1996 four right whales were sighted in the southeastern Bering Sea. Since then, sightings of a few individuals have been reported annually in the same area. Photo-identification and biopsy studies between 1996 and 2004 indicate that there are at least 23 individual right whales in the population, including three cow-calf pairs. The surviving population may number only a few tens of animals, making it one of the world's most endangered mammal populations (MMC 2005). In its 2003 stock assessment report, NMFS reported that it was unable to provide a reliable estimate of abundance. As a result, a PBR level for the population has not been calculated (NMFS 2005a).

Major Threats: The 1991 recovery plan identified vessel interactions, entrapment and entanglement in fishing gear, habitat degradation, and hunting as potential threats, but almost no information was available on the level of those threats (NMFS 1991a). The low abundance and scattered distribution of eastern North Pacific right whales confound assessments of the scale of current threats (NMFS 2005a).

Management Framework: The Northern Right Whale Recovery Team convened by NMFS in 1987 considered management needs for North Pacific right whales in developing the draft Northern Right Whale Recovery Plan (NMFS 1991a). However, the team was not reconvened after the plan was adopted, and no regional team has been established specifically for North Pacific right whales.

Critical Habitat: In February 2002 NMFS rejected a petition by the Center for Biological Diversity to designate most of the eastern Bering Sea as right whale critical habitat (MMC 2004). NMFS based its decision on a conclusion that essential features of critical habitat could not be identified, given available information. It therefore advised that it would continue to analyze the situation (68 Fed. Reg. 51758). In June 2005 in response to a lawsuit filed by the Center for Biological Diversity in 2004, a federal court in San Francisco found the NMFS decision not to designate critical habitat to be arbitrary and capricious, and it directed the Service to proceed with a critical habitat proposal. In late July 2006, NMFS published final rules to designating critical habitat in an area of about 36,000 sq mi in the southeastern Bering Sea and a small area south of Kodiak Island in the Gulf of Alaska (71 Fed Reg. 38277).

Recovery Plan: The 1991 recovery plan for northern right whales included a separate, although brief section on North Pacific right whales (NMFS 1991a). The plan noted that the lack of information on where North Pacific right whales occur precluded the identification of site-specific research and management actions. Upon identification of such areas, the recovery plan recommended that the following objectives be pursued:

- Initiate studies to determine the population size and monitor trends in abundance of the North Pacific right whale;
- Identify and protect habitats essential to the survival and recovery of North Pacific right whales;
- Collect and analyze information on the areas and seasons where potential conflicts exist between vessel traffic and North Pacific right whales and the types of vessels involved;
- Vigorously enforce whale protection laws;
- Continue the international ban on hunting and other directed lethal take;
- Reduce and eliminate injury and mortality caused by fisheries and fishing gear; and
- Maximize efforts to acquire scientific information from dead or stranded North Pacific right whales.

Although NMFS has published a revised recovery plan for North Atlantic right whales (NMFS 2005), it has not done so for North Pacific right whales.

Major Management Actions: Other than efforts to designate critical habitat, no management actions have been taken for North Pacific right whales. As indicated above, since 1996 NMFS has supported studies annually to better identify the number and distribution of right whales feeding in the southeastern Bering Sea in summer.

Staff and Funding Levels: Prior to the mid-1990s, no staff or funding was devoted specifically to North Pacific right whales by NMFS. Funding specifically for North Pacific right whales is not reported in the Fish and Wildlife Service's summary of federal expenditures on endangered species between 1998 and 2004 (FWS 2003b–d, 2005d–f). Based on information provided to the Marine Mammal Commission during its recent annual meetings, however, NMFS has provided between $100,000 and $200,000 per year since 1996 for various studies, including aerial and shipboard surveys, acoustic detection studies, satellite telemetry, and genetic sampling of right whales in Alaska. The Coast Guard has contributed ship time for studies, but its costs for doing so are unknown. NMFS estimates that it devoted at least 3.4 FTEs in staff effort on North Pacific right whale recovery work (0.6 by its regional offices and headquarters and 2.8 by its science centers) during 2005.[19]

Sei Whale

Population Status: Sei whales (*Balaenoptera borealis*) were hunted commercially in the early to mid-1900s. The species as a whole was listed as endangered throughout its worldwide range under the ESCA in 1970, and that designation was carried forward under the ESA. The IWC classifies the Nova Scotia population of sei whales and all populations in the North Atlantic as protection stocks for which all commercial catch limits are set at zero. Sei whales in the eastern

---

[19] P. Michael Payne, personal communication. 17 August 2005. Chief, Marine Mammals Division, Office of Protected Species, National Marine Fisheries Service, Silver Spring, MD 20910; John Bengtson, personal communication. 8 December 2006. National Marine Mammal Laboratory, National Marine Fisheries Service, Seattle, WA 98115.

North Pacific are also classified as protection stocks. Although the population structure of sei whales is not well understood, NMFS recognizes three populations in U.S. waters, based largely on historical whaling records: a Nova Scotia population in the western North Atlantic, an eastern North Pacific population, and a Hawaii population.

Nova Scotia Population: The distribution of the Nova Scotia population is centered in Canadian waters, but in spring and summer a portion of the population moves south to feed in U.S. waters of the Gulf of Maine and Georges Bank (NMFS 2006b). Generally, those whales remain offshore along the edge of the continental shelf, but occasionally they enter shallower waters, presumably in search of prey when food in offshore waters is insufficient. In 1977 the sei whale population in Canadian waters was estimated at 1,393 to 2,248 animals. Based on aerial surveys in the late 1970s and early 1980s, sei whale abundance between Cape Hatteras and Nova Scotia was estimated to be 280 whales. There are no more recent estimates, and information is insufficient to determine current population size, population trends, or the PBR level (NMFS 2006b).

Eastern North Pacific Population: The IWC recognizes one population of sei whales in the North Pacific (NMFS 2006a). In its stock assessment reports, however, NMFS considers whales off the Pacific coast of North America to be a distinct population separate from the population that occurs throughout the rest of the North Pacific. Commercial whaling in the North Pacific reduced sei whale abundance from an estimated pre-exploitation level of 42,000 whales to between 7,260 and 12,620 whales in 1974. Between 1947 and 1987 commercial whalers took 61,500 sei whales in the North Pacific, of which 410 were taken off central California. Shipboard surveys in 1996 and 2001 yielded an estimated abundance of 56 whales off California, Oregon, and Washington. Based on that estimate, NMFS calculates a PBR of 0.1.

Hawaiian Population: Although information on the population structure of sei whales in the North Pacific is insufficient to identify individual stocks with confidence, NMFS recently decided to prepare a separate stock assessment for sei whales in Hawaiian waters to avoid the risk of assuming them to be part of a single panmictic stock. Based on vessel surveys in 2002, the abundance of sei whales in U.S. waters around Hawaii was estimated to be 77 whales, with a PBR of 0.1.

Major Threats: Vessel collisions and entanglement in fishing gear are potential threats to sei whales. Off the northeastern U.S. coast, a few recent collision-related sei whale deaths have been recorded (Laist et al. 2001, NMFS 2006b). There were no documented deaths due to entanglement in fishing gear. No recent sei whale deaths or serious injuries have been recorded in the eastern North Pacific or Hawaiian waters from collisions or entanglement (NMFS 2006a).

Management Framework: NMFS has not established a recovery team or other management team for sei whales. The agency has limited its management actions to efforts to control commercial whaling through the IWC and the development of take reduction plans for large whale species along the U.S. Atlantic and Pacific coasts.

Critical Habitat: None designated.

Recovery Plan: Although a draft recovery plan for fin and sei whales was completed in 1998 (Reeves et al. 1998), it was not adopted (see fin whales above).

Major Management Actions: The IWC did not begin regulating commercial hunting for sei whales until 1970 (Reeves et al. 1998). Commercial hunting for the species was prohibited in the North Pacific in 1976 but continued in the North Atlantic until 1986 when the IWC's moratorium on all commercial whaling went into effect. Other than addressing the impact of commercial whaling through the IWC, NMFS management actions regarding sei whales have been limited largely to conducting section 7 consultations and the development and implementation of take reduction plans that apply to large whales in general.

Staff and Funding Levels: According to FWS annual expenditure reports (FWS 2003b–d, 2005d–f, 2006), funding for work on sei whales between 1998 and 2004 ranged from $3,600 in 2000 to $202,900 in 2003 (Table 20, Appendices C.1–7). Most reported expenditures have been by the U.S. Coast Guard for enforcement and reflect an apportionment of expenditures for ship time to enforce rules generally applicable to large whales. According to budget documents, NMFS allocated $994,000 in FY2003 for the recovery of endangered large whales (e.g., blue, bowhead, fin, sei, sperm, and North Pacific right whales, Appendix E). It is not clear how much, if any, of that funding was dedicated to sei whales. NMFS estimates that it devoted at least 0.2 FTE in staff effort on sei whale recovery work (all by its regional offices) during 2005.[20]

Table 20. Federal and state expenditures (in $ thousands) for the recovery of sei whales, 1998–2004 (Source: FWS 2003b–d; 2005d–f; 2006)

Fiscal Year	FWS	USGS	NMFS	USCG	Other Federal	Total Federal	State	Total State and Federal
1998	–	–	–	–	4	4	1	5
1999	–	–	–	–	4	4	–	4
2000	–	–	–	–	4	4	–	4
2001	–	–	–	–	12	12	–	12
2002	–	–	–	–	1	1	–	1
2003	–	–	–	199	4	203	–	203
2004	–	–	–	60	6	66	–	66

Sperm Whale

Population Status: Sperm whales (*Physeter macrocephalus*) were drastically reduced in numbers worldwide by commercial whaling in the 1800s and early 1900s. The species as a whole was listed as endangered throughout its range under the ESCA in 1970, and that designation was carried forward under the ESA. The IWC has classified sperm whales worldwide as protection stocks for which commercial catch limits have been set at zero. Information on the population structure of the species is limited. The IWC currently considers sperm whales in the North Atlantic to be single population and those in the North Pacific to be

---

[20] P. Michael Payne, personal communication. 17 August 2005. Chief, Marine Mammals Division, Office of Protected Species, National Marine Fisheries Service, Silver Spring, MD 20910.

divided into eastern and western populations. Abundance of sperm whales in the North Atlantic is unknown. For the eastern North Pacific Ocean, estimates include 22,700 whales for tropical latitudes and 24,000 (based on visual sightings) and 39,200 (based on visual sightings and acoustic data) for eastern temperate latitudes, although it is unclear whether whales from this area enter U.S. waters (Barlow and Taylor 1998). In contrast to the IWC, NMFS currently recognizes five sperm whale population stocks in U.S. waters for purposes of preparing stock assessment reports: a North Atlantic population, a northern Gulf of Mexico population, a California/Oregon/Washington population, a Hawaii population, and a North Pacific population.

North Atlantic Population: Sperm whales that occur off the U.S. Atlantic coast are likely part of a larger population (NMFS 2006b). Based on surveys carried out in 2004, the best available estimate of abundance for sperm whales in U.S. waters off the East Coast is 4,804 whales. The PBR level is 7. Data are insufficient to determine population structure or trends.

Northern Gulf of Mexico Population: Based on strandings, sightings, and historic whaling catches, sperm whales in the northern Gulf of Mexico are currently considered a distinct population for management purposes (NMFS 2006b). Pooled data from surveys conducted in 1996–2001 yield a best estimate of abundance of 1,349 whales in the northern Gulf of Mexico, and a PBR level of 2.2. Data are insufficient to determine population trends.

California/Oregon/Washington Population: Recent genetic analyses of sperm whales in the eastern North Pacific suggest that the whales along the California coast differ markedly from those sampled farther offshore (NMFS 2006a). Although there appear to be large numbers of sperm whales west and south of the U.S. Exclusive Economic Zone off the West Coast, it is not clear whether those whales enter U.S waters. The best available abundance estimate, which is derived from surveys in 1996 and 2001, is 1,233 sperm whales off California, Oregon, and Washington. The PBR level is 1.8. Data are insufficient to determine population trends.

Hawaii Population: Hawaii was the center of a sperm whale fishery in the 19th century (NMFS 2006a). Strandings and sound recordings document the continued presence of sperm whales in these waters. Preliminary results of genetic studies suggest a significant difference between whales sampled off the U.S. mainland coast and those off Hawaii (NMFS 2006a). Based on a shipboard survey in 2002, the abundance of sperm whales in the U.S. Exclusive Economic Zone around the Hawaiian archipelago is 7,082 whales resulting a PBR of 11. Information is insufficient to determine population trends.

North Pacific Population: The range of the North Pacific sperm whale population considered in NMFS stock assessment reports extends from British Columbia, Canada, through Alaska, west to Russia. Current information is not sufficient to estimate its abundance, trend, or PBR level (NMFS 2005a).

Major Threats: Sperm whales were hunted with varying degrees of intensity until the moratorium on commercial whaling went into effect in 1986–1987. Between 1800 and 1987 commercial whalers took at least 436,000 sperm whales worldwide (NMFS 2006a). The actual take may have been as high as one million. Although commercial harvests are currently banned worldwide under the IWC's moratorium on commercial whaling, the moratorium was adopted as a temporary measure and may be removed in the future, thereby raising the possibility of resumption in commercial hunting of sperm whales. Because of their offshore distribution, sperm whales have less exposure to many types of human impact than do some coastal species, but they are still vulnerable to entanglement in fishing gear, collisions with ships, chemical contaminants, and noise pollution (NMFS 2002b).

Entanglement and Entrapment in Fishing Gear: Although sperm whales are known to become entangled in gillnets and longlines, the frequency of such events appears to be very low. In recent years, there has been no evidence of entanglements for the northern Gulf of Mexico and Hawaii populations. In the North Atlantic, three sperm whale entanglements were documented between 1993 and 1998, but since then only one entanglement has been documented, suggesting a minimum annual rate of mortality and serious injury of 0.2 (NMFS 2006b). Along the Pacific coast, an average of one sperm whale per year was killed or seriously injured in offshore drift gillnets between 1997 and 2001 (NMFS 2006a). For waters off Alaska, the incidental mortality and serious injury rate based on known reports is 0.4 whale per year. These rates are less than 10 percent of calculated PBR levels and are considered insignificant and approaching zero.

Ship Strikes: Although there have been several reports of ship strikes involving sperm whales in areas such as the Canary Islands and parts of the Mediterranean Sea (Laist et al. 2001, NMFS 2002b), fewer than five collisions have been recorded between sperm whales and ships in U.S. waters (Jenson and Silber 2003). Highest risks appear to occur when sperm whales use habitats close to land where ship traffic is greater.

Contaminants: In some areas, high contaminant loads have been found in sperm whales (Ferber 2005). In the North Atlantic, levels of mercury and PCBs were low in sperm whales sampled, but cadmium levels were high (NMFS 2006b). Whether or how such contaminant levels affect sperm whales is not known.

Noise: Noise associated with oil and gas activities (particularly seismic surveys and drilling), military activities (particularly sonars used to detect submarines), and routine ship traffic may affect sperm whales (Mate et al. 1994). Such effects have been of particular concern in the Gulf of Mexico because of the extent of seismic surveys to locate and delineate oil and gas reserves.

Management Framework: NMFS is the lead federal agency responsible for managing sperm whales. Together with the Department of State, NMFS and other offices in NOAA develop and coordinate scientific advice and U.S. positions for meetings of the IWC. NMFS and the Minerals Management Service share responsibility for ensuring that noise and other possible impacts associated with offshore oil and gas exploration and development do not adversely affect sperm whales. No recovery team or other interagency management team has been established to oversee or assist management activities specifically related to sperm whales. However, sperm whales have been considered in some take reduction plans developed for large whales taken incidentally in commercial fisheries.

Critical Habitat: None designated.

Recovery Plan: A draft recovery plan for sperm whales was circulated for public comment early in the summer of 2006 (NMFS 2006d). The immediate and ultimate goals of the draft plan are to recover sperm whale populations to the point where they can be downlisted to threatened and delisted from the list of endangered species. A two-tier system of criteria is included in the draft plan for reclassification and delisting purposes. The first tier addresses population benchmarks and identifies the following standards:

- For reclassifying as threatened, the overall population in each ocean basin (1) must have remained stable or increased for at least 1.5 generations (26 years) or (2) must have satisfied a risk analysis standard of no more than a 1 percent chance of quasi-extinction in 100 years.
- For removing the species from the list, the overall population in each ocean basin (1) must have remained stable or increased for at least 3 generations (51 years) or (2) have less than a 10 percent probability of becoming endangered in 20 years.

The second tier describes standards relative to the five listing factors established by the ESA.

- *Destruction, modification, or curtailment of the species' habitat or range*: For downlisting, fishing interactions, vessel interactions, prey reduction, and effects of anthropogenic noise must have been assessed and needed management actions must have been initiated. For removal from the list, management actions must have been proven effective.
- *Overutilization for commercial, recreational, or educational purposes*: For downlisting, direct human kills must be managed on a sustainable basis by the IWC, and for removal from the list, those management actions must have been proven effective and consistent with MMPA standards for maintaining populations at OSP levels.
- *Disease or predation*: For both downlisting and removal from the list, assessments must have been undertaken showing that these factors are not appreciably affecting recovery.
- *Inadequacy of existing regulatory mechanisms*: For both downlisting and removal from the list, the IWC must be regulating directed take on a sustainable basis, and applicable authorities must be adequately regulating takes due to vessel collisions and fishery interactions.
- *Other natural or manmade factors*: For both downlisting and removal from the list, anthropogenic factors must have been investigated and determined not to be limiting recovery.

To meet these goals and criteria, the draft plan identifies nine objectives: (1) coordinate state, federal, and international recovery actions, (2) determine population discreteness and structure, (3) develop and apply methods to estimate population size and monitor trends in abundance, (4) conduct risk analyses for whales in each ocean basin, (5) identify and protect habitat essential to recovery, (6) identify and minimize human sources of injury and mortality, (7) determine and minimize detrimental effects of anthropogenic noise, (8) maximize efforts to acquire scientific information from dead, stranded, and entangled whales, and (9) develop a plan for monitoring the population after the species is removed from the list. Because sperm whales move across international borders, the draft plan stresses the importance of a multinational research and management approach.

Major Management Actions: A ban on pelagic whaling for sperm whales in the North Pacific was first adopted by the IWC in 1980. It was extended globally in 1986–1987 when the IWC adopted a moratorium on all commercial whaling and set catch quotas for all stocks at zero. Section 7 consultations between NMFS and the Minerals Management Service have examined the effects of oil and gas exploration and development on sperm whales in the Gulf of Mexico and have concluded that such activities are not likely to jeopardize their continued existence. Research is being undertaken in the Gulf of Mexico to improve information on possible noise-related effects. Implementation of a take reduction plan for drift gillnets along the Oregon/Washington/California coast in 1997 included measures, such as education of skippers and the use of pingers, designed to reduce the take of marine mammals, including sperm whales.

Staff and Funding Levels: According to NMFS budget documents, NMFS allocated $994,000 in FY2003 funding to the recovery of endangered large whales (Appendix E). It is not clear how much of this was devoted to sperm whales. NMFS estimates that it devoted at least 2.2 FTEs in staff effort on sperm whale recovery work (0.5 by its regional offices and headquarters and 1.7 by its science centers) during 2005.[21] Annual FWS reports on expenditures for endangered species (FWS 2003b–d, 2005d–f, 2006) indicate that total funding related to sperm whale research and conservation between 1998 and 2004 ranged from $1,200 in 2002 to $2.27 million in 2004 (Table 21, Appendices C.1–7). Almost all the reported funding for 2003 was for U.S. Coast Guard enforcement activities.

Table 21. Federal and state expenditures (in $ thousands) for the recovery of sperm whales, 1998–2004 (Source: FWS 2003b–d; 2005d–f; 2006)

Fiscal Year	FWS	USGS	NMFS	USCG	Other Federal	Total Federal	State	Total State and Federal
1998	–	–	–	–	4	4	1	5
1999	–	–	–	6	1	7	–	7
2000	–	–	–	–	3	3	–	3
2001	–	–	–	–	27	27	–	27
2002	–	–	–	–	1	1	–	1
2003	–	–	–	199	4	203	–	203
2004	6	–	–	60	2,203	2,268	2	2,270

In recent years, the Minerals Management Service and partner agencies and organizations have been assessing the effects of noise from seismic air guns used to explore for oil and gas reserves on sperm whale distribution and abundance in the Gulf of Mexico. Between 2002 and 2007 more than $10 million has been allocated or committed in support of this study.[22]

The draft sperm whale recovery plan projects future funding needs to implement each of the nine major management actions identified previously (NMFS 2006d). As shown in Table 22, funding

---

[21] P. Michael Payne, personal communication. 17 August 2005. Chief, Marine Mammals Division, Office of Protected Species, National Marine Fisheries Service, Silver Spring, MD 20910.

[22] Ann Jochens, personal communication. 12 June 2006. Texas A&M University, College Station TX 77843; William Lang, personal communication. 12 June 2006. Program Director, Division of Ocean Sciences, National Science Foundation, 4301 Wilson Blvd., Suite 725, Arlington, VA 22230.

needs were developed for each of the three ocean basins in which sperm whales occur and total $37.14 million over the next 20 years.

Table 22. *Projected funding needs (in $ thousands) to implement recovery activities for sperm whales in the 2006 draft sperm whale recovery plan (NMFS 2006d)*

Ocean Basin*	Action 1	Action 2	Action 3	Action 4	Action 5	Action 6	Action 7	Action 8	Action 9	Total
North Atlantic (2012)	250	500	9,000	100	525	385	520	2,623	75	13,950
North Pacific (2012)	220	500	13,500	100	525	385	520	2,650	75	4,780
Southern Ocean (2026)	220	250	3,000	200	475	180	410	–		4735

* Dates in parentheses are estimates of the earliest possible dates for meeting recovery criteria.

Beluga Whale, Cook Inlet Population

Population Status: Distinct populations of beluga whales (*Delphinapterus lecuas*) are found in five areas off Alaska: the Beaufort Sea, the eastern Chukchi Sea, the eastern Bering Sea, Bristol Bay, and Cook Inlet (NMFS 2005d). Studies indicate that Cook Inlet beluga whales comprise the most discrete and isolated population in U.S. waters and that most whales remain in the inlet year-round (NMFS 2005d). Before 1994 there were no regular, systematic surveys of beluga whales in Cook Inlet; however, based on an aerial survey count of 479 whales in August 1979 and on a correction factor for unobserved whales, NMFS estimates a population abundance of 1,300 whales at that time. In 1994 NMFS began comprehensive, systematic aerial surveys of beluga whales in Cook Inlet (NMFS 2005d). Between 1994 and 1998 the surveys documented a decline of 47 percent, from 653 to 347 animals (NMFS 2005d). Based on the 2003 survey results, their abundance was estimated at 357 whales. The most recent NMFS stock assessment report uses those results to calculate a PBR of 2 (NMFS 2005a). Beluga whales are an important subsistence resource for Alaska Natives, and subsistence hunting levels were severely limited beginning in 1999 because of the population's decline. Although the limited harvest was expected to allow the population to recover, the anticipated increase in population size has not occurred (Lowry et al. 2006).

In 1988 NMFS included the Cook Inlet beluga whale population on its list of candidate species for listing under the ESA (53 Fed. Reg. 33516). Although inclusion on that list did not, in itself, impose restrictions, it signaled that federal agencies should take beluga whales into account in their planning. In 1998 NMFS began the process of deciding whether to designate Cook Inlet beluga whales as depleted under the MMPA or as threatened or endangered under the ESA (64 Fed. Reg. 56258). In 1999 NMFS received two petitions to list the Cook Inlet beluga whales as endangered under the ESA; both petitions identified unregulated hunting as a major cause for the decline of the population. On 31 May 2000 NMFS announced a decision to deny the petitions and designated the Cook Inlet population as depleted under the MMPA (65 Fed. Reg. 34590).

Although NMFS denied the two petitions to list the population under the ESA, in 2006 NMFS began a reexamination of the merits of such a listing in view of the population's failure to increase since harvest limits were imposed (71 Fed. Reg. 14836).

Major Threats: In 1999 NMFS concluded that the cause of the decline was high levels of mortality from subsistence hunting by Alaska Natives—including whales that were both struck and landed and those that were struck but lost and presumed dead (65 Fed. Reg. 38778). Although the precise level of mortality due to hunting is uncertain, the estimated average number of animals killed annually in subsistence harvests between 1995 and 1997 was 87 whales (NMFS 2005a).

Beluga whales in Cook Inlet frequent shallow waters near developed coastal areas around Anchorage and ascend freshwater rivers. Because of this, they face a wide range of human-related threats in addition to subsistence hunting. These include vessel traffic and habitat alteration due to coastal development, as well as natural threats (NMFS 2004d; NMFS 2005a,d).

Natural Threats

- *Stranding Events*: Strandings of beluga whales are common on tidal mud flats in Cook Inlet, but whales often are able to free themselves on incoming tides. Between 1988 and 2004 NMFS recorded strandings of 804 beluga whales, including 129 reported mortalities (Vos and Shelden 2005). Of those strandings, 91 occurred between 1998 and 2004. Some strandings coincided with occurrences of killer whales in the inlet and may be the result of attempts to avoid predation.
- *Predation*: Cook Inlet beluga whales are preyed upon by killer whales (Shelden et al. 2003b). Although little is known about the level of predation, it could be significant, especially in light of the severely reduced size of the population.
- *Parasitism and Disease*: Little is known about the effects of disease on Cook Inlet beluga whales.
- *Habitat Capacity and Environmental Change*: Climate change may affect the availability of prey for beluga whales, chiefly salmon and eulachon, but to date there is no evidence that prey availability is a limiting factor.

Human-induced Threats

- *Subsistence Harvest*: Alaska Natives hunt Cook Inlet beluga whales for food and traditional handicrafts. Take levels for Cook Inlet beluga whales are now limited to those authorized through a co-management agreement with NMFS. Although the decline in Cook Inlet beluga whale abundance in the 1990s can be explained largely by the level of Native take, the population's failure to recover in recent years is apparently due to other factors.
- *Commercial Fishing*: Beluga whales in Cook Inlet may be taken incidentally in fisheries for shellfish, groundfish, herring, and salmon. The only records of beluga whale mortality in commercial fisheries are from the early 1980s. Observer coverage of these fisheries is limited, but no incidental mortality was reported by observers or in fishery logbooks between 1990 and 2000 (NMFS 2005a).

- *Pollution*: Cook Inlet beluga whales are exposed to many kinds of pollutants commonly found in urban and industrial areas. Sources include partially treated sewage and runoff, discharges from industrial activities, such as petroleum exploration, fish-processing facilities, mining and agricultural operations, accidental oil spills, and routine discharges from oil exploration and development operations. With the exception of copper, beluga whales in Cook Inlet show lower levels of contaminants in their tissues than beluga whale populations elsewhere in Alaska (NMFS 2005d).
- *Vessel Traffic*: Beluga whales are vulnerable to being struck by vessels, particularly near river mouths and other favored habitats that were once relatively isolated but are now accessible by boats.
- *Tourism and Whale-Watching*: Currently there are no vessel-based commercial whale-watching operations in upper Cook Inlet where beluga whales are most easily observed. NMFS has concluded that whale watching is not a substantial threat to Cook Inlet beluga whales (NMFS 2005d).
- *Coastal Development*: Beluga whales are found primarily in nearshore waters where they may come into conflict with development of adjacent lands and shallow waters. The effects of coastal development are poorly known, and NMFS is proposing that standards for coastal development be prepared, particularly in Knik Arm, an important summer feeding area for beluga whales near Anchorage (NMFS 2005d).
- *Noise*: Like other toothed whales, beluga whales use sound to communicate, locate prey, and navigate. In Cook Inlet, a wide variety of human activities generate noise that may affect beluga whales.
- *Oil and Gas*: Although oil and gas production in Cook Inlet is past its peak, about 238 wells are presently in production and approximately six new wells are drilled each year (NMFS 2005d). Both state and federal governments continue to offer leases for exploration and development. Oil spills could affect beluga whales directly or significantly alter their habitat.

Management Framework: Lead federal responsibility for managing beluga whales rests with NMFS. The management framework established by the MMPA provides an exemption for the taking of marine mammals by Alaska Natives for subsistence uses and the production of handicrafts. The Act allows limits on subsistence hunting only if a species has been designated as depleted. NMFS therefore had no authority to regulate hunting by Alaska Natives when the level of hunting increased in the mid-1990s (65 Fed. Reg. 38778). Because of concern about high levels of subsistence take, in 1999 the U.S. Congress enacted legislation (PL 106-31, section 3022, 113 Stat. 57, 100) establishing a moratorium on hunting Cook Inlet beluga whales unless authorized through a co-management agreement between Alaska Native organizations and NMFS. The moratorium was made permanent by legislation passed in 2000 (PL 106-553), and conforming regulations were adopted by NMFS (65 Fed. Reg. 17973). NMFS is currently developing a conservation plan under the MMPA to identify and help guide research and management work to recover the Cook Inlet beluga whale population (NMFS 2005d).

Critical Habitat: Critical habitat is not applicable because the Cook Inlet beluga whale population currently is not listed as endangered or threatened under the ESA. However, the draft conservation plan characterizes habitats in Cook Inlet according to their importance to the population (NMFS 2005d).

Recovery Plan: Because Cook Inlet beluga whales are not listed under the ESA, a recovery plan has not been developed for this population. However, in 2005 NMFS released a draft conservation plan for Cook Inlet beluga whales prepared under authority of the MMPA (NMFS 2005d). Its stated purpose is to recover the Cook Inlet beluga whale population to its OSP level. Based on current estimates of carrying capacity, it recommends that NMFS consider removing the Cook Inlet population from the list of depleted species when the population reaches 780 animals. The draft plan sets out three objectives for achieving this goal:

- Identify and eliminate or mitigate factors that are responsible for the decline of the Cook Inlet beluga whales or that may be preventing their recovery;
- Continue and, as necessary, expand research and management programs to monitor trends and detect natural or human-related factors affecting the Cook Inlet population of beluga whales and its habitat; and
- Assess the success of implementing conservation actions and high-priority studies identified in the plan.

Major Management Actions: In May 1999 President Clinton signed legislation establishing a moratorium on the taking of Cook Inlet beluga whales by Native subsistence hunters unless authorized by a cooperative agreement between NMFS and affected Alaska Native organizations (§3022 PL 106-31). That moratorium was to have expired in October 2000, but it was extended indefinitely by Public Law 106-553. In 2000 NMFS issued a proposed rule to establish harvest limitations under a formal rulemaking process set forth in the MMPA. Based on the recommendations of an administrative law judge and the findings of an environmental impact statement, NMFS published interim final regulations that set a harvest level of 1.5 whales per year for 2001–2004 (MMC 2005). Since 2000 NMFS has entered into cooperative agreements with the Cook Inlet Marine Mammal Council under which limited hunts have been authorized. The 2003 agreement calls for maintaining the beluga whale population at "levels that will allow for long-term sustainable harvests" (NMFS 2005d). In 2004, as required under a stipulation agreed to by the parties to the rulemaking, NMFS and the Council suspended the hunt because of the unusually high number of beluga whale deaths (20) recorded the previous year. The parties to the rulemaking also agreed that NMFS would develop a long-term harvest regime to govern subsistence taking after 2004 (MMC 2005). The long-term harvest plan has not been finalized.

Staff and Funding Levels: Because Cook Inlet beluga whales are not listed under the ESA, funding levels for this population are not reported in annual FWS expenditure reports for endangered and threatened species. The Marine Mammal Commission's survey of federally funded marine mammal research (Waring 2002) reports that federal expenditures for research on all beluga whale populations between FY1991 and FY2000 ranged from $160,000 in FY1991 to $781,000 in FY1995 (see Appendix F). The proportion devoted to Cook Inlet beluga whales is unknown. In 2000, the most recent year reported, the funding level was $351,000. The principal sources of funding were NMFS, the Navy, and the National Science Foundation. Between FY2002 and FY2004 NMFS allocated roughly $150,000 annually for research and management activities related to Cook Inlet beluga whales. NMFS estimates that it devoted at least 6.1 FTEs in staff effort on Cook Inlet beluga whale recovery work (2.3 by its regional offices and headquarters and 3.8 by its science centers) during 2005.[23]

---

[23] P. Michael Payne, personal communication. 17 August 2005. Chief, Marine Mammals Division, Office of Protected Species, National Marine Fisheries Service, Silver Spring, MD 20910.

The draft conservation plan (NMFS 2005d) projects cost estimates amounting to a total of $4.7 million for identified activities (including all activities ranked from priority 1 through 3) during the first five years of recovery work after plan adoption (Table 23). The estimates, however, are provided only for activities associated with objective 1 (i.e., identify and eliminate or mitigate factors responsible for the decline of the Cook Inlet beluga whales or which may be preventing their recovery). Costs associated with objectives 2 and 3 are not provided.

Table 23. *Projected funding needs (in $ thousands) to implement objective 1 during the first five years after adoption of the 2005 draft Cook Inlet beluga whale conservation plan (NMFS 2005d)*

Actions	Year 1	Year 2	Year 3	Year 4	Year 5	Total
Stranding events	103	164	103	91	108	569
Predation	6	8	10	12	14	50
Subsistence harvest	56	56	45	18	45	220
Commercial fishing	12	22	32	27	32	125
Vessel traffic	0	215	210	28	128	581
Tourism/whale-watching	38	63	41	31	35	208
Noise	20	40	40	20	20	140
Oil and gas activities	90	90	85	70	75	410
Research	72	137	78	118	80	485
Oil spills	60	110	100	75	75	420
Enforcement	70	65	70	63	67	335
Outreach and education	0	0	50	15	15	80
Marine discharges and pollution	10	10	15	15	20	70
Habitat alteration and coastal development	15	15	20	20	25	95
Knik Arm development	10	35	40	28	28	141
Legal/administrative support	150	170	140	150	150	760
TOTAL	722	1,200	1,079	781	917	4,699

Bottlenose Dolphin, Mid-Atlantic Coastal Population

Population Status: Mid-Atlantic coastal bottlenose dolphins (*Tursiops truncatus*) are a morphologically distinct group of dolphins that generally remains in waters less than 25 meters deep along the U.S. Atlantic coast from Long Island, New York, to Florida (NMFS 2002). Based on genetic analyses, photo-identification, satellite telemetry, and analyses of stable isotopes, at least seven management units have been identified within the population's range (i.e., northern migratory, northern North Carolina, southern North Carolina, South Carolina, Georgia, northern Florida, and central Florida) (NMFS 2006b).

In 1987–1988 a large die-off of at least 742 dolphins reduced the number of Atlantic coastal bottlenose dolphins by what was then thought to be more than half their abundance. As a result, NMFS designated the population as depleted under the MMPA in 1993. The proximate cause for the die-off was determined to be a neurotoxin produced by a red tide dinoflagellate, *Ptychodiscus brevis*. However, the affected dolphins also carried high levels of organochlorines and other contaminants that may have predisposed them to effects of the neurotoxin (54 Fed. Reg. 41654). Aerial surveys are the primary source of information on distribution and abundance of coastal bottlenose dolphins. Surveys since the 1987–1988 die-off suggest that their abundance is substantially greater than previously thought (NMFS 2002). Results of surveys, conducted in 2002, are shown in Table 24 (69 Fed. Reg. 65129).

Table 24. Estimates of abundance, bycatch, and potential biological removal for mid-Atlantic coastal bottlenose dolphin management units in 2002 (NMFS 2006a)

Management Unit	Abundance	Estimated Bycatch 2001–2002	Potential Biological Removal
SUMMER (May-October)			
Northern migratory	17,466	112	146.2
Northern North Carolina	7,079	8	40.8
Oceanic	6,160		32.6
Estuary	919		82.0
Southern North Carolina	4,787	0	19.9
Oceanic	3,646		18.6
Estuary	141		1.2
WINTER (November-April)			
Winter Mixed (Northern migratory, northern and southern North Carolina)	16,913	58	135.6
ALL YEAR			
South Carolina	2,325		19.6
Georgia	2,195		17.2
Northern Florida	448	0	N/a
Central Florida	10,652	6	N/a

Major Threats: Because they inhabit nearshore waters, mid-Atlantic coastal bottlenose dolphins are exposed to a number of anthropogenic and natural threats caused by interactions with commercial fisheries, red tides, contaminants, and focused recreational attention.

Incidental Catch in Fisheries: Perhaps the principal threat to coastal bottlenose dolphins is bycatch in coastal fisheries, primarily large-mesh gillnet fisheries (NMFS 2006a). Analyses indicate that bycatch rates are highest within state waters, particularly in North Carolina and Virginia, during winter. Among the fisheries of greatest concern are the mid-Atlantic coastal gillnet fishery, the Virginia pound net fishery, the mid-Atlantic beach seine fishery, the Atlantic blue crab trap fishery, the North Carolina inshore gillnet fishery, the North Carolina roe mullet stop net fishery, the North Carolina long-haul seine fishery, the southeast Atlantic gillnet fishery, and the southeastern U.S. Atlantic shark gillnet fishery (69 Fed. Reg. 65128) (see Appendix B and later discussion). Although no bycatch has been documented by observers for the summer southern North Carolina management unit, stranding data indicate that dolphins also are taken as bycatch in that area and time of year (69 Fed. Reg. 65129).

Red Tides: Neurotoxin poisoning associated with red tides appears to be an infrequent cause of major mortality for bottlenose dolphins; however, over the last 15 years at least six die-offs much smaller than the 1987–1988 event have been recorded (MMC 2004). Limited understanding about the population structure of coastal bottlenose dolphins and their abundance makes it impossible to accurately assess the impact of such die-offs.

Contaminants: Coastal bottlenose dolphins are exposed to a wide range of pollutants from land-based run-off. Like many other marine mammals that inhabit nearshore areas, bottlenose dolphins carry high levels of some contaminants. The direct and indirect effects of contaminants have not been established but may include impairment of immune function (a possible contributing factor in the large 1987–1988 die-off) and reproduction.

Tourism: Over the past decade, both legal and illegal commercial dolphin-watching ventures have encouraged close human interactions (e.g., feeding) with bottlenose dolphins. These activities have increased dramatically, particularly in the southeastern United States. A study by Samuels et al. (2003) concluded that dolphins are vulnerable to injury and death as a result of human contact and that important natural behaviors can be disrupted through such contact. For the last several years, NMFS has been considering regulations to govern such operations.

Management Framework: NMFS has lead federal responsibility for conserving mid-Atlantic coastal bottlenose dolphins under the authority of the MMPA. Section 118(f)(1) of the MMPA requires the preparation and implementation of take reduction plans for strategic marine mammal stocks that interact with category I or category II fisheries. Coastal bottlenose dolphin populations in the Atlantic qualify as strategic stocks because fishery-related incidental mortality exceeds current estimates of PBR levels for some management units and because the population is designated as depleted (NMFS 2006b). In February 1997 NMFS convened a take reduction team, but the team determined that information was insufficient to develop management measures. After further research and analyses, NMFS convened a new take reduction team in October 2001. That team met five times and submitted recommendations to NMFS in May 2002. The Service determined that those recommended measures would not meet the statutory requirement for reducing incidental mortality and serious injury to below the PBR level. No other teams exist specifically for the purpose of managing mid-Atlantic coastal bottlenose dolphins. The population is now managed according to a complex structure of "management units."

Critical Habitat: Critical habitat is not applicable because the mid-Atlantic coastal bottlenose dolphin population is not listed under the ESA.

Recovery Plan: Provisions for preparing a recovery plan are not applicable because the mid-Atlantic coastal bottlenose dolphin population is not listed under the ESA. However, when NMFS proposed designating the population as depleted under the MMPA in 1991, it advised that it would prepare a conservation plan (56 Fed. Reg. 40595). In May 2001 a draft conservation plan was provided to the Marine Mammal Commission, which subsequently submitted comments to NMFS (MMC 2004). However, a draft plan has not been circulated for public review.

Major Management Actions: In November 1988 the Center for Marine Conservation petitioned NMFS to designate the coastal bottlenose dolphin population as depleted under the MMPA (54 Fed. Reg. 41654). Proposed rules to do so were published in August 1991 (56 Fed. Reg. 40594) and adopted in 1993 (58 Fed. Reg. 17789). At the time, it was thought that there was only one coastal population distributed along the Atlantic coast. Although this is no longer believed to be the case, the stock structure remains uncertain, and the depleted designation remains in effect. The principal management focus has been on reducing incidental mortality and serious injury in coastal fisheries. In November 2004 NMFS proposed regulations based on recommendations prepared by the Bottlenose Dolphin Take Reduction Team (69 Fed. Reg. 65127). They called for restrictions on fishing areas, gillnet soak times, and amounts of gear, with specific measures differing by management unit. Other recommendations were made for education and outreach efforts and for research, particularly to improve understanding of population stock structure. Final rules implementing those measures were published in 2006 (71 Fed. Reg. 24775).

Staff and Funding Levels: Because mid-Atlantic coastal bottlenose dolphins are not listed under the ESA, estimated expenditures spent on this population are not reported in annual FWS expenditure reports required under the ESA. According to the Marine Mammal Commission's survey of federally funded marine mammal research (Waring 2002), expenditures for biological and population assessment research on bottlenose dolphins between FY1991 and FY2000 ranged from $822,000 in FY1997 to $2.5 million in FY1995 (Appendix F). This funding, however, is not restricted explicitly to the mid-Atlantic coastal population. The principal sources of funding were NMFS and the Navy.

NMFS estimates that it devoted at least 15.9 FTEs in staff effort on coastal mid-Atlantic bottlenose dolphin conservation (2.1 by its regional offices and headquarters and 13.8 by its science centers) during 2005.[24] NMFS budget documents indicate that it allocated $748,000 to coastal bottlenose dolphins in FY2001, $2 million in FY2002, $1.99 million in FY2003, and $3.96 million in FY2004 (Appendix E).

Killer Whale, Southern Resident Population

Status: The taxonomy of killer whales (*Orcinus orca*) is poorly known, but new information is being developed. Until recently, killer whales were considered to be a single species worldwide (69 Fed. Reg. 76674). Based on recent information, this is no longer believed to be the case. NMFS currently recognizes several distinct groups of killer whales in the North Pacific Ocean, including resident, transient, and offshore populations, each of which differs from the others in significant ways. A distinct group of southern resident killer whales occurs in waters straddling the U.S.-Canada border between Washington and British Columbia. This group is further divided into three pods designated J, K, and L.

In the late 1960s and early 1970s, 47 killer whales were removed for purposes of research and public display, reducing the southern resident population to about 70 animals (MMC 2002). The

---

[24] P. Michael Payne, personal communication. 17 August 2005. Chief, Marine Mammals Division, Office of Protected Species, National Marine Fisheries Service, Silver Spring, MD 20910.

population subsequently increased to a high of 99 whales in 1995 but then declined to 79 whales by 2001. The decline seems to have resulted from a decrease in fecundity and an increase in mortality of immature and mature females. In 2001 the Center for Biological Diversity and other environmental groups petitioned NMFS to list southern resident killer whales as threatened or endangered under the ESA (69 Fed. Reg. 76673). Based on findings by a biological review team, NMFS denied the petition, concluding that southern resident killer whales did not constitute a separate species or a distinct population segment under the Act. In May 2003, however, NMFS designated the population as depleted under the MMPA.

In response to litigation successfully challenging the decision on the initial ESA petition, NMFS reexamined the possibility of listing southern resident killer whales under the ESA. A new biological review team convened by NMFS concluded that southern resident killer whales meet the definition of a distinct population segment (Krahn et al. 2002). NMFS subsequently proposed listing the population as threatened (69 Fed. Reg. 76678). In taking this action, NMFS cited new results from population modeling studies that suggested, under the most optimistic recovery scenario, the population has a 0.1 to 3 percent probability of extinction in 100 years. Under the most pessimistic scenario, it was predicted to have a 39 to 67 percent probability of extinction in 100 years. In support of its proposal to list southern resident killer whales as threatened rather than endangered, NMFS cited evidence of a small increase in abundance since 2000 and noted that the recruitment of several juvenile male and female whales to breeding age was expected in the next few years (69 Fed. Reg. 76679). In 2005 NMFS took final action and decided to list the southern resident killer whale population as endangered, rather than threatened, under the ESA (70 Fed. Reg. 69903). According to the notice, the listing as endangered instead of threatened resulted from information received during the comment period and a reanalysis of threats facing the population. The count of southern resident killer whales in 2005 was 84 whales; its PBR level is calculated to be 0.8 (NMFS 2006a).

Major Threats: Although specific causes for the slow growth and periodic declines in abundance of southern resident killer whales remain unknown, a number of possible factors were identified by the most recent biological review (Krahn et al. 2002). Since the mid-1980s the abundance of salmon, a principal prey species for southern resident killer whales, has declined in Puget Sound. In addition, the whales have been found to have high levels of organochlorines, including PCBs and a chemical flame retardant, that has been associated with compromised immune systems and reproductive function in other species. Oil spills and noise and disturbance from vessel traffic, including whale-watching ventures, also are considered possible factors in the decline. Noise-related impacts associated with the operation of sonar by Navy vessels passing through the species' habitat also have been a source of concern. In support of its listing proposal, NMFS also cited concerns about the limited number of reproductive males and the lack of reproduction by some sexually mature females.

Management Framework: At present, no recovery team or other interagency management team has been convened specifically to oversee or assist NMFS in implementing recovery efforts for southern resident killer whales. In its proposal to list the population as threatened, NMFS announced that it would convene a recovery team if designation were to occur. In March 2005 NMFS released a preliminary draft conservation plan under the MMPA (NMFS 2005c).

Critical Habitat: In listing southern resident killer whales as endangered, NMFS declined to propose critical habitat, citing difficulty in identifying critical habitat for a group of animals whose foraging areas vary in time and space and which do not use specific breeding, nursing, or resting areas. In June 2006, however, NMFS proposed designating more than 2,500 square miles of inland waters in Puget Sound, the Strait of Juan de Fuca, and around the San Juan Islands as critical habitat. Final designation of the area was made in November 2006 (71 Fed. Reg. 69054).

Recovery Plan: In March 2005 NMFS released a preliminary draft conservation plan under the MMPA (NMFS 2005c). This preliminary draft plan, structured much like a recovery plan, identifies proposed actions to accomplish the following objectives:

- Monitor the status and trends of the southern resident killer whale population;
- Protect the population from factors that may contribute to its decline or reduce its ability to recover;
- Protect the population from additional threats that may disturb, injure, or kill the whales or affect habitat;
- Conduct research to facilitate and enhance conservation efforts;
- Develop public information and education programs;
- Respond to killer whales found stranded, sick, injured, or isolated, that pose a threat to the public, or that exhibit nuisance behaviors; and
- Promote transboundary and interagency coordination and cooperation.

Although NMFS has not announced plans to prepare a recovery plan for southern resident killer whales, the draft conservation plan presumably would provide a basis for doing so.

Canada's Department of Fisheries and Oceans has convened a recovery team for southern resident killer whales that includes representatives of the Washington Department of Fish and Wildlife and NMFS. The team has begun developing a recovery plan under Canadian authority (69 Fed. Reg. 76679).

Major Management Actions: In announcing its proposal to list the southern resident killer whales as threatened, NMFS described initial management needs including public education, outreach, and stewardship activities in cooperation with the Seattle Aquarium and the Whale Museum. A major focus of outreach efforts would be promoting responsible whale-watching behavior and enforcement in cooperation with the Washington Department of Fish and Wildlife (69 Fed. Reg. 76679). NMFS also noted that it would evaluate protective regulations available under the ESA. As noted above, NMFS designated southern resident killer whales as endangered in 2005 and designated critical habitat in November 2006.

Staff and Funding Levels: Because southern resident whales were not listed under the ESA until 2005, funding levels for this population have not been reported in past annual FWS expenditure reports for listed endangered and threatened species. However, budget documents indicate that NMFS allocated $746,000 in FY2003 and $1.5 million in FY2004 for actions related to recovery of southern resident killer whales. NMFS estimates that its headquarters, regional offices, and fisheries science centers devoted 7.1 FTEs to research and management activities (2.1 by its regional office and headquarters staff and 5 by its science centers) related to the southern resident killer whale population in 2005.[25] Projected funding needs to carry out tasks identified in the 2005 southern resident killer whale conservation plan during the first five years after adoption of the plan totaled $13.6 million (Table 25).

Table 25. *Projected funding needs (in $ thousands) to implement conservation activities for southern resident killer whales during the first five years after adopting the draft 2005 southern resident killer whale conservation plan (NMFS 2005c)*

Actions	Year 1	Year 2	Year 3	Year 4	Year 5	Total
MANAGEMENT						
Identify contaminant clean-up sites	30	30	–	–	–	60
Minimize risks from oil spills	20	–	–	–	–	20
Minimize disturbance from vessels	220	270	290	310	290	1,380
Develop public outreach programs	172	132	142	132	142	720
Respond to distressed/stranded whales	N/A	N/A	N/A	N/A	N/A	N/A
Pursue cooperation with Canada	10	230	200	240	160	840
RESEARCH AND MONITORING						
Monitor status and trends	20	100	100	100	100	420
Assess distribution and movements	419	975	1,025	1,025	1,025	4,469
Assess diet	112	190	190	190	190	872
Assess population dynamics	32	130	130	130	130	552
Determine metabolic rates	40	75	75	75	75	340
Assess changes in prey availability	–	200	200	200	200	800
Assess effects of noise	150	325	325	325	325	1,450
Assess effects of contaminants/disease	55	210	210	210	210	895
Assess genetic relationships	70	150	150	100	100	570
Improve research technology	50	50	50	50	50	250
TOTAL	1,400	3,067	3,087	3,087	2,997	13,638

Killer Whale, AT1 Group

Status: The AT1 group of killer whales is a genetically and socially distinct group of transient killer whales in the northern Gulf of Alaska. This group has been resighted annually in Prince William Sound and the Kenai Fjords area (NMFS 2005a). Like other transient killer whales, the AT1 whales are specialized feeders on marine mammals, particularly harbor seals (*Phoca vitulina*) and Dall's porpoises (*Phocoenoides dalli*). Although their range overlaps with other killer whale populations, they have never been observed to associate with whales from other groups.

---

[25] P. Michael Payne, personal communication. 17 August 2005. Chief, Marine Mammals Division, Office of Protected Species, National Marine Fisheries Service, Silver Spring, MD 20910; John Bengtson, personal communication. 8 December 2006. National Marine Mammal Laboratory, National Marine Fisheries Service, Seattle, WA 98115.

Under the MMPA, AT1 killer whales are considered part of a larger eastern North Pacific transient killer whale population (NMFS 2003a). The minimum population estimate for the eastern North Pacific population is 346 animals. Although some AT1 killer whales were first observed in 1978 in Prince William Sound, the group was not identified as a separate unit until 1984 (NMFS 2003). At that time, three individuals were identified as juveniles, indicating that reproduction had occurred in the previous eight years. In 1987, 9 of the 22 whales counted in the group were males. This is considered a very high percentage of males. All 22 whales were observed regularly until the *Exxon Valdez* oil spill in March 1989. Since that time, the population has steadily declined. The most recent abundance estimate is eight whales, including four aging females (NMFS 2005a). No new calves have been documented since 1984.

In November 2002 several conservation organizations submitted a petition to NMFS to designate the AT1 group of transient killer whales as depleted under the MMPA (68 Fed. Reg. 3483). In response, NMFS convened a status review group that subsequently concluded that AT1 killer whales had a distinct vocal dialect and pattern of movement and were genetically distinct from other transient killer whales (NMFS 2003). Based on those findings, NMFS concluded that AT1 killer whales constituted a population stock as defined by the MMPA and that the population of nine animals remaining at the time had declined to 41 percent of their presumed carrying capacity (i.e., the 22 whales documented in the late 1980s). In June 2004 NMFS issued a final rule designating the group as depleted under the MMPA (69 Fed. Reg. 31321).

Major Threats: Threats identified for AT1 killer whales by NMFS include the following:

Oil Spills: AT1 killer whales appear to have been harmed by the 1989 *Exxon Valdez* oil spill (NMFS 2003). Eleven members of the group have disappeared since the spill, and at least some of those animals are thought to have died because of it. The AB pod of resident killer whales in Prince William Sound also was observed swimming through the spill and, within two years, it lost 13 of its 36 members. Although steps have been taken to reduce the likelihood of large spills occurring in the future, such a threat will continue to exist as long as oil is transported through habitats used by these whales.

Environmental contaminants: Seven members of the AT1 group were found to have significantly higher levels of organochlorine concentrations than resident killer whales in the same area (NMFS 2003). The high levels are similar to those found in other North Pacific transient killer whales and are consistent with a diet that includes other top-level predators. Exposure to organochlorines may be contributing to the absence of observed reproduction in this group over the past 20 years.

Prey Availability: The abundance of harbor seals in Prince William Sound—a primary prey item for AT1 killer whales—declined 63 percent between 1984 and 1997 after the *Exxon Valdez* oil spill (NMFS 2003). This may have limited the whales' ability to find adequate food and compromised their health and reproduction.

Fisheries Interactions: Although a number of fisheries operate in the range of AT1 killer whales, incidental take and mortality of killer whales has been documented only for the Bering Sea groundfish trawl and longline fisheries (NMFS 2003).

<u>Whale-Watching and Vessel Traffic</u>: It appears that AT1 killer whales are not likely to be affected by the increase in whale-watching in Alaska (NMFS 2003). Most whale-watching activities in Prince William Sound and Kenai Fjords interact with resident killer whales. Although other types of vessel traffic also have increased, it is unknown whether or to what extent vessel noise might impair the ability of killer whales to navigate, forage, and communicate.

Management Framework: NMFS is the lead agency responsible for conserving killer whales. No interagency management teams have been established explicitly to oversee or assist with recovery of this group of killer whales.

Critical Habitat: Critical habitat is not applicable because the AT1 killer whale population is not listed as endangered or threatened under the ESA.

Recovery Plan: In designating AT1 killer whales as depleted in June 2004, NMFS announced its intent to develop a conservation plan under provisions of the MMPA (69 Fed. Reg. 31322). A draft plan had not been circulated for public review as of the compiling of this report.

Major Management Actions: No specific management actions for AT1 killer whales have been taken to date. Recovery work on this group of whales has been limited to research and monitoring by NMFS' National Marine Mammal Laboratory and contracted researchers to determine demographic parameters and monitor their abundance (69 Fed. Reg. 31322).

Staff and Funding Levels: Because AT1 killer whales are not listed under the ESA, funding levels for this population are not reported in annual FWS expenditure reports for endangered and threatened species. NMFS estimates that it devoted 0.5 FTE in staff effort (0.2 by its regional offices and headquarters and 0.3 by its science centers) to the AT1 group of killer whales.[26] No estimates of funding levels for research activities specific to this group of whales could be identified.

---

[26] P. Michael Payne, personal communication. 17 August 2005. Chief, Marine Mammals Division, Office of Protected Species, National Marine Fisheries Service, Silver Spring, MD 20910; John Bengtson, personal communication. 8 December 2006. National Marine Mammal Laboratory, National Marine Fisheries Service, Seattle, WA 98115.

IV. OVERVIEW AND TRENDS

STATUTORY PROTECTION PROVISIONS

The ESA and the MMPA provide the foundation for most marine mammal protection activities. For species listed as threatened or endangered, the ESA is generally more important. Among the most important provisions of the ESA are (1) a prohibition on the taking of listed species, including adverse modification of their critical habitat; (2) requirements for preparing and implementing recovery plans that identify necessary recovery actions and associated costs; and (3) requirements for all federal agencies to use their respective authorities to protect listed species and to consult with either NMFS or FWS if any actions they authorize, fund, or carry out are likely to jeopardize the continued existence of a listed species or adversely modify its critical habitat. In this regard, the Act authorizes the designation of areas as critical habitat if they contain biological or physical features essential for a species' survival.

The MMPA prohibits intentional as well as unintentional injury, death, or harassment of all marine mammals, including those listed as endangered or threatened. This prohibition is subject to some exceptions, such as non-wasteful taking by Alaska Natives for subsistence and handicraft purposes and for authorized scientific research and enhancement activities. The MMPA also provides exemptions for (1) taking small numbers of marine mammals incidental to activities other than commercial fishing if the taking is authorized by regulations, and (2) taking incidental to commercial fishing, provided that the take does not exceed a PBR level calculated specifically for the stock. For fisheries not achieving this standard, NMFS is required to convene a take reduction team and prepare a take reduction plan to reduce takes to below the PBR level. If a marine mammal stock falls below its OSP level, it also must be listed as "depleted." Besides further limiting the taking from stocks so listed, the Act authorizes the preparation of a conservation plan similar to a recovery plan under the ESA.

Other relevant legislation includes the Magnuson-Stevens Fishery Conservation and Management Act, which establishes national standards for harvesting fish and authorizes the development of fishery management plans. In part, national standards under this Act require that fishery management plans prevent overfishing while achieving an optimum yield that takes into account interactions with other species, such as marine mammals, and ecosystem elements. The Act also requires minimizing bycatch of marine mammals and other non-target species. Most fishery management plans, however, have not directly addressed the impact of fisheries on marine mammals.

Other important statutes include the National Environmental Policy Act, which requires the preparation of environmental impact statements for major federal actions that may affect the environment; the Outer Continental Shelf Lands Act, which guides the exploration and development of oil and gas reserves in federal waters and requires consideration of environmental effects on marine mammals and other species; and Title III of the Marine Protection, Research and Sanctuaries Act, which authorizes the designation and management of national marine sanctuaries that include marine areas of national significance, some of which are particularly important as marine mammal habitats.

The conservation of marine mammals, including listed species, also is subject to provisions of several international treaties. For example, the International Convention for the Regulation of Whaling established the International Whaling Commission, which recommends limits on commercial and subsistence harvests of whales by member countries. The Convention on International Trade in Endangered Species of Fauna and Flora establishes controls on international trade in wildlife species by its member countries.

POPULATION STATUS

The abundance of listed marine mammal populations varies widely. Some are among the world's rarest mammals, such as the AT1 group of killer whales (with eight individuals), eastern North Pacific right whales (numbering perhaps a few tens of animals), and North Atlantic right whales (numbering about 300 animals). Other populations are far larger but have experienced alarming declines in recent decades. For instance, the eastern North Pacific population of northern fur seals has declined from more than two million to an estimated 688,028 animals, while western Steller sea lions, which numbered more than 150,000, now number about 38,000 animals. Excluding Caribbean monk seals—which are widely considered to be extinct—the 21 listed marine mammal taxa include 7 with known or probable declining trends, 8 that have shown signs of increasing over the past 25 years, and 6 whose population trends are unknown.

SPECIES PROTECTION PROGRAMS

As of December 2006, 14 marine mammal species and populations occurring regularly in U.S. waters were recognized as endangered under the Endangered Species Act and four others were listed as threatened (Lowry et al. 2007). By virtue of these listings, all 18 taxa are automatically classified as depleted under the MMPA. Four other marine mammal taxa were independently listed as depleted.

Differences in the behavior, distribution, and preferred habitats of these marine mammals present a wide variety of recovery challenges. Some large whales annually migrate thousands of miles across the jurisdictions of several countries and are exposed to diverse threats including entanglement in fishing gear, contamination by pollutants, and collisions with vessels. The movements of other marine mammals, such as Florida manatees, Hawaiian monk seals, and southern sea otters, are comparatively limited, with animals remaining largely or entirely under U.S. jurisdiction. Those taxa tend to be limited to coastal waters where, again, human activities can have profound effects on population growth and survival.

A significant development for marine mammal conservation programs in recent years has been an improvement in the understanding of population structure through new genetic studies and better data on species distribution and ecology. The implications of this new information have yet to be fully reconciled with current assessments of the conservation status and recovery goals for the listed marine mammals. For example, although humpback whales are listed as a single species and classified as endangered worldwide, at least four separate populations have now been identified in U.S. waters alone. Furthermore, there appear to be at least six subpopulations of humpback whales whose use of discrete feeding grounds suggests that they would not be readily repopulated by whales from different subpopulations if they were to be reduced. Similar behavioral patterns appear to isolate groups of killer whales and Florida manatees. To integrate rapidly advancing understanding of stock structure into recovery programs, management agencies are struggling to reassess and revise recovery priorities, goals, and conservation strategies to conform to this new understanding. Failure to understand and account for population structure can lead to poorly directed management actions, ineffective recovery effort, and the loss of ecologically significant species groups.

THREATS TO MARINE MAMMAL SPECIES AND POPULATIONS

In the 19th and 20th centuries, commercial hunting greatly reduced most of the listed marine mammal taxa, and it was thought that cessation of hunting would allow the species to recover fully. Because marine mammals tend to be long-lived and to reproduce slowly, their recovery from severe depletion is a long process at best and, in some cases, will take more than 100 years even after factors limiting population growth have been controlled. Some species and populations have shown signs of recovery since directed harvests ended. After decades of protection, the eastern Pacific population of gray whales recovered to near-pre-exploitation levels, allowing it to be removed from the endangered species list in 1994. Since passage of the ESA and MMPA, several other listed species also have shown varying degrees of recovery, including some populations of humpback whales, blue whales, sperm whales, and fin whales, Guadalupe fur seals, and Florida manatees. In a few cases—particularly for populations that were reduced to very low levels—a variety of factors is preventing or slowing recovery, and it often is not clear which factors are most influential.

The most prevalent impediments to the growth of listed marine mammal taxa in U.S. waters include incidental entanglement in fishing gear, ship strikes, reduction in prey availability, entanglement in marine debris, and the effects of natural biotoxins. Other factors that have been important for at least some species are subsistence harvests, coastal development, contaminants, oil spills, disturbance and harassment by people, climate change, predation, disease, entrapment in physical structures, and loss or degradation of key habitats (see Appendix G). The significance of different types of stresses varies by species and population. For example, entanglement in marine debris is a serious threat to Hawaiian monk seals but a relatively minor threat to Florida manatees and great whales. Entrapment in floodgates and navigation locks poses a threat unique to Florida manatees. Ship strikes and collisions with smaller vessels affect a number of species but have had their greatest effect on Florida manatees and North Atlantic right whales. Mid-Atlantic bottlenose dolphins are most affected by fishery interactions, contaminants, and disease. Although significant progress has been made in reducing incidental injury and mortality of many marine mammals in fisheries, direct (e.g., entanglement in active fishing gear) and indirect (e.g., removal of marine mammal prey items) interactions continue to impede the recovery of a number of listed marine mammals.

Examples of significant natural threats to species are male mobbing and shark predation on Hawaiian monk seals, cold winter weather and periodic red tides on Florida manatees and bottlenose dolphins, and outbreaks of disease on bottlenose dolphins. In some cases, causes of decline remain unknown or subject to controversy (e.g., southwest Alaska sea otters, northern fur seals, and Steller sea lions) despite directed study. In many cases involving natural threats, human-related factors may have subtle underlying influences. For example, red tide-related die-offs may be indirectly related to effects of contaminants that impair animal immune systems, and the frequency or intensity of red tides themselves may be related to pollution from land run-off or, potentially, changes in ocean temperature and currents secondary to climate change. Similarly, cold stress in some manatees may be related to the location and reliability of warm-water outfalls created by power plants and used by manatees during winter.

MANAGEMENT FRAMEWORK

Although NMFS and FWS exercise lead responsibility for marine mammals under their respective jurisdictions, the conservation of many endangered, threatened, and depleted marine mammal taxa rely on a much broader group of federal, state, and non-governmental partners. The activities of these agencies and groups often are organized through recovery teams, take reduction teams, implementation teams, Alaska Native organizations, and other formal and informal advisory groups.

The most elaborate example of this approach is the Florida manatee recovery program. Although FWS and the Florida Fish and Wildlife Conservation Commission carry out most formal regulatory aspects of the program and USGS and the Florida Fish and Wildlife Research Institute undertake most manatee research, the current manatee recovery team includes more than 140 members from 60 agencies and groups. The team's activities are coordinated through 12 working groups and task forces. The cooperative efforts of these organizations help address many of the tasks identified in the recovery plan that the lead agencies could not undertake alone, given limited resources. However, the breadth of involvement also presents an enormous organizational challenge.

Cooperative programs with large numbers of partners also exist for North Atlantic right whales and Steller sea lions. Somewhat less complex, but no less crucial, partnerships exist for bowhead whales, Hawaiian monk seals, and southern sea otters. In some cases, other agencies or organizations play key decision-making roles in recovery efforts. For instance, the North Pacific Fishery Management Council has developed and incorporated measures to reduce fishery impacts on western Steller sea lions into its groundfish fishery management plans, and the Alaska Eskimo Whaling Commission allocates and enforces Native subsistence catch quotas for bowhead whales. Congress also has played an important role in many recovery programs by directing appropriations to species or projects and, in a few cases, by enacting legislation designed to address species-specific management issues. Examples of the latter include statutory provisions authorizing the translocation of southern sea otters and legislation prohibiting the subsistence hunting of Cook Inlet beluga whales except as provided in co-management agreements.

Conservation programs for many listed species, however, are far less developed. For example, blue whales, sperm whales, fin whales, sei whales, and Guadalupe fur seals receive very little species-specific management attention from NMFS or other agencies. Because the United States is a member of the IWC, NMFS and the Department of State have actively represented U.S. interests at IWC meetings to promote protection of whales from commercial exploitation. Also, the National Marine Sanctuary Program has supported research and public education regarding marine mammals that occur in national marine sanctuaries.

CRITICAL HABITAT

Although the ESA now requires designating critical habitat for species or populations that are listed, such areas have not been designated for most listed marine mammals. This is partly because this requirement was not in effect when most marine mammals were first listed. In addition, data to identify such areas are not available for some species, and both NMFS and FWS have been reluctant to dedicate resources to this purpose for species already listed. Where such efforts have been made, it has often been in response to litigation to compel such designations. Only 7 of the 18 marine mammal taxa currently listed have had critical habitat designated (i.e., North Atlantic and North Pacific right whales, southern resident killer whales, Hawaiian monk seals, eastern and western Steller sea lions, and Florida manatees).

RECOVERY PLANS AND TEAMS

Recovery plans or conservation plans have been completed and adopted for 9 of the 18 marine mammal taxa listed as endangered or threatened under the ESA and one of the four taxa listed only as depleted under the MMPA (Table 26). In a few cases, these plans have been updated periodically to reflect new information and issues. For example, the Florida manatee recovery plan has been updated three times at roughly five-year intervals, and the recovery plans for northern right whales and southern sea otters have both been revised once since initial adoption. Recovery plans for Hawaiian monk seals and Steller sea lions and the conservation plan for northern fur seals are currently being updated for the first time. Recovery plans for humpback whales and Antillean manatees are more than a decade old and have not been updated. Draft recovery plans also have been developed or initiated for four other taxa (fin whales, sperm whales, sei whales, and southwest Alaska sea otters), but no plans have been developed or planned for three taxa (bowhead whales, Guadalupe fur seals, and Caribbean monk seals). With regard to the four taxa listed only as depleted under the MMPA, a conservation plan was adopted for one (the Pribilof Islands population of northern fur seals) and draft plans are in varying stages for the other three. A draft conservation plan for mid-Atlantic bottlenose dolphins was prepared several years ago but has not been circulated for pubic review, a draft conservation plan for Cook Inlet beluga whales was released in 2005, and an intent to prepare a draft conservation plan for AT1 killer whales was announced in 2004.

The different recovery and conservation plans vary greatly in content. The goals of recovery plans developed prior to the mid-1990s were generally qualitative and often called for increasing populations to undefined levels that would allow downlisting or delisting with adequate levels of protection for the species and its habitats. Recent plans (e.g., for North Atlantic right whales and Florida manatees) reflect the 1994 amendments to the ESA that require objective, measurable criteria for determining when species have recovered. Those plans generally have far more specific goals, such as downlisting or delisting the species after specific quantitative criteria have been met. In such cases, however, meeting the quantitative benchmarks merely triggers a qualitative analysis of the five listing factors set forth in the ESA and to date, with the exception of Florida manatees, no analyses have been undertaken to measure progress against identified criteria.

Table 26. *Status of recovery plans and conservation plans prepared under the Endangered Species Act and Marine Mammal Protection Act for endangered, threatened, and depleted marine mammals.*

Common Name	Adopted Plans	Draft Plans	Plans Currently under Development or Revision
Florida Manatee	1980, 1989, 1991, 1996, 2001		Revision
Puerto Rican Manatee	1986		
Caribbean Monk Seal			
Hawaiian Monk Seal	1983	2006	
Western Steller Sea Lion	1992	2006	
Blue Whale	1998	2006	
Western Arctic Bowhead Whale			
Fin Whale		1998, 2006	
Humpback Whale	1991		
North Atlantic Right Whale	1991, 2005		
North Pacific Right Whale	1991		
Sei Whale		1998	
Sperm Whale		2006	
Southern Resident Killer Whale		2005	
Southern Sea Otter	1982, 2003		
Southwest Alaska Sea Otter			Development
Guadalupe Fur Seal			
Eastern Steller Sea Lion	1992		Revision
Eastern North Pacific Northern Fur Seal		1993	Revision
Cook Inlet Beluga Whale		2005	
Mid-Atlantic Coastal Bottlenose Dolphin			Development
AT1 Killer Whale			

Although causes of population declines and obstacles to recovery are not always apparent, all of the recovery and conservation plans provide thorough analyses of known and suspected or potential conservation threats as they are understood at the time the plans are written. As most plans are developed by teams of stakeholders and scientists and are made available for public comment, the plan development process provides an important opportunity for reaching agreement on conservation issues and needs and for encouraging and directing involvement by concerned agencies and groups. Developed plans also vary in the degree to which they focus on reducing the factors contributing to the unfavorable status of listed species. In most cases, initial recovery plans have focused more on identifying research priorities to clarify and provide a more informed basis for management actions.

Approved recovery plans typically outline sets of prioritized tasks that provide a basis for projecting funding needs over a five-year period. The funding needs invariably exceed levels the lead agencies expect to provide but have served to encourage, justify, and guide cooperative involvement and funding by partner agencies and organizations. Periodic plan revisions have provided renewed opportunities for encouraging and guiding partner agencies and groups in light of new information and progress. However, because many taxa either do not yet have approved recovery or conservation plans or have plans that are more than 10 years old, the benefits of provisions for preparing plans under the ESA and MMPA have not been used to their fullest extent for all listed taxa.

The role and composition of recovery teams has varied by species and over time. As noted above, the recovery team for Florida manatees has evolved from a small team composed principally of scientists to one that now includes more than 150 members representing management agencies, industry and environmental groups, academia, and the public. This shift reflects a change in focus from research to provide information for decision-making to one of coordinating a wide range of research, monitoring, and recovery activities performed by many different institutions. Similarly, the recovery teams initially convened by NMFS for Hawaiian monk seals were composed principally of scientists, but recent membership changes have reduced the number of scientists and increased representation from involved agencies and stakeholders. However, because the lead agencies have convened teams for only a few listed taxa, the provisions authorizing them to establish teams have been underused.

MANAGEMENT ACTIONS

In most cases, recovery program management measures—particularly regulations—have been developed through an adaptive management approach. That is, management measures have been adopted incrementally and remain in effect until they are determined to be insufficient, at which time they are supplemented or replaced with new measures. This approach reflects agency desires to minimize the risk of imposing unnecessary measures. However, it also can result in management programs that develop too slowly and are ineffective or minimally effective. Adaptive management presumes an ability to measure the effectiveness of implemented measures. Effectiveness is usually evaluated by one of two methods: (1) monitoring trends in overall population abundance or particular population parameters (e.g., rates of mortality) in response to a particular measure, and (2) studies to assess the extent to which relevant stakeholders use or comply with recommended or required measures.

The North Atlantic right whale recovery program typifies the adaptive management approach although, in this case, one that has been unsuccessful. To reduce entanglement in fishing gear, NMFS adopted a take reduction plan in 1997 that relied largely on requirements for modifying fishing gear. As observed right whale entanglements continued with little evidence of a decline, NMFS has had to make frequent minor and major changes to its plan. However, instead of implementing fundamentally different approaches with a higher probability of addressing entanglement risks, adopted changes have relied on expanded requirements for the same gear modifications, so far resulting in little or no progress. To reduce right whale deaths due to ship collisions, NMFS initially relied on public outreach and voluntary actions by vessel operators. Initial outreach efforts were supplemented by mandatory ship reporting measures in the late 1990s to ensure that vessel operators transiting key habitats were aware of available information on right whales, collision risks, and avoidance measures. As those measures failed to reduce the frequency of collision-related right whale deaths, steps were initiated to develop a fundamentally different approach involving new speed and routing requirements. Adaptive management also has been used incrementally to better effect for expanding the scope of restrictions on fisheries interacting with southern sea otters and Steller sea lions and for boat speed limits to protect Florida manatees. In the Steller sea lion case, however, the changes in management were driven more by litigation than by recognition of and response to inadequate protection measures.

The scope and scale of recovery programs for listed marine mammals varies greatly depending on many factors including the types of threats, the adequacy of information with which to design management measures, public interest, and available funding. As indicated in the following section on staffing and funding, roughly 95 percent of the funding allocated to the 18 taxa listed as endangered or threatened has been devoted to 7 taxa (Florida manatees, California sea otters, Hawaiian monk seals, eastern and western Steller sea lions, North Atlantic right whales, and humpback whales). For the other 11 listed taxa (Puerto Rico manatees, southwest Alaska sea otters, Caribbean monk seals, Guadalupe fur seals, North Pacific right whales, bowhead whales, blue whales, fin whales, sei whales, sperm whales, and southern resident killer whales), recovery programs involve limited studies to assess population trends and limited management actions. Management efforts for large whales generally involve programs that cover multiple taxa simultaneously (e.g., take reduction plans addressing several species and participation in the IWC management program). Funding levels for the four taxa listed only as depleted under the MMPA are moderate to small. In general, no single factor or set of factors explains the disparate scope of recovery efforts.

For many of the taxa receiving the most funding, interactions with commercial fisheries have been and may continue to be the major issue (i.e., North Atlantic right whales, mid-Atlantic coastal bottlenose dolphins, Steller sea lions, Hawaiian monk seals, and southern sea otters). Management measures to address fishery interactions with listed marine mammals have frequently involved biological opinions prepared pursuant to section 7 of the ESA and lawsuits filed by environmental groups to compel greater protection for listed marine mammals. Adopted management actions have focused on the design of fishing gear, voluntary or mandatory use of fishing gear modifications, time/area fishing closures, fishery observer programs, disentanglement programs, and, in the case of southern sea otters, attempts to exclude animals from certain areas. In several cases, NMFS has convened take reduction teams composed of fishermen, government agency officials, conservationists, and other interests to recommend take reduction plans under the MMPA for reducing incidental injury and mortality. Although work to develop plans for non-listed marine mammals appears to have resulted in added protection in some cases (e.g., Gulf of Maine harbor porpoises), efforts to develop plans for listed taxa, such as North Atlantic right whales and bottlenose dolphins, have been less successful. In the case of North Atlantic right whales, entanglement rates have not declined since the take reduction plan was first implemented in 1997 despite periodic efforts to reconvene and expand the take reduction team and to implement significant plan modifications. In the case of bottlenose dolphins, limits on available information have delayed plan adoption. In these cases, it appears that MMPA provisions requiring the formation of take reduction teams and the preparation of take reduction plans have not been effective and that alternative approaches for identifying needed measures may be needed.

The depletion of prey resources by commercial fisheries also is a significant issue for some listed taxa (e.g., Steller sea lions and Hawaiian monk seals). Such indirect fishery interactions are nominally addressed in fishery management plans under the Magnuson-Stevens Fishery Conservation and Management Act, but our understanding of such potential impacts and efforts to investigate them have been inadequate to date. Following litigation concerning the effects of management plans for fisheries that might affect Steller sea lions, the North Pacific Fishery Management Council and NMFS limited fishing in or near certain sea lion habitats (e.g., rookeries and foraging areas), but they have not addressed the large-scale question of whether fishing under a maximum sustainable yield-based paradigm is safe for marine ecosystems. With regard to possible effects of lobster fishing on Hawaiian monk seals, the Western Pacific Fishery Management Council and NMFS rejected management recommendations by the Marine Mammal Commission for nearly 10 years until litigation and uncertainty as to the status of the lobster stock compelled NMFS to close the fishery entirely. Although efforts to address such indirect interactions are consistent with directives that fishery management plans establish optimal yield levels that take into account ecological factors, such efforts have been inconsistent at best and suggest that clearer guidance and direction are needed.

As a general matter related to both incidental taking in fishing gear and effects on prey availability, federal managers appear particularly reluctant to consider creating or modifying time/area closure provisions to address interactions with marine mammals. Although such actions are invariably controversial, time/area closures are routinely adopted and used to manage targeted fish stocks. However, most fishery management councils and NMFS have given little consideration to integrating time/area closure systems to benefit both marine mammal conservation and fish conservation objectives at the same time. A broader approach in preparing fishery management plans to adopt closure systems that attempt to meet conservation benefits for both fish stocks and marine mammals would be a positive step toward addressing conservation needs for marine mammals.

In several cases, state agencies have appeared more willing than federal agencies to establish fishery closures to protect marine mammals. For example, over the last decade, the state of California has excluded trap and net fishing from important sea otter habitats. In 2005 the state of Hawaii restricted all types of fishing in state waters of the Northwestern Hawaiian Islands to protect marine life, including Hawaiian monk seals.

Several listed taxa, particularly large whales and Florida manatees, are affected by vessel collisions. To reduce collision risks for whales, federal managers have relied largely on outreach and voluntary actions by mariners. The most ambitious efforts in this regard have focused on North Atlantic right whales that use calving grounds off Florida and Georgia and feeding grounds off New England. Those efforts advise vessel operators on ways to reduce collision risks and provide them with real or near-real time reports of whale sighting locations. Because these efforts have not reduced observed levels of collision-related right whale deaths, NMFS is developing regulatory measures to restrict vessel speeds and routing in key right whale habitats. Such rules have already been developed by the state of Florida and FWS to protect Florida manatees. Some of those rules have been contentious and subject to legal challenges. FWS and the state also have sought to reduce boat collisions with manatees by limiting or conditioning permits for marinas and other watercraft facilities in manatee habitat and by encouraging comprehensive manatee protection plans as part of county growth management plans.

Other management issues common to many listed marine mammal taxa are entanglement in marine debris and harassment by human activities. The taxa most affected by marine debris appear to be Hawaiian monk seals and the Pribilof Islands population of northern fur seals. Management actions to reduce marine debris impacts have included efforts to disentangle individual animals, public education to foster proper disposal practices, and volunteer beach clean-ups. Dedicated at-sea clean-up efforts also have been undertaken to remove hazardous debris from reefs adjacent to monk seal pupping beaches in the Northwestern Hawaiian Islands. To date, pleas for voluntary action to properly dispose of trash does not appear to have reduced debris levels. Efforts to reduce human disturbance have generally focused on keeping people some minimal distance away from animals. For example, NMFS has established a 100-yard minimum approach distance for humpback whales in Hawaii and Alaska and a 500-yard minimum approach distance for North Atlantic right whales. The agency also has developed non-binding whale-watching guidelines specific to each of its regions of the county. For Florida manatees, FWS has established no-entry manatee sanctuaries at warm-water refuges where manatees can avoid attention by swimmers and divers. To minimize disturbance of Hawaiian monk seals on beaches in the main Hawaiian Islands, volunteers working with NMFS and the state of Hawaii post temporary safety zones around hauled-out animals to keep beachgoers at a proper distance. These measure have had varying degrees of success.

For several listed marine mammal taxa, management programs include or encourage steps to purchase land or set aside areas whose development or use could adversely affect marine mammals or their habitat. Both the state of Florida and FWS have acquired tens of thousands of acres of land adjacent to waterways heavily used by Florida manatees. The importance of the Midway Islands as monk seal pupping habitat was a factor prompting the U.S. Navy to transfer the area to FWS for use as a national wildlife refuge. In several cases, marine areas have been designated as national marine sanctuaries largely or in part because of their importance as habitat for listed marine mammals (e.g., the Hawaiian Islands Humpback Whale National Marine Sanctuary, the Stellwagen Bank National Marine Sanctuary, and the Papahānaumokuākea Marine National Monument).

Another element common to management programs for several listed taxa (e.g., southern sea otters, Hawaiian monk seals, and Florida manatees) is direct intervention to improve survival rates or reduce risks (e.g., head start programs, translocations, and rescue/rehabilitation programs). Because of logistical limitations, direct intervention programs are generally not feasible for large whales (with the exception of disentanglement efforts noted previously). In the late 1980s FWS implemented a program to relocate southern sea otters outside their existing range in California to establish a new colony at an offshore island that would reduce the risk of a catastrophic event, such as an oil spill, affecting the entire remaining population. Between 1981 and 1993 NMFS attempted to increase the survivorship of Hawaiian monk seal pups at French Frigate Shoals and Kure Atoll by taking them into captivity for brief periods and then releasing them back into the wild. Injured and distressed Florida manatees are routinely brought into captivity for rehabilitation and release back into the wild.

STAFFING AND FUNDING

Staffing and funding are significant factors affecting the scope of recovery programs. Both have increased substantially since directed management programs were first required by the MMPA and ESA in the 1970s. NMFS estimates that it spent 131.4 FTEs in staff time on research and management activities for the 18 listed species and populations under its jurisdiction during 2005. Of this, 32.7 FTEs were by headquarters and regional office staffs for management purposes and 98.7 by the staff of fisheries science centers principally for research (Table 27) (Payne and Bengtson pers. comm.[27]). Seventy percent of that staff time was devoted to four taxa: North Atlantic right whales, western Steller sea lions, Hawaiian monk seals, and mid-Atlantic bottlenose dolphins. Nearly three-quarters of the remaining staff effort was devoted to four other taxa: southern resident killer whales, humpback whales, eastern Steller sea lions, and beluga whales. FWS and USGS allocated at least 30.9 FTEs in staff effort to the four listed marine mammals under jurisdiction of the Department of the Interior, most of which was devoted to the recovery efforts for Florida manatees.

Information on funding allocated to listed marine mammals is fraught with limitations. The most systematic and useful sources of information were (1) annual administrative reports prepared by FWS and USGS pursuant to a requirement of the MMPA (FWS 1981–1996, FWS and National Biological Service 1996, FWS and USGS 1997–2004), and (2) annual reports on recovery program expenditures for all endangered and threatened species prepared by FWS pursuant to a requirement in the ESA (FWS 2003b–d, 2005d–f, 2006). NMFS also prepared annual administrative reports pursuant to MMPA requirements through the early 2000s; however, its reports did not provide information on species-specific funding allocations. Annual MMPA administrative reports by FWS and USGS were more useful, but those also do not summarize total costs by species and address only the listed marine mammals under Department of the Interior jurisdiction (i.e., manatees and sea otters) and combine budget data for some categories for all marine mammals. Requirements for those reports have since been eliminated. Recent National Oceanic and Atmospheric Administration budget books also provide line-item summaries of appropriations that include information for some species, but many relevant line-items list only receiving organizations, and it is not clear what taxa or what work is being addressed. The Marine Mammal Commission's annual surveys of federally funded marine mammal research provide species-specific information on research projects but do not address funding for management activities and are organized by agency rather than species.

Perhaps the single most useful source of funding data are the FWS annual reports of expenditures for all endangered and threatened species. Those reports include a species-by-species summary of all "reasonably identifiable federal expenditures primarily for the conservation of endangered and threatened species," including expenditures by states receiving grants under section 6 of the ESA. In part, the reports identify taxa-specific funding levels by federal and state agencies for the listed marine mammals that receive the most funding. They do not, however, itemize costs for listed marine mammals that receive low levels of funding (generally those less than $1 million) or are not listed as endangered or threatened (i.e., species listed only as depleted under the MMPA). They also do not necessarily reflect costs that are not clearly related to a specific species. In this regard, agencies providing funding data have broad latitude in determining how they tabulate their expenditures. As a result, accounting methods differ across agencies. For example, budget data for the Coast Guard, whose enforcement and

---

[27] P. Michael Payne, personal communication. 17 August 2005. Chief, Marine Mammals Division, Office of Protected Species, National Marine Fisheries Service, Silver Spring, MD 20910; John Bengtson, personal communication. 8 December 2006. National Marine Mammal Laboratory, National Marine Fisheries Service, Seattle, WA 98115.

support activities accounted for half of all reported expenditures on listed marine mammals in 2003, include all costs for ship operations (e.g., fuel costs, depreciation, and crew salaries) while on missions whose primary objective relates to listed species. Other agencies, however, apparently may not include such administrative and overhead costs. It also is unclear whether and how cost accounting methods by reporting agencies have changed over time, the extent to which participating agencies may have changed, or to what degree agency staff salaries are reflected. Notwithstanding such limitations, FWS reports provide the most comprehensive source of funding data available for listed marine mammals.

Table 27. *Estimated number of full time equivalent staff positions (FTEs) devoted to marine mammal protection programs by the National Marine Fisheries Service and the Fish and Wildlife Service in fiscal year 2005 (P. M. Payne and J. Bengtson pers. comm.).*

Species	NMFS Regional Offices & Headquarters	NMFS Fisheries Science Centers	Fish and Wildlife Service	U.S. Geological Survey	Total
Florida Manatee	–	–	11.25	13.36	24.61
Puerto Rican Manatee	–	–	1.00	0.75	1.75
Caribbean Monk Seal	0	0	–	–	0
Hawaiian Monk Seal	1.20	21.00	–	–	22.20
Western Steller Sea Lion	1.10	13.30	–	–	14.40
Blue Whale	0.35	1.18	–	–	1.53
Western Arctic Bowhead Whale	0.60	3.50	–	–	4.10
Fin Whale	0.60	0.28	–	–	0.88
Humpback Whale	1.80	5.30	–	–	7.10
North Atlantic Right Whale	16.00	13.20	–	–	29.20
North Pacific Right Whale	0.60	2.80	–	–	3.40
Sei Whale	0.20	0	–	–	0.20
Sperm Whale	0.53	1.70	–	–	2.23
Southern Resident Killer Whale	2.10	4.95	–	–	7.05
AT1 Killer Whale	0.20	0.25	–	–	0.45
Southern Sea Otter	–	–	2.00	?	2.00+
Guadalupe Fur Seal	0	0.20	–	–	0.20
Eastern Steller Sea Lion	1.30	5.13	–	–	6.43
Eastern North Pacific Fur Seal	1.70	8.40	–	–	10.10
Cook Inlet Beluga Whale	2.30	3.78	–	–	6.08
Mid-Atlantic Coastal Bottlenose Dolphin	2.10	13.75	–	–	15.85
Southwest Alaska Sea Otter	–	–	2.50	?	2.50+
TOTAL FTEs	32.68	98.72	16.75+	14.11+	162.16+

Based on those reports, federal expenditures for ESA-listed marine mammal taxa increased steadily from $8.5 million in 1998 to a high of $82.6 million in 2003, and then declined to $71.2 million in 2004 (Table 28). During that same period, expenditures by states receiving ESA section 6 grants increased from $40,100 to $8.9 million. Much of this increase can be attributed to funding for Steller sea lions. Excluding funds for that species, reported expenditures for the other ESA-listed marine mammals increased from $2.9 million to $17.1 million between 1998 and 2000 and then increased at a slower rate, reaching $28.6 million in 2004. For most listed marine mammals, more than half of all funding has been devoted to research and monitoring. The high expenditures on research reflect the fundamental need for demographic and biological data. Such data are essential for making and justifying management decisions in environmental impact statements, recovery and conservation plans, budget documents, and other decision-making records. For several listed marine mammals (e.g., AT1 killer whales, several great whales, and Guadalupe fur seals), research and monitoring studies are virtually the only activities funded.

Funding for marine mammal taxa listed under the ESA is heavily weighted toward a few taxa (Figure 1). Of the $82.6 million in federal and state expenditures reported during the peak funding year of 2003, 91 percent was allocated to four taxa: western and eastern Steller sea lions ($49.5 million and $5.3 million, respectively), North Atlantic right whales ($11.8 million), and Florida manatees ($9.8 million). More than half of the remaining funds were allocated to three other taxa: Hawaiian monk seals ($2.1 million), humpback whales ($1.6 million), and southern sea otters ($1.4 million). The remaining $1 million was distributed among the other nine ESA-listed taxa and was reported principally by the Coast Guard for enforcement. Overall, more than half of all reported expenditures for ESA-listed marine mammals in 2003 ($42.9 million) was reported by the Coast Guard for enforcement, principally related to Steller sea lions and North Atlantic right whales. Excluding Coast Guard funds from the 2003 total, federal and state expenditures totaled $39.6 million, with 88 percent allocated to eastern and western Steller sea lions ($14.9 million), North Atlantic right whales ($10.7 million), and Florida manatees ($9.85 million). An additional 12 percent was allocated to Hawaiian monk seals, southern sea otters and humpback whales. Only 0.4 percent of the funding by agencies other than the Coast Guard in 2003 was spent on the other nine listed taxa. Overall, federal agencies accounted for nearly all spending on all listed marine mammal taxa except Florida manatees, where the state of Florida has provided more than 60 percent of reported expenditures since the 1990s.

Funding levels for species listed only as depleted are less clear. Funding for bottlenose dolphins has exceeded $2 million in some years, but funding for Cook Inlet beluga whales, AT1 killer whales, and the eastern North Pacific fur seal population has rarely, if ever, exceeded about $200,000 to $400,000 annually.

During the period 2001–2004 expenditures reported by NMFS for listed marine mammals declined from $40.7 million to $32.6 million; those reported by FWS remained relatively steady at between about $2 million to $2.5 million (Figure 2). At the same time, Congress earmarked increasing amounts of funding to both agencies for various activities on specific taxa. Most notable in this regard were earmarks for Steller sea lions and North Atlantic right whales. A significant amount of the congressional earmarks was targeted to non-federal research organizations for research and monitoring activities. Although data have not been compiled for

2004 and 2005, congressional appropriations to NMFS and FWS for work on marine mammal recovery programs have been further reduced. As a result of recent budget cuts and increasing numbers of earmarks, the ability of NMFS and FWS to allocate funds among taxa on a discretionary basis is very limited.

Table 28. **Total estimated federal and state expenditures on endangered and threatened species in fiscal years 1998–2005. Numbers in parentheses are state funding levels; all amounts are in $ thousands.**

Species	FY 98	FY 99	FY 00	FY 01	FY 02	FY 03	FY 04
West Indian Manatee (Florida + Puerto Rico taxa)	1,565 (13)	4,351 (1,945)	9,743 (5,923)	9,373 (5,936)	8,571 (5,929)	9,799 (5,969)	9,862 (5,945)
Southern Sea Otter	495 (0)	615 (156)	624 (35)	1,094 (35)	1,066 (35)	1376 (40)	734 (20)
Caribbean Monk Seal	10 (0)	0 (0)	0 (0)	8 (0)	0 (0)	0 (0)	0 (0)
Hawaiian Monk Seal	1,156 (0)	1,105 (0.4)	1,267 (14)	2,121 (14)	2,197 (14)	2,145 (15)	2,321 (0)
Steller Sea Lion (East + West taxa)	3,079 (19)	7,234 (8)	13,113 (6)	46,783 (2,338)	55,998 (2,496)	–	–
Eastern Steller Sea Lion	–	–	–	–	–	5,297 (1,203)	10,811 (1,203)
Western Steller Sea Lion	–	–	–	–	–	49,514 (1,200)	31,746 (1,200)
Guadalupe Fur Seal	0 (0)	2 (0)	2 (0)	0 (0)	0 (0)	0 (0)	0 (1)
Blue Whale	4 (1)	125 (0)	6 (0)	1 (0)	8 (0)	203 (0)	67 (2)
Bowhead Whale	1 (1)	(0) (3)	3 (3)	25 (25)	7 (0)	204 (0)	190 (0)
Fin Whale	5 (1)	13 (0.3)	5 (1)	24 (2)	13 (1)	206 (1)	72 (3)
Humpback Whale	361 (41)	492 (8)	567 (11)	740 (11)	890 (11)	1,615 (18)	666 (7)
Northern Right Whale (N. Pacific + N. Atlantic taxa)	1,460 (1)	3,273 (290)	4,872 (127)	6,036 (145)	8,393 (280)	11,802 (123)	12,370 (504)
Sei Whale	5 (1)	4 (0)	4 (0)	12 (0)	1 (0)	203 (0)	66 (0)
Sperm whale	5 (1)	7 (0)	3 (0)	27 (0)	1 (0)	203 (0)	2,270 (2)
TOTAL (All Marine Mammals)	$8,505 (81)	$17,222 (2,410)	$30,207 (2,410)	$66,244 (8,505)	$77,147 (8,765)	$82,567 (8,570)	$71,175 (8,887)
Percent of funding relative to all listed taxa	2.2% (0.5%)	2.6% (4.3%)	5.8% (6.1%)	10.2% (11.1%)	10.7 (11.7%)	12.1% (12.6%)	9% (14.5%)

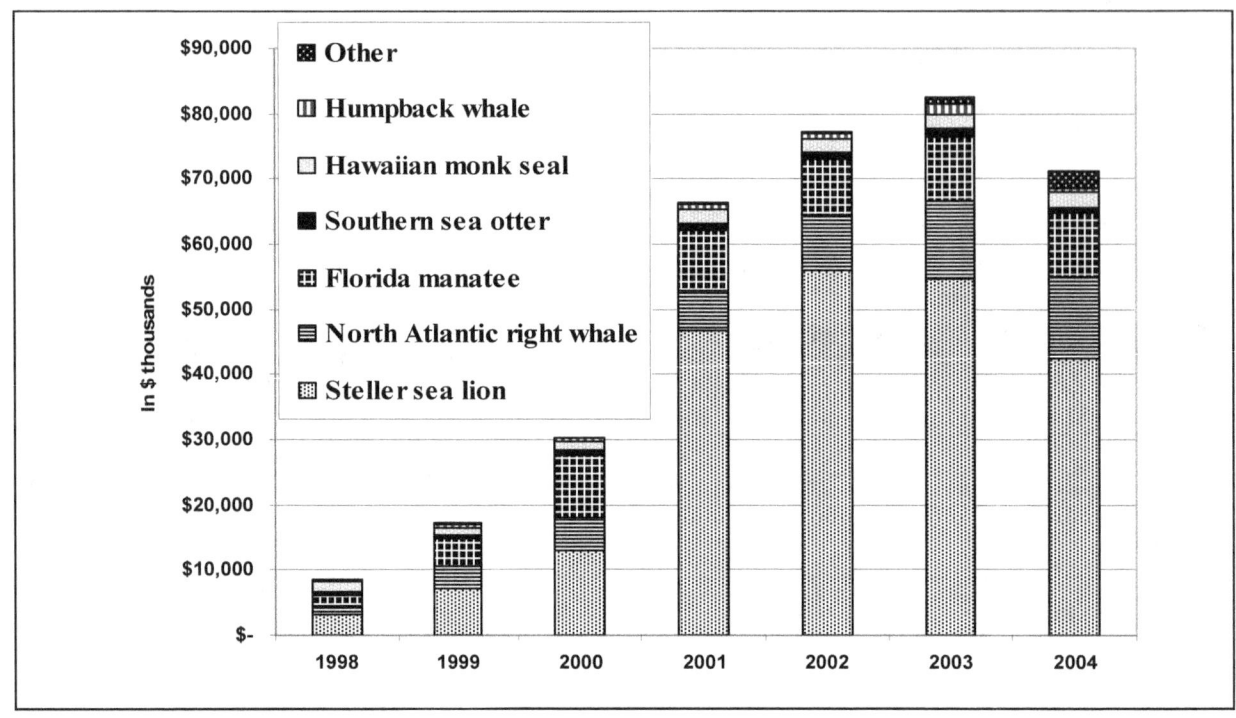

Figure 1. **Expenditures for recovery activities on all taxa listed as endangered or threatened by species and by year, 1998–2004**

Recent trends in congressional funding for endangered marine mammal programs pose at least two major challenges for lead agencies. First, appropriated funding has not been sufficient to address all high-priority needs identified in recovery and conservation plans. Second, the increasing proportion of funding appropriated as earmarks limits the agencies' ability to respond to new information and issues. Although most earmarks have usefully addressed important research and management needs, they have reduced the ability of the lead agencies, particularly NMFS, to allocate funds based on its best assessment of greatest need or opportunity. In addition, although earmarks often allow the start-up of new programs, they do not provide a basis for carrying out long-term research or management work. As a result, modifications to existing recovery programs are difficult, and the implementation of new recovery initiatives for species and populations that may be equally or even more endangered than those receiving the most funding is limited. In addition, for those species that do receive significant funding, it is very difficult for the agencies to plan and support multi-year commitments that often are essential to achieve program goals.

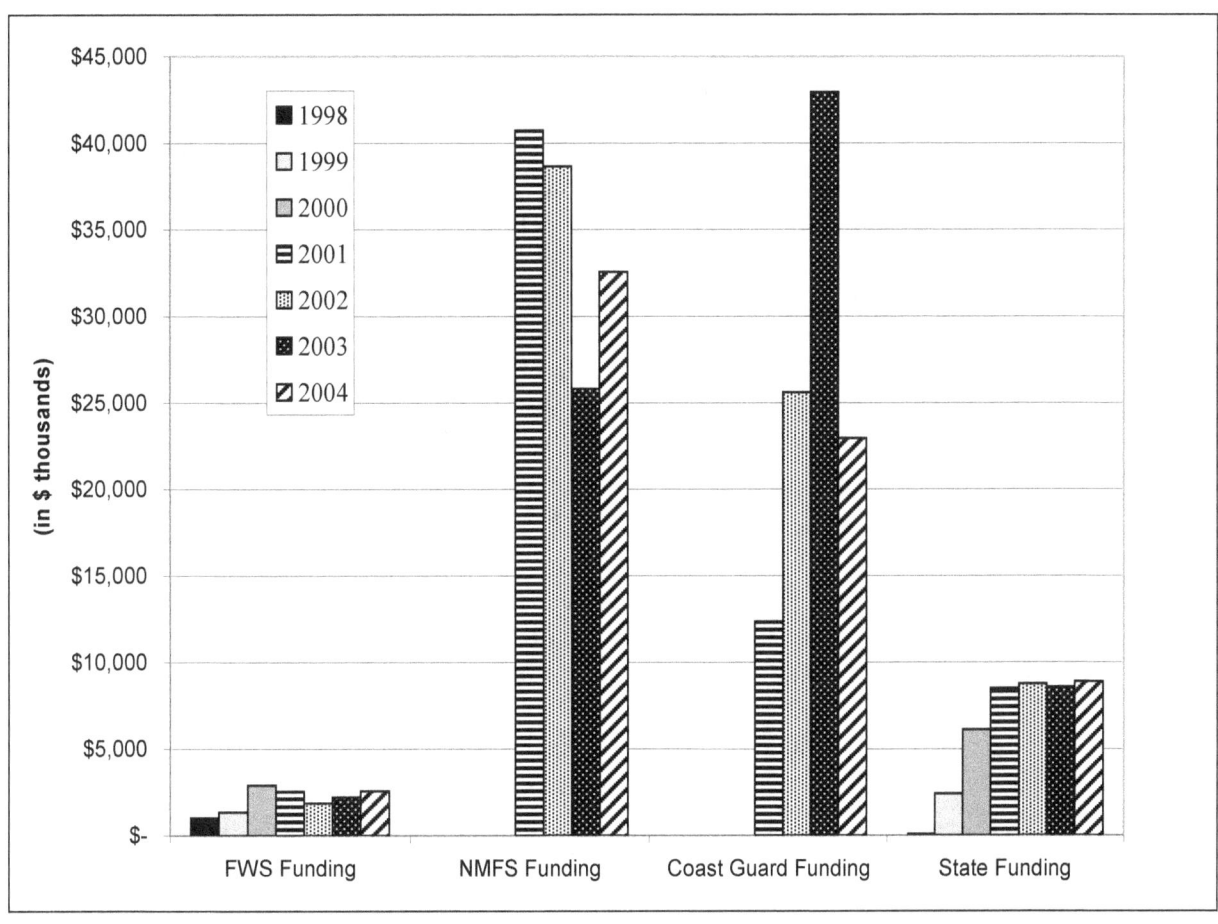

Figure 2. ***Expenditures for recovery activities on all taxa listed as endangered or threatened by agency and by year, 1998–2004. (Data for NMFS and USCG were not reported separately prior to 2001)***

Where resources have been available, recovery efforts for threatened, endangered, and depleted marine mammal populations have become increasingly sophisticated. In some cases, improved research techniques have better defined factors responsible for population declines or failure to recover. In other cases, resolution of such causes has remained elusive. For most taxa, improved information, particularly with regard to stock structure, has made it clear that the task of recovery is far more complex than previously thought. Managers must consider not just a single, broadly distributed species but multiple populations and subpopulations, each of which may be affected by different threats and human activities in a variety of ways that are not always apparent. This has made scientific and political decisions concerning how to mitigate the impact of human activities more difficult.

Pressures on marine mammal populations, not to mention other marine wildlife, are clearly increasing as human demands for food, waste disposal, and economic development continue to grow. Although recovery programs for listed marine mammals have made great strides in addressing these issues, and some listed species are making good progress toward recovery, constraints on funding levels and agency flexibility loom as significant impediments in addressing pressing needs for other species.

V. ACKNOWLEDGMENTS

The authors wish to thank the staff of the National Marine Fisheries Service and the Fish and Wildlife Service for their patience and assistance with innumerable requests for information. In particular, we would like to thank P. Michael Payne of the National Marine Fisheries Service and Deborah Crouse of the Fish and Wildlife Service for helping to coordinate many of the responses made during the preparation of this report. Although many people with both agencies and the Marine Mammal Commission reviewed and commented on various sections of this report, we express a special thanks to Lloyd Lowry, Suzanne Montgomery, and Timothy Ragen for their careful reviews of multiple drafts. Special thanks also go to Wilhelmina Innes for her help in preparing the appendices and various tables in the body of the report.

VI. REFERENCES

Baker, C. S., and L. M. Herman. 1989. Behavioral responses of summering humpback whales to vessel traffic: experimental and opportunistic observations. Technical report NPS-NR-TRS-89-01 to the National Park Service. U.S. Department of the Interior, Gustavus, AK. 50 pp.

Baker, J. D., and T. C. Johanos. 2004. Abundance of the Hawaiian monk seal in the main Hawaiian Islands. Biological Conservation 116:103–110.

Barlow, J., and B. L. Taylor. Unpubl. Preliminary abundance of sperm whales in the northeastern temperate Pacific estimated from a combined visual and acoustic survey. Paper SC/50/CAWS20 presented to the International Whaling Commission, June 1998.

Bartholomew, G. A. 1950. A male Guadalupe fur seal on San Nicolas Island, California. Journal of Mammalogy 31:175–180.

Bean, M. J., and M. J. Rowland. 1997. The Evolution of National Wildlife Law. Praeger Publishers, Westport, CT.

Braun, R. C., and P. K. Yochem. 2006. Workshop to evaluate the potential for use of morbillivirus vaccination in Hawaiian monk seals. Final report prepared for the Marine Mammal Commission, Bethesda, MD. 35 pp.

Calambokidis, J., and J. Barlow. 2004. Abundance of blue and humpback whales in the eastern North Pacific estimated by capture-recapture and line transect methods. Marine Mammal Science 20:65–85.

Calkins, D. G., and K. B. Schneider. 1985. The sea otter (*Enhydra lutris*). Pp. 37–45 *in* J. Burns, K. J. Frost, and L. F. Lowry (eds.). Marine mammal species accounts. Alaska Department of Fish and Game. Game Technical Bulletin 7.

Caswell, H., M. Fujiwara, and S. Brault. 1999. Declining survival probability threatens the North Atlantic right whale. Proceedings of the National Academy of Science 96:3308–3313.

Clark, J. A., J. M. Hoekstra, P. D. Boersman, and P. Kareiva. 2002. Improving U.S. Endangered Species Act Recovery Plans: key findings and recommendations of the SCB recovery plan project. Final report to the FWS, Washington, DC March 2002. Cited in National Marine Fisheries Service (NMFS). 2004. Interim Endangered and Threatened Species Recovery Planning Guidance. October 2004. http://www.nmfs.noaa.gov/pr/recovery/guidance.htm.

Crouse, D. T., L. A. Mehrhoff, M. J. Parkin, D. R. Elam, and L. Y. Chen. 2002. Endangered species recovery and the SCB study: A U.S. Fish and Wildlife Service perspective. Ecological Applications V. 12, No. 3, pp.719–723. Cited in National Marine Fisheries Service (NMFS). 2004. Interim Endangered and Threatened Species Recovery Planning Guidance. October 2004. http://www.nmfs.noaa.gov/pr/recovery/guidance.htm.

DeMaster, D., R. Angliss, J. Cochrane, P. Mace, R. Merrick, M. Miller, S. Rumsey, B. Gaylor, G. Thompson, and R. Waples. 2004. Recommendations to NOAA Fisheries: ESA Listing Criteria by the Quantitative Working Group, 10 June 2004. U.S. Dep. Commerce, NOAA Tech. Memo. NMFS-F/SPO-67, 85p. http://spo.nmfs.noaa.gov/tm/.

Department of Commerce and Department of the Interior (DOC DOI 1996). 1996. Secretarial Order on American Indian Tribal Rights, Federal-Tribal Trust Responsibilities, and the Endangered Species Act. Order 513, May 13, 1996.

Doroff, A. M., J. A. Estes, M. T. Tinker, D. M. Burns, and T. J. Evans. 2003. Sea otter population declines in the Aleutian Archipelago. Journal of Mammalogy 84(1):55–64.

Estes, J. A. 1990. Growth and equilibrium in sea otter populations. Journal of Animal Ecology 59:385–401.

Estes, J. A., M. T. Tinker, T. M. Williams, and D. F. Doak. 1998. Killer whale predation linking oceanic and nearshore ecosystems. Science 282:473–476.

Ferber, D. 2005. Sperm whales bear testimony to worldwide pollution. Science 309:1166.

Fish and Wildlife Service and National Marine Fisheries Service (FWS and NMFS). 1994a. Interagency Cooperative Policy for Peer Review in Endangered Species Activities. 59 Fed.Reg. 34270.

Fish and Wildlife Service and National Marine Fisheries Service (FWS and NMFS). 1994b. Interagency Cooperative Policy on Information Standards Under the Endangered Species Act. 59 Fed.Reg. 34271.

Fish and Wildlife Service and National Marine Fisheries Service (FWS and NMFS). 1994c. Interagency Cooperative Policy on Recovery Plan Participation and Implementation Under the Endangered Species Act. 59 Fed.Reg. 34272.

Fish and Wildlife Service and National Marine Fisheries Service (FWS and NMFS). 1994d. Interagency Cooperative Policy for the Ecosystem Approach to the Endangered Species Act. 59 Fed.Reg. 34274.

Fish and Wildlife Service and National Marine Fisheries Service (FWS and NMFS). 1994e. Interagency Cooperative Policy Regarding the Role of State Agencies in Endangered Species Act Activities. 59 Fed.Reg. 34275.

Fleischer, L. A. 1987. Guadalupe fur seal, *Arctocephalus townsendi*,. Pp 43–48 *in* J.P. Croxall and R.L. Gentry (eds). Status, biology, and ecology of fur seals. Proceedings of an international symposium and workshop. Cambridge, England, 23–27 April 1984. U.S. NOAA Technical Report NMFS 51. National Marine Fisheries Service. U.S. Department of Commerce.

Fowler, C. M. 1982. Interactions of northern fur seals and commercial fisheries. *In* Transactions of the 47th North American Wildlife and Natural Resources Conference. Wildlife Management Institute. Washington, DC.

Fowler, C. M. 1985. An evaluation of the role of entanglement in the population dynamics of northern fur seals on the Pribilof Islands. *In* Proceedings of the Workshop on the Fate and Impact of Marine Debris, 27–29 November 1984. U.S. Department of Commerce. NOAA Tech Memo, NMFS-NOAA- TM-MNMF-SWFC-54.

Gilmartin, W.G. 1983. Recovery Plan for the Hawaiian Monk Seal, *Monachus schauinslandi*. National Marine Fisheries Service, Southwest Region. March 24, 1983.

Groombridge, B. (ed.). 1994. 1994 IUCN Red List of Threatened Animals. IUCN, Gland, Switzerland.

Haubold, E. M, C. Deutsch, and C. Fonnesbeck. 2005. Preliminary biological status review of the Florida manatee (*Trichechus manatus latirostris*). Florida Fish and Wildlife Conservation Commission. Fish and Wildlife Research Institute. St. Petersburg, FL.

Hawaiian Monk Seal Recovery Team. 2005. Draft Recovery Plan for the Hawaiian Monk Seal. October 2005. Prepared for the Office of Protected Resources, National Marine Fisheries Service. Silver Spring, MD.

Hubbs, C. L. 1956. The Guadalupe fur seal still lives! Zoonoz. San Diego Zoological Society 29(12):6–9.

Jameson, R. J, K. W. Kenyon, A. Johnson, and H. M. Wight. 1982. History and status of translocated sea otter populations in North America. Wildlife Society Bulletin 10(2):100–107.

Jensen, A. S., and G. K. Silber. 2003. Large whale ship strike database. NOAA Technical Memorandum NMFS-OPR-25. Office of Protected Resources. National Marine Fisheries Service. U.S. Department of Commerce, Silver Spring, MD. 37 pp.

Kenyon, K. W. 1972. Man versus the monk seal. Journal of Mammalogy 53(4):687–696.

Kenyon, K. W. 1977. Caribbean monk seal extinct. Journal of Mammalogy 58(1):97–98.

Krahn, M. M. et al. 2002. Status review of southern resident killer whales (*Orcinus orca*) under the Endangered Species Act. U.S. Dept. Commerce, NOAA Tech. Memo. NMFS-NWFSC-54, 133 pp.

Kraus, S. D. M. W. Brown, H. Caswell, C. W. Clark, M. Fujiwara, R. D. Kenny, A. R. Knowlton, S. Landry, C. A. Mayo, W. A. McLellan, M. J. Moore, D. J. Nowacek, D A. Papst, A. J. Read, and R. M. Rolland. 2005. North Atlantic right whales in crisis. Science: 309: 561–562.

Lafferty, K. D., and L. R. Gerber. 2002. Good medicine for conservation biology: the intersection of epidemiology and conservation theory. Conservation Biology 16:593–604.

Laist, D. W., and C. Shaw. 2006. Preliminary Evidence that Boat Speed Restrictions Reduce Deaths of Florida Manatees. Marine Mammal Science 22(2):472–479.

Laist, D. W., and J. E. Reynolds. 2005a. Florida Manatees, warm-water refuges, and an uncertain future. Coastal Management 33:279–295.

Laist, D. W., and J. E. Reynolds. 2005b. Influence of power plants and other warm water refuges on Florida manatees. Marine Mammal Science 21(4):739–764.

Laist, D. W., A. R. Knowlton, J. G. Mead, A. S. Collet, and M. Podesta. 2001. Collisions between ships and whales. Marine Mammal Science 17(1:35–75.

Lefebvre, L., W. M. Marmontel, J. P. Reid, G. B. Rathbun, and D. P. Domning. 2001. Status and biogeography of the West Indian manatee. Chapter 23 in C. Woods (ed.). Patterns of West Indian Biogeography. CRC Press. 35 pp + Figs.

Lowry, L., D. W. Laist, and E. Taylor. 2007. Endangered, Threatened, and Depleted Marine Mammals in U.S. Waters: A Review of Species Classification Systems and Listed Species. Report to the Marine Mammal Commission, Bethesda MD. 79 + viii pp.

Lowry, L., G. O'Corry-Crowe, and D. Goodman. 2006. *Delphinapterus leucas* (Cook Inlet population). *In*: IUCN 2006. 2006 IUCN Red List of Threatened Species.

Marine Mammal Commission (MMC). 1991. Marine Mammal Commission Annual Report: Calendar Year 1990. Marine Mammal Commission. National Technical Information Service. NTIS PB91-164236. 280 pp.

Marine Mammal Commission. 2001. Annual Report to Congress 2000. Bethesda, MD. http://www.mmc.gov.

Marine Mammal Commission. 2002. Annual Report to Congress 2001. Bethesda, MD. http://www.mmc.gov.

Marine Mammal Commission. 2003. Annual Report to Congress 2002. Bethesda, MD. http://www.mmc.gov.

Marine Mammal Commission. 2004. Annual Report to Congress 2003. Bethesda, MD. http://www.mmc.gov.

Marine Mammal Commission. 2005. Annual Report to Congress 2004. Bethesda, MD. http://www.mmc.gov.

Marine Mammal Commission. 2006. Annual report to Congress 2005. Bethesda MD. http://www.mmc.gov.

Marine Mammal Commission. 2007. Report of the Workshop on Assessing the Population Viability of Endangered Marine Mammals in U.S. Waters. Marine Mammal Commission, Bethesda, MD. 37 pp.

Mate, B. R., K. M. Stafford, and D. K. Ljungblad. 1994. A change in sperm whale (*Physeter macrocephalus*) distribution correlated to seismic surveys in the Gulf of Mexico. Journal of the Acoustical Society of America. 96:3268–3269.

National Marine Fisheries Service. 1991a. Recovery Plan for the Northern Right Whale (*Eubalaena glacialis*). Prepared by the Right Whale Recovery Team for the National Marine Fisheries Service, Silver Spring, MD.

National Marine Fisheries Service. 1991b. Recovery Plan for the Humpback Whale (*Megaptera novaeangliae*). Prepared by the Humpback Whale Recovery Team for the National Marine Fisheries Service, Silver Spring, MD.

National Marine Fisheries Service. 1992. Final Recovery Plan for Steller Sea Lions (*Eumetopias jubatus*). Prepared by the Steller Sea Lion Recovery Team for the National Marine Fisheries Service. Silver Spring, MD.

National Marine Fisheries Service. 1993. Final Conservation Plan for the Northern Fur Seal (*Callorhinus ursinus*). Prepared by the National Marine Mammal Laboratory/Alaska Fisheries Science Center, Seattle, Washington, and the Office of Protected Resources, National Marine Fisheries Service, Silver Spring, MD.

National Marine Fisheries Service. 2003. Status Review of the AT1 Group of killer whales from the Prince William Sound and Kenai Fjords area. http://www.fakr.noaa.gov/protectedresources/whales/killerwhales/at1statreview0703.pdf.

National Marine Fisheries Service. 2004a. Interim Endangered and Threatened Species Recovery Planning Guidance. http://www.nmfs.noaa.gov/pr/recovery/guidance.htm.

National Marine Fisheries Service. 2004b. Report to Congress: Review of Commercial Fisheries' Progress Toward Reducing Mortality and Serious Injury of Marine Mammals Incidental to Commercial Fishing Operations. 18 pp + appendix.

National Marine Fisheries Service. 2004c. Environmental Assessment and Regulatory Impact Review for the Implementation of the Zero Mortality Rate Goal of the Marine Mammal Protection Act.

National Marine Fisheries Service. 2004d. Record of Decision for Subsistence Harvest Management of Cook Inlet Beluga Whales: Final Environmental Impact Statement. http://www.fakr.noaa.gov/protectedresources/whales/beluga/cibrod2004.pdf.

National Marine Fisheries Service 2005a. Alaska Marine Mammal Stock Assessments, 2005. NOAA Tech. Memorandum NMFS-AFSC-161. A U.S. Department of Commerce. Alaska Fisheries Science Center. Seattle, WA. 250 pp. http://www.nmfs.noaa.gov/pr/sars/species.htm

National Marine Fisheries Service. 2005b. Recovery plan for the North Atlantic Right Whale (*Eubalaena glacialis*). U.S. Department of Commerce. National Marine Fisheries Service. Silver Spring, MD. http://www.nmfs.noaa.gov/pr/PR3/recovery.html.

National Marine Fisheries Service. 2005c. Preliminary Draft: Conservation Plan for Southern Resident Killer Whales (*Orcinus orca*). Silver Spring, MD. http://www.nwr.noaa.gov/mmammals/whales/CPPSKW.html.

National Marine Fisheries Service. 2005d. Draft Conservation Plan for the Cook Inlet Beluga Whale (*Delphinapterus leucas*). Silver Spring, MD. http://www.fakr.noaa.gov/protectedresources/whales/beluga/mmpa/draft/conservationplan032005.pdf.

National Marine Fisheries Service 2006a. U.S. Pacific marine mammal stock assessments: 2005. NOAA Tech. Memorandum NMFS-SWFSC-388. U.S. Department of Commerce. Southwest. Fisheries Science Center. La Jolla, CA. 317 pp. http://www.nmfs.noaa.gov/pr/sars/species.htm

National Marine Fisheries Service 2006b. U.S. Atlantic and Gulf of Mexico marine mammal stock assessments: 2005. NOAA Tech. Memorandum NMFS-NE-194. U.S. Department of Commerce. Northeast Fisheries Science Center. Woods Hole, MA. 352 pp. http://www.nmfs.noaa.gov/pr/sars/species.htm

National Marine Fisheries Service. 2006c. Draft recovery plan for the fin whale (*Balaenoptera physalus*). Office of Protected Resources. National Oceanic and Atmospheric Administration. Silver Spring, MD. http://www.nmfs.noaa.gov/pr/recovery/plans.htm.

National Marine Fisheries Service. 2006d. Draft recovery plan for the sperm whale (*Physeter macrocephalus*). Office of Protected Resources. National Marine Fisheries Service. National Oceanic and Atmospheric Administration. Silver Spring, MD. http://www.nmfs.noaa.gov/pr/recovery/plans.htm

National Marine Fisheries Service 2006e. Draft revision of the recovery plan for the Hawaiian monk seal (*Monachus schauinslandi*). Office of Protected Resources, National Oceanic and Atmospheric Administration, Silver Spring, MD. http://www.nmfs.noaa.gov/pr/recovery/plans.htm

National Ocean Service. 2004. Proposed Northwestern Hawaiian Islands National Marine Sanctuary: Advice and Recommendations on Development of Draft Fishing Regulations Under the National Marine Sanctuaries Act Section 304(a: (5). http://hawaiireef.noaa.gov/designation/fishing2004.html.

NOAA Fisheries. 2000. Annual Report: Administration of the Marine Mammal Protection Act of 1972, 1999–2000. http://www.nmfs.noaa.gov.

NOAA Fisheries. 2003. Priorities for the 21st Century: NOAA Fisheries' Strategic Plan for FY2003 – FY2008. http://www.nmfs.noaa.gov.

National Research Council. 2003. The Decline of the Steller Sea Lion in Alaskan Waters: Untangling Food Webs and Fishing Nets. National Academy Press, Washington, DC.

O'Shea, T. J., R. R. Reeves, and A. K. Long. 1999. Marine mammals and persistent ocean contaminants: proceedings of the Marine Mammal Commission Workshop, Keystone, Colorado, 12–15 October 1998. Marine Mammal Commission. Bethesda, MD. 150 pp.

Ohsumi, S., and S. Wada. 1974. Status of whale stocks in the North Pacific, 1972. Report of the International Whaling Commission. 25:114–126.

Polovina, J. J. 2005. Climate variation, regime shifts, and implications for sustainable fisheries. Bulletin of Marine Science 76(2):233–244.

Ragen, T. J., and D. M. Lavigne. 1999. The Hawaiian monk seal: biology of an endangered seal. Pp. 224–245 *in* J.R. Twiss and R.R. Reeves (eds). Conservation and Management of Marine Mammals. Smithsonian Institution Press. Washington, DC.

Rathbun, G. B, N. Carr, T. Carr, and C. A. Woods. 1985. The distribution of manatees and sea turtles in Puerto Rico, with emphasis on Roosevelt Rhodes Naval Station. NTIS PB 85-151847 AS. National Technical Information Service. Springfield, VA. 83 pp.

Rathbun, G. B, and E. Possardt. 1986. Recovery Plan for the Puerto Rico Population of the West Indian (Antillean) Manatee (*Trichechus manatus manatus* L.). U.S. Fish and Wildlife Service, Atlanta, GA.

Rathbun, G. B., and R. L. Wallace. 2000. Florida manatee. Pp. 107–111 *in* R.P. Reading and B. Miller (eds). A Reference Guide to Conflicting Issues. Greenwood Press. Westport, CT.

Reeves, R. R., G. Silber, and P. M. Payne. 1998. Draft Recovery Plan for the Fin Whale *Balaenoptera physalus* and Sei Whale *Balaenoptera borealis*. Prepared for the Office of Protected Resources, National Marine Fisheries Service, Silver Spring, MD.

Reeves, R. R., P. J. Clapham, R. L. Brownell, Jr., and G. K. Silber. 1998. Recovery Plan for the Blue Whale (*Balaenoptera musculus*). Prepared for the Office of Protected Resources, National Marine Fisheries Service, Silver Spring, MD.

Reeves, R. R., A. J. Read, L. Lowry, S. K. Katona, and D. J. Boness 2007. Report of the North Atlantic Right Whale Program Review, 13–17 March 2006, Woods Hole, MA. Available from the Marine Mammal Commission, Bethesda MD. 67 pp.

Rotterman, M. L., and T. Simon-Jackson. 1988. Sea otter. Pp. 237–275 *in* J. W. Lentfer (ed.). Selected marine mammals of Alaska. Species accounts with research and management recommendations. Prepared for the Marine Mammal Commission. PB88-178462. National Technical Information Service. Springfield, VA. 275 pp.

Samuels, A., L. Bijder, R. Constantine, and S. Heinrich. 2003. A review of swimming with wild cetacean with a special focus on the Southern Hemisphere. *In* N. J. Gales, M. Hindell, and R. Kirkwood (eds.) Marine Mammals and Humans: Towards a Sustainable Balance. Melbourne University Press.

Shelden, K. E. W., D. J. Rugh, D. P. DeMaster, and L. R. Gerber. 2003a. Evaluation of Bowhead Whale Status: Reply to Taylor. Conservation Biology 17(3):918–920.

Shelden, K. E. W., D. J. Rugh, B. A. Mahoney, and M. E. Dahlheim. 2003b. Killer whale predation on a beluga whale in Cook Inlet, Alaska: implications for a depleted population. Marine Mammal Science 19(3):529–544.

Shelden, K. E. W., and D. J. Rugh. 1995. The Bowhead Whale, *Balaena mysticetus*: Its Historic and Current Status. Marine Fisheries Review 56(3–4):1–20.

Stevick, P. N., J. Allen, P. J. Clapham, N. Friday, S. K. Katona, F. Larsen, J. Lien, D. K. Mattila, P. J. Palsboll, J. Sigurjonsson, T. D. Smith, N. Oien, and P. S. Hammond. 2003. North Atlantic humpback whale abundance and rate of increase four decades after protection from whaling. Marine Ecology Progress Series 258: 263–273.

Thomas, N. J. and L. H. Creekmore. 2005. Southern Sea Otter Health and Mortality: Questions Surrounding the Population Decline. http://www.werc.usgs.gov/otters

Thomas, N. J. and R. A. Cole. 1996. The Risk of Disease and Threats to the Wild Population. Endangered Species Update 13:12:24.

U.S. Coast Guard. 2004. 2004 Report: Mission-Programs. http://www.uscg.mil/CG_2004_html/goals.html#LMR.

U.S. Congress. 2004. Conference report to accompany H.R. 4818 making appropriations for foreign operations, export financing, and related programs for the fiscal year ending September 30, 2005, and for other purposes. Conference report to accompany H.R. 4818. 108th Congress, 2d session. House Report 108–792.

U.S. Fish and Wildlife Service.1981–1996. Administration of the Marine Mammal Protection Act of 1972. Annual reports from 1980–1993 (Series). U.S. Department of the Interior. Washington, D.C.

U.S. Fish and Wildlife Service. 1982. Southern sea otter recovery plan. Fish and Wildlife Service. Unit i. Denver, CO. 66 pp.

U.S. Fish and Wildlife Service. 1994a. West Indian manatee (*Trichechus manatus manatus*) Antillean stock. Stock Assessment Report prepared by the Jacksonville Field Office. Jacksonville, FL.

U.S. Fish and Wildlife Service. 1994b. Conservation Plan for the Sea Otter in Alaska. Marine Mammals Management, Anchorage, AK.

U.S. Fish and Wildlife Service. 1995. Southern sea otter (*Enhydra lutris nereis*) California stock. Stock Assessment Report prepared by the Fish and Wildlife Service. Sacramento, CA

U.S. Fish and Wildlife Service. 2000. West Indian manatee (*Trichechus manatus manatus*) Florida stock. Stock Assessment Report prepared by the Jacksonville Field Office. Jacksonville, FL.

U.S. Fish and Wildlife Service. 2001. Florida Manatee Recovery Plan: Third Revision. http://www.fws.gov/northflorida/Manatee/manatees.htm#Manatee%20Recovery%20Plan

U.S. Fish and Wildlife Service. 2002. Endangered Species Recovery Program: Frequently Asked Questions. http://endangered.fws.gov/recovery.

U.S. Fish and Wildlife Service. 2002b. Consultations with Federal Agencies: Section 7 of the Endangered Species Act. http://endangered.fws.gov.

U.S. Fish and Wildlife Service. 2002c. Delisting a Species: Section 4 of the Endangered Species Act. http://endangered.fws.gov/recovery.

U.S. Fish and Wildlife Service. 2002d. Recovery Report to Congress: Fiscal Years 2001–2002. http://endangered.fws.gov/recovery.

U.S. Fish and Wildlife Service. 2002e. Sea Otter (*Enhydra lutris*) Southwest Alaska Stock, Stock Assessment Report. http://www.nmfs.noaa.gov/pr/PR2/Stock_Assessment_Program/individual_sars.html.

U.S. Fish and Wildlife Service. 2003a. Final Revised Recovery Plan for the Southern Sea Otter (*Enhydra lutris nereis*). FWS, Region 1, Portland, OR.

U.S. Fish and Wildlife Service. 2003b. Federal and State Endangered and Threatened Species Expenditures: Fiscal Year 2000. U.S. Department of the Interior. Endangered Species Program. Washington, DC. http://www.fws.gov/endangered/expenditures/19982000.html.

U.S. Fish and Wildlife Service. 2003c. Federal and State Endangered and Threatened Species Expenditures: Fiscal Year 1999. U.S. Department of the Interior. Endangered Species Program. Washington, DC. http://www.fws.gov/endangered/expenditures/19982000.html

U.S. Fish and Wildlife Service. 2003d. Federal and State Endangered and Threatened Species Expenditures: Fiscal Year 1998. U.S. Department of the Interior. Endangered Species Program. Washington, DC. http://www.fws.gov/endangered/expenditures/19982000.html.

U.S. Fish and Wildlife Service. 2003e. Three-Year Summary of Federal and State Endangered and Threatened Species Expenditures: Fiscal Years 1998–2000. U.S. Department of the Interior. Endangered Species Program. Washington, D.C. http://www.fws.gov/endangered/expenditures/19982000.html.

U.S. Fish and Wildlife Service. 2004. ESA Basics: 30 Years of Protecting Endangered Species. http://endangered.fws.gov/.

U.S. Fish and Wildlife Service. 2004b. Listing a Species as Threatened or Endangered: Section 4 of the Endangered Species Act. February 2004. http://endangered.fws.gov.

U.S. Fish and Wildlife Service. 2004c. Partnerships With States: Tools for Helping Communities and Landowners Conserve Species Habitat. http://endangered.fws.gov.

U.S. Fish and Wildlife Service. 2005a.: Translocation of southern sea otters. draft supplemental environmental impact statement. Ventura Fish and Wildlife Office. Ventura, CA. 242 pp + appendices.

U.S. Fish and Wildlife Service. 2005b. Species Information on Threatened and Endangered Animals and Plants. http://www.fws.gov/endangered/wildlife.html.

U.S. Fish and Wildlife Service. 2005c. Service seeks public input for manatee five-year review. Press release. April 14, 2005.

U.S. Fish and Wildlife Service. 2005d. Federal and State Endangered and Threatened Species Expenditures: Fiscal Year 2003. U.S. Department of the Interior. Endangered Species Program. Washington, DC. http://www.fws.gov/endangered/pubs/expenditurereports.html.

U.S. Fish and Wildlife Service. 2005e. Federal and State Endangered and Threatened Species Expenditures: Fiscal Year 2002. U.S. Department of the Interior. Endangered Species Program. Washington, DC. http://www.fws.gov/endangered/pubs/expenditurereports.html.

U.S. Fish and Wildlife Service. 2005f. Federal and State Endangered and Threatened Species Expenditures: Fiscal Year 2001. U.S. Department of the Interior. Endangered Species Program. Washington, DC. http://www.fws.gov/endangered/pubs/expenditurereports.html.

U.S. Fish and Wildlife Service. 2006. Federal and State Endangered and Threatened Species Expenditures: Fiscal Year 2004. U.S. Department of the Interior. Endangered Species Program. Washington, DC. http://www.fws.gov/endangered/expenditures/19982000.html.

U.S. Fish and Wildlife Service and National Biological Service. 1996. Administration of the Marine Mammal Protection Act of 1972: January 1 1994 to December 31 1994. U.S. Department of the Interior. Washington, DC.

U.S. Fish and Wildlife Service and the National Marine Fisheries Service. 1998. Endangered Species Act Consultation Handbook: Procedures for Conducting Section 7 Consultations and Conferences. http://www.fws.gov/endangered/consultations/s7hndbk/toc-glos.pdf.

U.S. Fish and Wildlife Service and U.S. Geological Survey. 1997–2004. Administration of the Marine Mammal Protection Act of 1972. Annual reports from 1995–2000 (Series) U.S. Department of the Interior. Washington, D.C.

U.S. Geological Survey. 2004. California Sea Otter Numbers Climb for Second Consecutive Year. Press release: June 16, 2004.

U.S. Geological Survey. 2005a. Manatee use patterns and benthic habitat characterization in Puerto Rico. Project #2070A7R, Task 15. http://cars.er.usgs.gov/basis/projects.

U.S. Geological Survey. 2005b. Manatee Biology, Ecology, and Adaptive Management. Project #2070A7R. http://cars.er.usgs.gov/basis/projects.

Vos, D. J., and K. E. W. Shelden. 2005. Unusual mortality in the Cook Inlet beluga (*Delphinapterus leucas*) population. Northwestern Naturalist 86:59–65.

Waring, G.H. 2002. Survey of Federally-Funded Marine Mammal Research and Studies, FY74 – FY00. Final Report to the Marine Mammal, Bethesda, MD.

Wendell, F. E, R. A. Hardy, and J. A. Ames. Unpublished. Assessment of the accidental take of sea otters, *Enhydra lutris*, in gill and trammel nets. Marine Research Branch, California Department of Fish and Game. 30 pp.

Western Ecological Research Center. 2004. Sea Otter Studies. http://www.werc.usgs.gov

Wiley, D. N, R. A. Asmutis, T. D. Pitchford, and D. P. Gannon. 1994. Stranding and mortality of humpback whales, *Megaptera novaeangliae*, in the mid-Atlantic and southeast United States, 1985–1992. Fishery Bulletin, U.S. 93:196–205.

Wilson, D. E., M. A. Bogan, R. L. Brownell, Jr., M. Burdin, and M. K. Maminov. 1991. Geographic variation in sea otters, *Enhydra lutris*. Journal of Mammalogy 72(1):22–36.

VII. APPENDICES

Appendix A. Major Federal Statutory Protection Measures

MARINE MAMMAL PROTECTION ACT

Passage of the Marine Mammal Protection Act (MMPA) in 1972 marked a dramatic departure from previous regimes for managing living marine resources (Bean and Rowland 1997). Rather than aiming to manage marine mammals for their maximum sustainable yield, the Act established as its primary objective "…to maintain the health and stability of the marine ecosystem." As consistent with this objective, the Act also established a goal "…to obtain an OSP keeping in mind the carrying capacity of the habitat." The Act defines OSP as "the number of animals which will result in the maximum productivity of the population or the species, keeping in mind the carrying capacity of the habitat and the health of the ecosystem of which they form a constituent element." This definition was further refined by NMFS in regulations as "a population size, which falls within a range from [the carrying capacity of the] ecosystem to the population level that results in maximum net productivity." Thus, rather than establishing a management regime focused on maximizing economic returns, it sought to assure that marine mammals are maintained as vital, functioning parts of a healthy marine environment.

The Act vested the Secretaries of Commerce and the Interior with responsibility for implementing its provisions. The Secretary of Commerce, acting through the National Marine Fisheries Service, has primary authority for all species in the order Cetacea (whales and porpoises), as well as all species in the order Pinnipedia (seals and sea lions) except walruses. The Commerce Secretary also implements the Act's provisions on incidental take of all marine mammals in commercial fisheries. The Secretary of the Interior, acting through the U.S. Fish and Wildlife Service, exercises authority for the Act's application to manatees, dugongs, polar bears, sea and marine otters, and walruses. The Act also established the Marine Mammal Commission, whose primary responsibility is to provide an independent source of advice and oversight to the Services and other federal and state agencies with regard to the Act's implementation. In assigning these responsibilities, the Act pre-empts state laws or regulations relating to the taking of marine mammals unless authorized through a process by which management authority can be transferred to individual states.

Moratorium on Taking and Relevant Exceptions

A central feature of the MMPA is its moratorium on "taking" and importing of marine mammals. This moratorium is subject to exceptions, exemptions, and waivers, whose number and breadth has grown as Congress has amended the Act (Bean and Rowland 1997). In defining "take," Congress included both intentional and unintentional capture, killing, and harassment of marine mammals. Harassment, in turn, has been defined to include actions that have the potential to injure or disturb a marine mammal or marine mammal stock in the wild.

Native Exemption: Section 101(b) of the Act exempts Alaska Indians, Aleuts, and Eskimos from the Act's prohibitions on taking when the taking is for subsistence purposes or for purposes of creating and selling authentic Native articles of handicrafts and clothing and the taking is not accomplished in a wasteful manner. Native takes of depleted species may be limited by regulation. Section 119 of the Act, adopted in 1994, authorizes the Secretaries of Commerce and the Interior to "…enter into cooperative agreements with Alaska Native organizations to conserve marine mammals and provide co-management of subsistence use by Alaska Natives."

Permits for Scientific Research, Public Display, Enhancement, and Photography: The MMPA authorizes the Services to issue permits for the taking or importation of marine mammals for the purposes of scientific research, public display, or enhancing the survival or recovery of a species or population. Amendments in 1994 provided additional authorization to grant permits for the taking of marine mammals in the course of educational or commercial photography.

The 1994 amendments to the MMPA also authorized the Services to issue letters of general authorization for research that may disturb but not injure a marine mammal or marine mammal population (MMC 2005). Such general authorizations are not allowed for activities that involve the taking of endangered or threatened species, which remain subject to separate ESA permitting requirements.

Small-Take Authorizations: Section 101(a)(5) of the MMPA directs NMFS and FWS to authorize the taking of small numbers of marine mammals incidental to activities other than commercial fishing (MMC 2005), provided that certain findings are made. In 1986 Congress amended the Act to allow the taking of marine mammals from depleted species and populations, as well as from non-depleted species and populations (MMC 2005). There are three basic types of such small-take authorizations:

- Authorization for most types of small takes require the promulgation of regulations that identify permissible methods of taking and specify reporting and monitoring requirements. The Services must determine that the taking will have a negligible impact on the affected populations and will not have an unmitigable adverse impact on the availability of such populations for subsistence purposes. Authorizations, under section 101(a)(5)(A), may be effective for as long as five years.
- In 1994 Congress added section 101(a)(5)(D) to streamline such authorizations if the taking will involve harassment only. Such authorizations do not require the promulgation of regulations but are subject to public notice and comment. Such authorizations may be issued for no longer than one year at a time.
- In 2003 Congress revised the small-take provisions as they apply to "military readiness activities." Among other things, it removed the small numbers and geographic specificity limitations and required the consideration of several factors such as personal safety and practicality in designing mitigation measures.

The Marine Mammal Commission generally comments on all such applications and associated regulations.

Taking Incidental to Commercial Fishing: In passing the MMPA, Congress set a goal of reducing the mortality and serious injury of marine mammals incidental to commercial fisheries "to insignificant levels approaching a zero mortality and serious injury rate" (NMFS 2004c). In amending the Act in 1994, Congress set a deadline of April 30, 2001, for achieving the goal of insignificant levels of incidental mortality and serious injury incidental to fisheries. Section 118(b) includes four elements (NMFS 2004b):

- Fisheries must reduce incidental mortality and serious injury to insignificant levels approaching zero;
- Fisheries that do reduce their levels of incidental mortality and serious injury to insignificant levels shall not be required to make further reductions;
- NMFS must review the progress of all commercial fisheries in meeting this goal and identify fisheries where additional information is required in order to assess the level of incidental mortality in a fishery; and
- If a fishery is not meeting the goal of zero mortality and injury rate, NMFS must use the mechanisms in section 118(f), including the convening of take reduction teams and the preparation, approval, and implementation of take reduction plans.

The 1994 amendments also included a mechanism (section 101(a)(5)(E)) for authorizing limited incidental take of marine mammals listed under the Endangered Species Act if NMFS or FWS determine that:

- The incidental mortality and serious injury will have a negligible impact on the species or stock;
- A recovery plan has been or is being developed under the ESA; and
- If required, a monitoring program has been established under section 118.

The MMPA allows intentional lethal taking of marine mammals in commercial fishery operations only if it is "imminently necessary in self-defense or to save the life of another person in immediate danger." Fishermen may intentionally take marine mammals by nonlethal means to deter them from damaging gear, catch, or other property under certain circumstances (MMC 2002). Section 101(a)(4) requires that the two Services publish guidelines on how to deter marine mammals safely (MMC 2002), but neither agency has yet published and finalized such guidelines.

Sections 117 and 118 of the MMPA require NMFS to carry out a comprehensive program to reduce interactions between marine mammals and commercial fishing operations (NOAA Fisheries 2000). That program includes—

- the preparation of stock assessment reports,
- convening of scientific review groups,
- publishing a list of fisheries,
- convening take reduction teams to develop take reduction plans, and
- meeting short- and long-term goals for reducing incidental takes of marine mammals.

Stock Assessment Reports: Section 117 requires marine mammal stock assessment reports to be prepared for all marine mammal stocks in U.S. waters. These reports are to be updated periodically based on use of the "best scientific information available."

The MMPA defines a population stock as "a group of marine mammals of the same species or smaller taxa in a common spatial arrangement that interbreed when mature." NMFS has interpreted this to mean "a management unit that identifies a demographically isolated biological population" (NMFS 2003b). A stock may be delineated based on its distribution and movements or population trends, as well as differences in morphology, genetics, contaminant and natural isotope loads, parasites, and oceanographic habitats. Reproductive isolation is proof of demographic isolation, according to the Service. (As a policy matter, the Service considers this definition to be different from the ESA definition of a distinct population segment, which it interprets as requiring that a population not only be distinct but that it represent an important component of the evolutionary legacy of the species [i.e., that it constitute an evolutionarily significant unit] in order to qualify for listing as endangered or threatened.)

Stock assessment reports must include a determination of the stock's potential biological removal (PBR) level. PBR is defined as the maximum number of animals—not including natural mortalities—that may be removed from a marine mammal population while still allowing that population to reach or maintain its OSP level. The stock assessment reports also must identify those stocks that are to be considered "strategic stocks." These include stocks with levels of human-caused mortality that exceed PBR, as well as any stock listed as endangered or threatened under the ESA, declining and likely to be listed as such in the foreseeable future, or listed as depleted under the MMPA (NMFS 2004b). Of the 145 marine mammal stocks assessed in 1995, 47 were determined to be strategic stocks (MMC 2002). The MMPA requires that assessments of strategic stocks be reviewed at least annually and those of other stocks be reviewed at least once every three years.

Under the MMPA, a species is designated as depleted when it falls below its OSP or if it is listed as endangered or threatened under the ESA. Once a species is determined to be depleted, a conservation plan may be developed to guide research and management actions to restore the species. As of June 2005, five marine mammal stocks had been designated as depleted independently of listing under the ESA.[28] They are the North Atlantic coastal bottlenose dolphin, the eastern spinner dolphin, the North Pacific or northern fur seal, the northeastern offshore spotted dolphin, and the Cook Inlet beluga whale.

Of these five depleted populations, NMFS has prepared draft conservation plans for North Atlantic coastal bottlenose dolphins and Cook Inlet beluga whales.

Scientific Review Groups: Under section 117 of the Act, the Secretary of Commerce established three regional scientific review groups—one each for Alaska, the Pacific Coast and Hawaii, and the Atlantic coast including the Gulf of Mexico (NOAA Fisheries 2000). Besides reviewing draft stock assessments, the review groups advise NMFS on a wide range of issues, including population status, trends, stock identity and dynamics, necessary research on marine mammals stocks, and methods to reduce incidental mortality and injury.

---

[28] The Hawaiian monk seal and the bowhead whale also were designated depleted under a separate action although both species also now qualify by virtue of their endangered status.

List of Fisheries: Section 118 requires NMFS to publish annually a list of fisheries that places all U.S. commercial fisheries into one of three categories based on the level of incidental serious injury and mortality of marine mammals (69 Fed. Reg. 48407). The list of affected species generally is based on observer data, logbook data, stranding reports, and reports of fishermen. Since 1996 some fisheries have been classified as category II fisheries by analogy to other gear types that are known to injure or kill marine mammals rather than on documented interactions (NOAA Fisheries 2000).

Fisheries are classified according to the impact of all fisheries on each marine mammal population, then the impact of individual fisheries on each population, measured as a ratio of the number of animals killed or injured to the PBR level (69 Fed. Reg. 48408).

- *Category I Fisheries*: Annual mortality and serious injury in a given fishery is greater than or equal to 50 percent of the PBR level.
- *Category II Fisheries*: Annual mortality and serious injury in a given fishery is between 1 and 50 percent of the PBR level, and the total number of deaths and serious injuries from all fisheries is greater than 10 percent of the stock's PBR level.
- *Category III Fisheries*: Annual mortality and serious injury in a given fishery is less than or equal to 1 percent of the PBR level or the total annual mortality and serious injury across all fisheries is less than or equal to 10 percent of the stock's PBR level.

In 2004 NMFS identified 7 category I fisheries, 34 category II fisheries, and 174 category III fisheries (69 Fed. Reg. 48407). Of the seven category I fisheries, six were listed as taking endangered, threatened, or depleted species (see Appendix B). Another 19 category II fisheries and 26 category III fisheries were listed as taking endangered, threatened, or depleted species of marine mammals.

Owners of vessels or gear engaging in a category I or II fishery are required by section 118(c)(3) to register with NMFS to engage lawfully in those fisheries or to be authorized to take a marine mammal incidental to their fishing operations (69 Fed. Reg. 48409). Participants in category III fisheries are not required to register with NMFS. Regardless of the category of a fishery, participants are required by law to report to NMFS all incidental injuries and mortalities occurring during commercial fishing operations (69 Fed. Reg. 48409). The Service defines injury as a wound or other physical harm, as well as the ingestion of or entanglement in fishing gear. Participants in category I and II fisheries are required to take on board an observer upon request by NMFS.

Zero Mortality Rate Goal: As mentioned above, the MMPA has always included a goal of reducing incidental mortality and serious injury to insignificant levels approaching a zero rate. However, Congress did not provide clear guidance in the interpretation of the so-called zero mortality rate goal, which includes zero serious injury. In July 2004 NMFS finalized a rule defining the threshold below which the rate of mortality or serious injury should be considered insignificant (69 Fed. Reg. 43338). Under the final rule, the agency set the threshold at 10 percent of a marine mammal stock's PBR level. In cases where the Service has inadequate information to determine population abundance or the rate of mortality and serious injury, it treats such stocks as experiencing incidental mortality and serious injury above insignificant levels (NMFS 2004c). Stocks treated in this manner include the northeastern Pacific fin whale, the North Pacific sperm whale, and the Hawaiian monk seal.

Take Reduction Plans: Section 118 of the MMPA requires that NMFS develop and implement a take reduction plan where a strategic stock of marine mammals interacts with a category I or II fishery and allows for development of take reduction plans for other category I fisheries where any stock of marine mammals interacts with a category I fishery that results in a high level of mortality and serious injury across a number of marine mammal stocks (NMFS 2004b).

The immediate goal of a take reduction plan is to reduce, within six months of its implementation, the incidental mortality and serious injury rate in a fishery to levels less than the PBR level for all affected marine mammal stocks. The overall goal is to reduce this rate to insignificant levels approaching a zero mortality and serious injury rate within five years of implementation. In seeking to achieve the latter goal, NMFS must take into account the economics of the fishery, the availability of existing technology, and existing fishery management plans.

Where human-caused mortality and serious injury is believed to be equal to or greater than the stock's PBR level, a take reduction team must prepare a take reduction plan within six months of the finding (MMC 2004). If NMFS has insufficient funds to prepare and implement all required take reduction plans, it gives priority to marine mammal stocks with mortality and serious injury rates greater than the stock's PBR level, stocks with a small population size, and stocks with the highest rate of decline (NMFS 2004c).

Four of the six take reduction teams convened by NMFS concerned fisheries that involved marine mammal populations listed as endangered or threatened under the ESA include the Pacific Offshore Cetacean, Atlantic Offshore Cetacean, Atlantic Large Whale, and Atlantic Bottlenose Dolphin teams.

ENDANGERED SPECIES ACT

In 1973 Congress passed a major revision of earlier versions of the endangered species legislation passed in 1966 and 1969, which had required the listing of species but provided no meaningful protection (FWS 2004). The principal purposes of the Endangered Species Act (ESA) of 1973 are to conserve "the ecosystems upon which endangered and threatened species depend" and to conserve and recover listed species. The Act placed responsibility for implementation in the hands of the Secretary of the Interior and the Secretary of Commerce, who delegated this authority to FWS and NMFS. Unlike the MMPA, the ESA allows states to adopt state laws and regulations relating to the taking of listed species, provided that those laws and regulations are more restrictive than those applicable under the Act. States may enter into cooperative agreements with the Services for carrying out certain recovery and other functions.

Like the MMPA, the ESA contemplates not only the conservation of individual species but also of the ecosystems upon which they depend. The aim of the Act is to employ all methods necessary "to bring any endangered species or threatened species to the point at which the measures provided pursuant to this Act are no longer necessary." To this end, the Act places a positive duty upon federal agencies to conserve endangered and threatened species and to promote their recovery (Bean and Rowland 1997).

In 1978 Congress added a requirement for the preparation of recovery plans[29] to aid in achieving the Act's goal of restoring endangered and threatened species so that the protections of the Act would no longer be needed (Bean and Rowland 1997). Later amendments provided greater detail on the contents and timing of such plans, as discussed later.

Prohibitions on Taking Endangered and Threatened Species and Exceptions

The ESA makes it unlawful to "take" an endangered species (FWS 2004). The Act defines take as "to harass, harm, pursue, hunt, shoot, wound, kill, trap, capture, or collect or attempt to engage in any such conduct." The Services have defined "harm" by regulation as "an act which actually kills or injures wildlife" (64 Fed. Reg. 60727). Such an act "may include significant habitat modification or degradation where it actually kills or injures wildlife by significantly impairing essential behavioral patterns, including breeding, feeding, or sheltering." The Secretary of the Interior also defined harass as "an intentional or negligent act or omission which creates the likelihood of injury to wildlife by annoying it to such an extent as to significantly disrupt normal behavior patterns which include, but are not limited to, breeding, feeding, or sheltering." NMFS has not defined these terms (FWS and NMFS 1998).

None of the prohibitions described here apply to activities affecting threatened species unless the appropriate Service issues regulations to that effect (Bean and Rowland 1997). The Services may issue prohibitions applicable to all threatened species or applicable only to individual threatened species.

Like the MMPA, the ESA includes exemptions to the prohibition on taking endangered species, which have expanded over time (Bean and Rowland 1997):

Native Exemption: From the beginning, the ESA provided an exemption to certain Alaska Natives and non-native permanent residents of Alaska Native villages to take listed species primarily for subsistence purposes and to sell non-edible byproducts when made into authentic Native handicrafts (Bean and Rowland 1997). The appropriate Service may regulate the harvest of listed species if it finds that the taking "materially and negatively affects" the species.

Permits for Scientific Research: The ESA authorizes the Services to issue permits allowing otherwise prohibited acts for the purposes of scientific research or enhancement of a population. Before issuing such permits, the Services must find that the activity will not "operate to the disadvantage" of the species.

Incidental Taking of Listed Species: In 1982 Congress provided authority to permit the taking of an endangered species incidental to an otherwise lawful activity (Bean and Rowland 1997).

---

[29] The Fish and Wildlife Service defines recovery as the process by which the decline of an endangered or threatened species is arrested or reversed and threats removed or reduced so that the species' survival in the wild can be assured (FWS 2004).

Such permission may be granted only if there is an acceptable plan and funding to mitigate the takings and only if the takings will not "appreciably reduce the likelihood of the survival and recovery of the species in the wild."

Incidental taking may also be authorized through a so-called "section 7(b)(4) statement" for federal actions that are subject to consultation under section 7(a)(2) of the ESA. If the Service determines that the "no-jeopardy" standard has been met and the authorized level of incidental taking will not jeopardize the continued existence of the species, it is to specify the level of taking that is allowed and set forth reasonable and prudent measures and related conditions designed to minimize the impact. For listed marine mammals, an incidental take statement may not be issued unless that taking has also been authorized under section 101(a)(5) of the MMPA.

Listing Categories and Processes

Fundamental to the structure of the ESA are two classifications of species: endangered and threatened (Bean and Rowland 1997). An endangered species is one that is in danger of extinction throughout all or a significant portion of its range. A threatened species is one that is likely to become endangered in the foreseeable future. In order to be listed, a species must be determined to be endangered or threatened because of any of five factors:

- The present or threatened destruction, modification, or curtailment of the species' habitat or range;
- Overutilization for commercial, recreational, scientific, or educational purposes;
- Disease or predation;
- The inadequacy of existing regulatory mechanisms;
- Other natural or manmade factors affecting the species' survival.

The listing of a species is the result of a rulemaking, which results in placing a species on the "List of Endangered and Threatened Wildlife," published at 50 C.F.R. § 17.11.

Once a species is placed on the list as endangered, all protective measures of the Act apply to the species and its habitat. Section 9 of the Act prohibits any person subject to the jurisdiction of the United States from, among other things, taking, importing, exporting, shipping in commerce in the course of a commercial activity, selling, or offering for sale any endangered species. In 1994 the Services adopted a policy of establishing a procedure at the time of listing that would identify activities that would or would not constitute a violation of the prohibitions on taking found in section 9 of the Act.

Prohibitions applicable to threatened species are established through regulations published pursuant to section 4(d) of the Act. These "protective regulations" need not, but often do include all of the prohibitions applicable to endangered species under section 9.

All species of plants and animals, except pest insects, are eligible for listing. The Act defines "species" broadly to include subspecies as well as distinct population segments of vertebrate species. The Services adopted a policy in 1996 that interpreted the term "distinct population segment" (61 Fed. Reg. 4722). This interpretation includes three elements:

- Discreteness of the population segment in relation to the remainder of the species to which it belongs;
- The evolutionary significance of the population segment to the species to which it belongs; and
- The population segment's conservation status in relation to the Act's standards for listing.

A population segment may be considered discrete if it is markedly separated from other populations of the same taxon by physical, physiological, ecological, or behavioral factors or is delimited by international government boundaries within which differences in management and other factors may be significant. Determining whether a population segment is significant may be based upon such findings as persistence of the population in an ecological setting unusual or unique for the taxon.

Recovering threatened or endangered species may sometimes benefit from reintroduction of the species into areas of its former range. Under section 10(j), the ESA defines such experimental populations as a geographically described group of reintroduced plants or animals that is isolated from other existing populations of the species (FWS 2002). Regardless of the species' designation elsewhere, an experimental population is considered threatened.

As of August 2006, 1,879 species were listed, including 1,310 in the United States. Of the 566 animal species with U.S. distribution, 410 species are listed as endangered and 156 as threatened. This includes 16 marine mammal species (see Table A-1).

Table A-1.   Marine mammals in U.S. waters listed as endangered or threatened under the ESA

Common Name	Scientific Name	Where Listed
Endangered		
West Indian manatee	*Trichechus manatus*	Entire range
Northern sea otter	*Enhydra lutris kenyoni*	Southwest Alaska DPS
Steller sea lion	*Eumetopias jubatus*	Western population
Caribbean monk seal	*Monachus tropicalis*	Entire range
Hawaiian monk seal	*Monachus schauinslandi*	Entire range
Blue whale	*Balaenoptera musculus*	Entire range
Fin whale	*Balaenoptera physalus*	Entire range
Sei whale	*Balaenoptera boreali*	Entire range
Humpback whale	*Megaptera novaeangliae*	Entire range
Bowhead whale	*Balaena mysticetus*	Entire range
Right whale	*Eubalaena glacialis*	Entire range
Gray whale	*Eschrichtius robustus*	Western Pacific Ocean
Sperm whale	*Physeter catodon*	Entire range
Threatened		
Southern sea otter	*Enhydra lutris nereis*	California (except experimental population at San Nicolas Island)
Steller sea lion	*Eumetopias jubatus*	Eastern population
Guadalupe fur seal	*Arctocephalus townsendi*	Entire range

Candidate Lists: Periodically, the Services publish a list of U.S. species that appear to meet the definitions for threatened or endangered (FWS 2004). As of June 2005, 44 marine species were on the species of concern list, two of which were marine mammals. The Cook Inlet population of beluga whales was originally placed on the candidate list in 1988; the southern resident population of killer whales was placed on the candidate list in 2001. Because of the large number of candidates and limited resources to conduct reviews, in the late 1970s the Services began developing systems for setting priorities among candidate species. In 1983 FWS adopted a priority system based on three criteria: the degree or magnitude of threat, the immediacy of the threat, and the taxonomic distinctiveness of the species (monotypic genus, then species, subspecies, variety, or vertebrate population).

Although the Services may initiate the listing process, individual citizens may also petition to have a species considered for listing under section 4(b) of the ESA. Within 90 days of receiving a petition, FWS or NMFS must publish a finding as to whether there is "substantial information" indicating a listing may be warranted. If the Service finds that a listing may be warranted, it must, within one year, make a finding as to whether the listing is or is not warranted. If, after the year, the Service finds that a listing is warranted, it may issue a proposed rule to list the species or, if other listing activities have a higher priority, it may defer issuing a proposed rule. In these latter cases, the Service must annually find whether the listing is warranted and either propose a rule to list the species, find that a listing is not warranted, or that it remains precluded by other, higher-priority listing actions.

Downlisting or Delisting Species: Every five years the Services review the status of listed species, as required by section 4(c)(2) of the Act. The Services base this review on goals for downlisting and delisting identified in recovery plans prepared for listed species. Based on this review, the Services may determine that a species may warrant downlisting or delisting (48 Fed. Reg. 43103). In considering whether to downlist or delist a species, the Service must follow the same process as when considering whether to list a species, including assessment of the status of the species and of existing threats and issuance of a proposed rule. To delist a species, the Services must determine that the species is not threatened by any of the five factors noted earlier. If a species is delisted, the Service must monitor the species for at least five years.

Designation of Critical Habitat

The ESA requires designation of critical habitat for listed species, with some exceptions (FWS 2004). Critical habitat includes geographic areas "on which are found those physical or biological features essential to the conservation of the species and which may require special management considerations or protection." Those features include the following:

- Space for individual and population growth and for normal behavior;
- Food, water, air, light, minerals, or other nutritional or physiological requirements;
- Cover or shelter;
- Sites for breeding, reproduction, and rearing of offspring, and
- Generally, habitats that are protected from disturbance or are representative of the historic geographical and ecological distribution of the species.

Designation of critical habitat must take into account possible economic impacts. An area may be excluded if the benefits of exclusion outweigh the benefits of designation and if the exclusion will not result in the extinction of the species (NMFS 2004). If it is found that designation would increase the degree of threat to a species (e.g., by informing would-be collectors of its location) or that the designation would not benefit the species, critical habitat does not have to be designated. Section 7(a)(2) of the Act requires that federal agencies avoid the destruction or adverse modification of critical habitat, whether or not the species currently uses that habitat.

Preparation of Recovery Plans

Unless the Secretary of the Interior or the Secretary of Commerce finds that a recovery plan will not promote the conservation of a listed species, the ESA requires the development and implementation of such a plan. Section 4(f)(1)(B) specifies the contents of a recovery plan as follows:

- a description of such site-specific management actions as may be necessary to achieve the plan's goal for the conservation and survival of the species;
- objective, measurable criteria which, when met, would result in a determination…that the species may be removed from the list; and,
- estimates of the time required and the cost to carry out those measures needed to achieve the plan's goal and to achieve intermediate steps toward that goal.

Although recovery plans do not have the force of regulation, they do serve as the principal tool for guiding each species' recovery process (NMFS 2004).

The agencies may appoint recovery teams to assist in the development and implementation of recovery plans, and those teams may include non-agency participants. As of June 2005 recovery plans had been adopted for 8 of the 16 marine mammal populations listed previously in this report, with separate plans prepared for Florida and Puerto Rico populations of the West Indian manatee and a single plan addressing both the eastern and western Steller sea lion populations.

In October 2004 NMFS issued interim guidance on recovery planning for listed species (NMFS 2004). In it, the Service emphasizes an ecosystem approach to recovery planning that encompasses the health of a species' habitat and ecosystem rather than simply the species' abundance and range (NMFS 2004). Similarly, the guidance calls for a shift in focus from simply increasing a species' numbers to alleviating threats that are contributing to the endangered or threatened status of a species or are likely to do so in the future. According to the guidance, a recovery plan should include an assessment of threats that determines the relative importance of each. The first step in the process is preparing a recovery outline based on currently available information. The recovery outline includes a preliminary strategy for guiding initial recovery actions and for making determinations regarding critical habitat, consultation, and take (NFMS 2004). The plan also is to identify recovery priorities using guidelines adopted by the Services in 1990 (55 Fed. Reg. 24296). Using this protocol, species are ranked on a scale from a high of 1 to a low of 12 regarding the magnitude of threat, recovery potential, and conflict with development projects or other economic activity. The recovery outline must also include a vision statement and a brief action plan.

A plan's recovery strategy should identify key facts and assumptions and specific objectives, together with their priority and timing, and recovery criteria—measurable and objective targets or values by which progress toward achievement of recovery objectives, especially the reduction or elimination of threats, can be measured. In determining priorities for recovery actions, a plan must use the following criteria (55 Fed. Reg. 24296):

- <u>Priority Action 1</u>: Actions that must be taken to prevent extinction or to prevent the species from declining irreversibly;
- <u>Priority Action 2</u>: Actions that must be taken to prevent a significant decline in a species' population or habitat quality or in some other significant impact short of extinction; and
- <u>Priority Action 3</u>: All other actions necessary to provide for full recovery of the species.

NMFS guidance requires that recovery plans describe actions and identify the length of time to complete the action, the responsible parties, and estimates of the costs. Regarding the last element, the guidance calls for estimating costs for the first five to ten years and until full recovery is achieved. Although citing the Act's requirement to identify costs, the guidance acknowledges the difficulty of estimating costs far into the future. Finally, NMFS guidance requires review of recovery plans after the five-year review of a listed species.

For a species listed as endangered or threatened and as depleted, a recovery plan required by the ESA generally serves also as the conservation plan required by the MMPA. Besides the components of a recovery plan identified here, a recovery plan should include information identified in Senate Report 100-92, according to the Service's guidance (NMFS 2004):

- an assessment of the status of the species or population and its essential habitat;
- a description of the nature, magnitude, and causes of any population declines or loss of essential habitat;
- an assessment of existing and possible threats to the species and its habitat;
- a discussion of critical information gaps;
- a description and discussion of research and management that could be undertaken to meet the objectives of the plan; and
- a schedule for implementing the research and management actions.

The guidance also calls for including goals and criteria for delisting under the ESA as well as goals and criteria for attaining OSP levels as required by the MMPA. Recovery plans must also include any take reduction plans developed under the MMPA, as well as any plans regarding rescue, rehabilitation, and captive breeding.

Section 7 Consultations and Obligations of Federal Agencies

Section 7 of the ESA contains several provisions that are designed to protect threatened and endangered species and designated critical habitat in the United States, its territorial seas, and the high seas. Section 7(a)(1) of the Act directs NMFS, FWS, and all other federal agencies to use their authorities to promote the conservation of threatened and endangered species. Section 7(a)(2) requires federal agencies to engage in consultations with NMFS, FWS, or both to insure that any action they authorize, fund, or carry out is not likely to jeopardize the continued existence of threatened or endangered species or result in the destruction or adverse modification of critical habitat that has been designated for these species.

There are several forms of consultation, but the most common forms are "informal" and "formal." Informal consultations are designed to determine if formal consultation on a federal action is required. Federal agencies can, however, work with the Services during an informal consultation to modify a particular action to eliminate the likelihood of adversely affecting listed resources. As a result, they may avoid having to consult formally on the action. If, however, a federal action is likely to adversely affect listed resources, agencies are generally required to engage in a formal consultation with the Services. Formal consultations are designed to determine if federal actions are likely to jeopardize the continued existence of threatened or endangered species or result in the destruction or adverse modification of critical habitat (FWS and NMFS 1998).

Formal consultations generally conclude when the Services provide a federal agency with their "biological opinion" on an agency action. Biological opinions, which document the Services' conclusions on an action and the reasons and evidence that led them to their conclusions, can conclude that an action is or is not likely to jeopardize the continued existence of threatened or endangered species or is or is not likely to result in the destruction or adverse modification of critical habitat that has been designated for these species. If the Services conclude that a federal action is likely to jeopardize the continued existence of threatened or endangered species or result in the destruction or adverse modification of critical habitat, they are required to work with federal agencies and any applicants to develop and recommend "reasonable and prudent alternatives" to the original proposal that are not likely to jeopardize the species or result in the adverse modification of critical habitat.

When the Services conclude that a federal action is not likely to jeopardize threatened or endangered species or result in the destruction or adverse modification of critical habitat, or when they can recommend reasonable and prudent alternatives that avoid these outcomes, but the action is still likely to "incidentally take" a threatened or endangered species, the Services are required to include an "incidental take statement" in their biological opinions. These statements exempt "take" associated with an action from the normal prohibitions of the Act. To receive these exemptions, federal agencies must (1) comply with reasonable and prudent measures and terms and conditions that the Services include in their incidental take statements and (2) for listed marine mammals, obtain an incidental take authorization under section 101(a)(5) of the MMPA.

Most federal agencies that operate in coastal and marine waters of the United States, its territorial seas, or the high seas—the U.S. Navy, U.S. Coast Guard, the Army Corps of Engineers, and NOAA, among others—engage in consultations with the Services to insure that their operations are not likely to jeopardize threatened or endangered species or result in the destruction or adverse modification of critical habitat designated for these species. NMFS engages in consultations on its fishery management plans and other actions related to its oversight of fisheries. The Minerals Management Service engages in consultations with the Services on oil and gas or mineral leasing, exploration, development, and production on the outer continental shelf. The U.S. Navy, National Science Foundation, Minerals Management Service, NOAA, and other federal agencies that fund research in the territorial seas of the United States or the high seas engage in consultations with the Services.

Before NMFS or FWS issues any permits for scientific research on ESA-listed marine mammals —or activities that are taken to enhance the propagation or survival of these species—in the United States, its territorial seas, or the high seas, those permits undergo formal section 7 consultation.

OTHER AUTHORITIES

National Environmental Policy Act

Under the National Environmental Policy Act, major federal actions that may have significant effects on the environment trigger a requirement for the preparation of an environmental impact statement that must describe any unavoidable adverse environmental effects, alternatives to the action, and the relationship between short-term uses of the environment and the maintenance and enhancement of long-term productivity. In recent years, these requirements have played a significant role in the evaluation of the impact of major fisheries off Alaska on endangered Steller sea lions.

Magnuson-Stevens Fishery Conservation and Management Act

The Magnuson-Stevens Fishery Conservation and Management Act of 1976 established a regional system for the development and conservation of marine fisheries in the Exclusive Economic Zone. Unlike the MMPA, the Magnuson-Stevens Act did not preempt state management authority for fisheries that occur primarily in state waters. The Act vested the Secretary of Commerce, acting through NMFS, with authority to review, approve, disapprove, and implement fishery management plans developed by regional fishery management councils. The regional councils include representatives of various sectors of the commercial and recreational fishing industry, other interests, state fisheries managers, and several federal agencies.

The Act establishes 10 national standards that fishery management plans must meet. National Standard 1 calls for preventing overfishing "while achieving, on a continuing basis, the optimum yield from each fishery for the United States fishing industry."[30] The optimum yield is a catch level that takes into account factors including ecological interactions with other species and ecosystem components. National Standard 9 calls for minimizing bycatch, to the extent practicable, and where bycatch cannot be avoided, minimizing mortality. Although amendments in 1996 changed some provisions to make management more risk-averse and cognizant of ecosystems, managers have remained largely focused on production and yield.

---

[30] The term "optimum," with respect to the yield from a fishery, means the amount of fish that—
   (A) will provide the greatest overall benefit to the Nation, particularly with respect to food production and recreational opportunities, and taking into account the protection of marine ecosystems;
   (B) is prescribed as such on the basis of the maximum sustainable yield from the fishery, as reduced by any relevant economic, social, or ecological factor; and
   (C) in the case of an overfished fishery, provides for rebuilding to a level consistent with producing the maximum sustainable yield in such fishery.

Since 1977 regional fishery management councils have developed many fishery management plans, which have been reviewed and implemented by the Service. To varying degrees, the councils have increasingly taken into account the impact of fisheries on marine mammals. However, these considerations remain incompletely addressed in most cases.

National Marine Sanctuary Program

The National Marine Sanctuary Program in the National Ocean Service, established under the Marine Protection, Research, and Sanctuaries Act of 1972, authorizes the Secretary of Commerce to designate and manage areas of the marine environment with special national significance due to their conservation, recreational, ecological, historical, scientific, cultural, archeological, educational, or esthetic qualities. The Act also directs the Secretary to facilitate all public and private uses of those resources that are compatible with the primary objective of resource protection. The sanctuary program may regulate activities identified at the time a sanctuary is designated or during regular revisions of sanctuary management plans. The appropriate fishery management council must be given the opportunity to draft any fishery-related regulations if the sanctuary managers determine that fishery management measures are needed to meet the sanctuary's goals.

Of 13 existing sanctuaries, the following are relevant to the conservation of listed species of marine mammals: Channel Islands, Monterey Bay, Gulf of the Farallones, and Cordell Bank off California, Olympic Coast off Washington, Hawaiian Islands Humpback Whale, Flower Garden Banks off Texas/Louisiana, Florida Keys, Gray's Reef off Georgia, and Stellwagen Bank off Massachusetts. The National Marine Sanctuary Program also is responsible for managing the Papahānaumokuākea Marine National Monument, which includes lands and waters in the Northwestern Hawaiian Islands.

Outer Continental Shelf Lands Act

The Outer Continental Shelf Lands Act (OCSLA) establishes federal jurisdiction over submerged lands seaward of state boundaries. The Act authorizes the Secretary of the Interior to grant leases for purposes of oil and gas exploration and development under conditions that ensure safe and environmentally sound activities. The Act calls for the development of five-year leasing programs, individual lease sales, geological and geophysical exploration, and plans for the exploration, development, and production of lease resources. The Act stipulates that economic, social, and environmental values of renewable and non-renewable resources are to be considered in the management of the outer continental shelf. Lease conditions may stipulate measures designed to avoid and monitor possible effects on marine mammals.

The Minerals Management Service in the Department of the Interior has primary responsibility for the OCSLA program. All stages of the exploration and development process are subject to environmental review, including section 7 consultations under the ESA and small take provisions of the MMPA. In support of these reviews, the department has in the past provided substantial funding for research regarding marine mammal populations, behavior, habitats, and other relevant matters.

International Convention for the Regulation of Whaling

Soon after the end of World War II, the United States led efforts to build on earlier international treaties for the management of commercial whaling. These efforts culminated in 1946 when the International Convention for the Regulation of Whaling was concluded (Bean and Rowland 1997). The convention established the International Whaling Commission (IWC) composed of one representative from each signatory nation. The IWC Schedule recommends species and stocks of whales to be protected, seasons or closed areas, size and catch limits, and methods of whaling. Amendments to the IWC Schedule require support by three-fourths of the members. In July 1982 the IWC agreed to a moratorium on commercial whaling, which went into effect in 1986. Most countries currently abide by the moratorium although some have continued to catch whales under a formal exception to the rule or provisions that allow them to catch whales for scientific research purposes.

The National Oceanic and Atmospheric Administration and the Department of State's Bureau of Oceans and International Environmental and Scientific Affairs are responsible for preparing and representing U.S. positions at IWC meetings.

Convention on International Trade in Endangered Species of Wild Fauna and Flora

The Convention on International Trade in Endangered Species of Wild Fauna and Flora was concluded in 1973. The Convention has 169 parties, including the United States. It establishes a system for listing species on one of three appendices. Appendix I includes species threatened with extinction for which commercial trade is prohibited or strictly limited. Appendix II includes species for which trade must be controlled in order to avoid utilization incompatible with their survival. Appendix III includes those species that receive special regulatory protection by at least one member country.

In general, Appendix I species may be imported only for other than commercial purposes and if the trade will not be detrimental to the survival of the species. Appendix II species may be exported for commercial purposes only if the export will not be detrimental to the survival of the species.

FUNDING FOR RESEARCH AND MANAGEMENT ACTIVITIES

Federal funding for the conservation of listed marine mammal species can be examined from at least four independent sources: (1) an annual report on expenditures for species listed under the ESA compiled by the Fish and Wildlife Service, (2) congressional appropriation documents, (3) individual agency budget documents, and (4) a federal survey of marine mammal funding compiled by the Marine Mammal Commission. Determining expenditures by federal and state agencies for recovery of listed species of marine mammals is severely confounded by inconsistencies in the way cost estimates are reported by different agencies, changes in how costs are reported over time, and lumping of funding among various categories that may or may not be limited to marine mammals. The most systematically gathered source of information is an annual report on endangered species expenditures prepared by the Fish and Wildlife Service, but even this suffers from several flaws described later. Public budget documents vary in their organization and detail by agency and by year. Congressional appropriation documents frequently include line-item appropriations for specific species or purposes; however, these are often pass-through funds for external organizations, have little relevance for determining internal agency expenditures, and may or may not be reported consistently from year to year. Agency program staffs generally have limited knowledge of all expenditures for individual species.

ESA Annual Report

Section 18 of the ESA, adopted in 1988, requires that the Fish and Wildlife Service report annually on expenditures for the conservation of threatened and endangered species. The Service assembles the report from annual submissions by all involved federal agencies (FWS 2003a). The Service has provided little guidance on how agencies are to develop their cost estimates and what guidance has been provided has changed somewhat over time. The Service has limited capacity to evaluate and verify these reports, and the estimates it receives may factor in varying costs and are accepted with little or no checking.

The most recent report covers FY2003, when agencies reported $1.2 billion in total expenditures, $785 million of which was ascribed to individual species and $101 million devoted to related land acquisition (FWS 2003a). The balance of expenditures was for activities that benefited a number of listed species or supported general implementation of the Act. The median expenditure that year for individual species with at least $100 in expenditures was $20,100, with 95 species receiving more than $1 million. The maximum expenditure for any individual species was $49.5 million for the western population of Steller sea lions, $39.9 million of which was reported by the Coast Guard for enforcement. Annual expenditures reported for Steller sea lions and other individual listed species of marine mammals between 1998 and 2003 are shown in Appendices C.1–6. Total expenditures for marine mammals in 2003 reached $83.7 million. The second highest total for a marine mammal, and ninth overall for all listed species, was for northern right whales at $11.8 million. After western Steller sea lions and right whales, the marine mammal species receiving the largest expenditures were West Indian manatees ($9.8 million), eastern Steller sea lions ($5.3 million), Hawaiian monk seals ($2.1 million), humpback whales ($1.6 million), and southern sea otters ($1.3 million).

Expenditures for other endangered marine mammals (blue whales, bowhead whales, fin whales, sei whales, and sperm whales) amounted to a little more than 1 percent of all expenditures allocated for the recovery of listed marine mammals. Although federal expenditures account for nearly all governmental spending on most listed marine mammals, state funding in 2003 accounted for more than half of all funding for the recovery of southern sea otters and the West Indian manatee in Florida. Expenditures for listed species of marine mammals grew from 2 to 12 percent of all expenditures for terrestrial and aquatic species of plants and animals.

Since 2001 it has been much easier to track the reported expenditures of individual agencies by species (See Appendices C.4–6). In 2003 the Coast Guard expenditures for enforcement of regulations concerning nine listed species (West Indian manatees, Steller sea lions, blue whales, bowhead whales, fin whales, humpback whales, right whales, sei whales, and sperm whales) amounted to nearly 60 percent ($42.9 of $74 million) of all federal expenditures for listed marine mammals.[31] By comparison, total Coast Guard expenditures in 2001 for marine mammal enforcement amounted to $12.3 million, of which $11.1 million was dedicated to Steller sea lions. The Coast Guard estimate includes the total cost for operating vessels (e.g., all crew and amortized maintenance costs) during periods when marine mammal enforcement is logged as the vessel's primary mission. During the same period (i.e. 2001–2003), expenditures for listed marine mammal species reported by NMFS declined from $40.7 million to $25.8 million and FWS reported a decline from $2.5 million to $2.2 million.

The funding for Steller sea lion and North Atlantic right whale conservation illustrates a broader feature of federal and state expenditures for listed species—namely disproportionate funding. For example, in 2003, about 1.6 percent of all listed species received roughly half of the funding that could be reasonably attributed to individual species (FWS 2003a). Those species that received separate appropriations from Congress or state legislatures are generally the species that attract the greatest public interest and enjoy the support of members of Congress on key committees.

Congressional Budget Allocations

In fiscal years 2004 and 2005 Congress made dozens of separate appropriations for individual marine mammal species (Table A-2) and, within these appropriations, allocations to specific programs or institutions (House of Representatives Report 108-792 [2004]). These included allocations for Cook Inlet beluga whale research, the Beluga Whale Committee, bowhead whale spatial studies, research on the southern resident population of killer whales, right whale activities, state cooperative plans on right whales, Hawaiian monk seals, and Steller sea lions.

Table A-2.   *Species-Specific Congressional Appropriations (in $ thousands) for Marine Mammals, 2001–2005*

Species/Population	FY2001 Enacted	FY2002 Enacted	FY2003 Enacted	FY2004 Enacted	FY2005 Request
Steller sea lions	35,054	32,145	18,233	17,683	13,846
North Atlantic right whales	4,989	6,850	9,936	12,193	5,850
Beluga whales	225	375	373	370	375
Hawaiian monk seals	798	825	820	816	825
Manatees	0	0	248	248	0
Bottlenose dolphins	748	2,000	1,987	3,958	0
North Pacific southern resident killer whales	0	0	746	1,458	0
Endangered large whales	0	0	994	(10)	1,000

FWS has entered into cooperative agreements with individual states regarding implementation of the ESA. In FY2002 the Service awarded roughly $106 million to states under five types of endangered species grants (FWS 2002). In 2004 this amount declined to $86.5 million, most of which was spend on land acquisition (USFWS 2004c).

---

[31] According to Coast Guard budget documents, operating expenses for living marine resources enforcement amounted to $347 million in 2003 and was set to rise to $497.9 million in 2005 (USCG 2004).

Agency Budget Documents: Another source of information is agency budget documents. Only NMFS budget information was easily available for this study (see Appendix E). Budget allocations (in thousands of dollars) for individual listed species for the period 2001–2005 are shown on the preceding page.

Marine Mammal Commission Survey of Federally-Funded Research

The Marine Mammal Commission carries out a survey of federally funded marine mammal research and studies. The most recent report in this series covers the period FY1974–FY2000 (Waring 2002). Like FWS annual report on endangered species expenditures, this report was derived from agency reports, which vary in completeness and accuracy by agency and by year. In particular, agencies sometimes encounter difficulties in separating administrative, management, enforcement, and research costs.

Like other sources of information presented in this report, this source documents substantial increases in funding for several species. Funding for stock assessment and biological research for northern right whales grew from $641,000 in FY1991 to $3.1 million in FY2000. Similar research on Hawaiian monk seals grew from $493,000 to $1.9 million during the same period, while Steller sea lion research funding grew from $4,000 to $4.2 million. Northern fur seal research funding grew similarly from $6,000 in FY1991 to $2.0 million in FY2000.

APPENDIX B

YEAR 2004 CATEGORY I, II, AND III FISHERIES AFFECTING SPECIES LISTED AS ENDANGERED, THREATENED, OR DEPLETED

Table B – 1. 2004 Category I Fisheries Affecting Species Listed as Endangered, Threatened, or Depleted
(Source: 69 FR 48407–48423)

Gear	Area	Estimated Number of Vessels/Persons 2004/2000	Endangered Species	Threatened Species	Depleted Species
Coastal gillnet	Mid-Atlantic	>655	Humpback whale		Bottlenose dolphin, coastal
Sink gillnet	Northeast U.S.	341	North Atlantic right whale, humpback whale, fin whale		
Large pelagic longline	Atlantic Ocean, Caribbean, Gulf of Mexico	<200	Humpback whale		
Lobster trap/pot	Gulf of Maine, Mid-Atlantic	13,000	North Atlantic right whale, humpback whale, fin whale		
Angel shark/halibut and other species large-mesh set gillnet	California	58		Southern sea otter	
Longline/set line for swordfish, tuna, billfish, mahi mahi, wahoo, oceanic sharks	Hawaii	140	Humpback whale, sperm whale		

Table B – 2. 2004 Category II Fisheries Affecting Species Listed as Endangered, Threatened, or Depleted

(Source: 69 FR 48407–48423)

Gear	Area	Estimated Number of Vessels/Persons 2004/2000	Endangered Species	Threatened Species	Depleted Species
Inshore gillnet	North Carolina	94			Bottlenose dolphin, coastal
Anchored float gillnet	Northeast U.S.	133	Humpback whale		
Gillnet	Southeast Atlantic	779			Bottlenose dolphin, coastal
Shark gillnet	Southeast U.S. Atlantic	6	North Atlantic right whale		Bottlenose dolphin, coastal
Atlantic blue crab pot	Florida	>16,000	West Indian manatee		
Atlantic mixed species pot	Atlantic coast	Unknown	Fin whale, humpback whale		
Haul seine	Mid-Atlantic	25			Bottlenose dolphin, coastal
Long-haul seine	North Carolina	33			Bottlenose dolphin, coastal
Roe mullet stop net	North Carolina	13			Bottlenose dolphin, coastal
Pound net	Virginia	187			Bottlenose dolphin, coastal
Salmon drift gillnet	Alaska, Bristol Bay	1,903		Steller sea lion	Northern fur seal
Salmon set gillnet	Alaska, Bristol Bay	1,014			Northern fur seal

Table B – 2. 2004 Category II Fisheries Affecting Species Listed as Endangered, Threatened, or Depleted (continued)

Gear	Area	Estimated Number of Vessels/Persons 2004/2000	Endangered Species	Threatened Species	Depleted Species
Salmon drift gillnet	Alaska, Cook Inlet	576			Beluga whale
Salmon drift gillnet	Alaska Peninsula and Aleutian Islands	164			Northern fur seal
Salmon set gillnet	Alaska Peninsula and Aleutian Islands	116	Steller sea lion, humpback whale		
Salmon drift gillnet	Alaska, Prince William Sound	541	Steller sea lion		Northern fur seal
Salmon drift gillnet	Southeast Alaska	481	Humpback whale	Steller sea lion	
Purse seine	Southeast Alaska	416	Humpback whale		
Thresher shark/swordfish drift gillnet	California and Oregon	113	Sperm whale, fin whale, humpback whale	Steller sea lion	Northern fur seal

143

Table B – 3. 2004 Category III Fisheries Affecting Species Listed as Endangered, Threatened, or Depleted (continued)

(Source: 69 FR 48407–48423)

Gear	Area	Estimated Number of Vessels/Persons 2004/2000	Endangered Species	Threatened Species	Depleted Species
Gillnet	Caribbean	>991	West Indian manatee, West Antillean		
Inshore gillnet	Delaware	60	Humpback whale		
Inshore gillnet	New York, Long Island Sound	20	Humpback whale		
Inshore gillnet	Rhode Island, southern Massachusetts, New York Bight	32	Humpback whale		
Shrimp trawl	Southeastern Atlantic, Gulf of Mexico	>18,000			Bottlenose dolphin, coastal
Monkfish trawl	Atlantic	Unknown			Bottlenose dolphin, coastal
Menhaden purse seine	Mid-Atlantic	22	Humpback whale		
Tub trawl groundfish bottom longline/hook-and-line	Gulf of Maine	46	Humpback whale		
Tuna, shark, swordfish hook-and-line, and harpoon	Gulf of Maine	26,223	Humpback whale		

Table B – 3. 2004 Category III Fisheries Affecting Species Listed as Endangered, Threatened, or Depleted (continued)

Gear	Area	Estimated Number of Vessels/Persons 2004/2000	Endangered Species	Threatened Species	Depleted Species
Herring stop seine/weir	Gulf of Maine	50	North Atlantic right whale, humpback whale		
Haul/beach seine	Caribbean	15	West Indian manatee, West Antillean		
Blue crab trap and pot	Gulf of Mexico	4,113	West Indian manatee, Florida		
Salmon gill net	Alaska, Cook Inlet	745	Steller sea lion		
Miscellaneous finfish set gillnet	Alaska	3	Steller sea lion		
Salmon set gillnet	Alaska, Prince William Sound	30	Steller sea lion		
Salmon troll	Alaska	2,335	Steller sea lion	Steller sea lion	
Halibut longline/set line	Alaska	3,079	Steller sea lion		
Atka mackerel trawl	Alaska, Aleutian Islands	8	Steller sea lion		
Flatfish trawl	Alaska, Aleutian Islands	26	Steller sea lion		

Table B – 3. 2004 Category III Fisheries Affecting Species Listed as Endangered, Threatened, or Depleted (continued)

Gear	Area	Estimated Number of Vessels/Persons 2004/2000	Endangered Species	Threatened Species	Depleted Species
Pollock trawl	Alaska, Bering Sea	120	Steller sea lion, humpback whale		
Groundfish trawl	California, Oregon, Washington	585	Steller sea lion		Northern fur seal
Sablefish pot	Alaska	6	Humpback whale		
Lobster, prawn, shrimp, rock crab, fish pot	California	608		Southern sea otter	
Lobster trap	Hawaii	15	Hawaiian monk seal		
Bottomfish hand line and jig	Hawaii	434	Hawaiian monk seal		
Tuna hand line and jig	Hawaii	144	Hawaiian monk seal		

NOTE: Many other species are taken in these fisheries that are not endangered, threatened, or depleted.

APPENDIX C

FEDERAL AND STATE EXPENDITURES FOR LISTED SPECIES OF MARINE MAMMALS

Appendix C.1. Federal and state expenditures (in $ thousands) for listed species of marine mammals in 1998 (Source: USFWS 1998)

Species	FWS	USGS	NMFS	Other Federal	Total Fedeal	State	Total State and Federal	% Total By Species
West Indian manatee	927	526	–	99	1,551	13	1,565	18.40
Southern sea otter	97	389	–	9	495	–	495	5.82
Caribbean monk seal	–	–	–	10	10	–	10	0.11
Hawaiian monk seal	–	–	1,504	12	1,516	–	1,516	17.82
Guadalupe fur seal	–	–	–	–	–	–	–	–
Steller sea lion (eastern and western populations)	–	–	3,040	20	3,060	19	3,079	36.20
Blue whale	–	–	–	3	3	1	4	0.05
Bowhead whale	–	–	–	–	–	1	1	0.02
Fin whale	–	–	–	4	4	1	5	0.06
Humpback whale	–	–	240	80	320	41	361	4.24
Northern right whale	2	–	1,100	357	1,458	1	1,460	17.16
Sei whale	–	–	–	4	4	1	5	0.06
Sperm whale	–	–	–	4	4	1	5	0.06
Total expenditures for listed marine mammal species	**1,025**	**915**	**5,884**	**602**	**8,424**	**81**	**8,505**	**100.00**
Total expenditures for all listed species (marine mammals and others)	54,123	5,855	28,151	278,188	366,316	16,338	382,654	
Marine mammal expenditures as percentage of expenditures for all listed species	1.9%	15.6%	20.9%	0.2%	2.3%	0.5%	2.2%	

Appendix C.2. Federal and state expenditures (in $ thousands) for listed species of marine mammals in 1999 (Source: USFWS 2003c)

Species	FWS	USGS	NMFS	USCG	Other Federal	Total Federal	State	Total State and Federal	% Total By Species	Total State and Federal $ Excl. USCG	% Total By Species Excl. USCG
West Indian manatee	1,145	526	–	619	117	2,407	1,945	4,351	25.27	3,732	28.53
Southern sea otter	95	317	–	–	47	459	156	615	3.57	615	4.70
Caribbean monk seal	–	–	–	–	–	–	–	–	–	–	–
Hawaiian monk seal	–	–	1,052	48	4	1,104	0.4	1,105	6.42	1,057	8.08
Guadalupe fur seal	–	–	–	–	2	2	–	2	0.01	2	0.02
Steller sea lion (eastern and western populations)	–	–	4,879	2,291	56	7,226	8	7,234	42.00	4,943	37.78
Blue whale	120	–	–	–	5	125	–	125	0.73	125	1.00
Bowhead whale	–	–	–	–	–	–	3	3	0.01	3	0.02
Fin whale	–	–	–	9	4	13	0.3	13	0.07	4	0.03
Humpback whale	–	–	131	277	76	484	8	492	2.85	215	1.64
Northern right whale	–	–	1,542	892	549	2,983	90	3,273	19.00	2,381	18.20
Sei whale	–	–	–	–	4	4	–	4	0.02	4	0.03
Sperm whale	–	–	–	6	1	7	–	7	0.04	1	0.01
Total expenditures for listed marine mammal species	1,360	843	7,604	4,142	865	14,813	2,410	17,222	100.00	13,082	100.00
Total expenditures for all listed species	52,749	5,428	36,195	23,740	227,063	345,175	91,907	437,082			
Marine mammal expenditures as % of expenditures for all listed species	2.6%	15.5%	21.0%	17.4%	0.4%	4.3%	2.6%	3.9%			

Appendix C.3. Federal and state expenditures (in $ thousands) for listed species of marine mammals in 2000 (Source: USFWS 2003b)

Species	FWS	USGS	NMFS	USCG	Other Federal	Total Federal	State	Total State and Federal	% Total By Species	Total State and Federal Excl. USCG	% Total By Species Excl. USCG
West Indian manatee	2,727	466	–	461	166	3,820	5,923	9,743	32.25	9,282	43.87
Southern sea otter	174	403	–	–	13	589	35	624	2.07	624	2.95
Caribbean monk seal	–	–	–	–	–	–	–	–	–	–	–
Hawaiian monk seal	–	–	1,210	–	43	1,253	14	1,267	4.19	1,267	5.99
Guadalupe fur seal	–	–	–	–	2	2	–	2	0.01	2	0.01
Steller sea lion (eastern and western populations)	–	–	5,243	7,810	54	13,107	6	13,113	43.41	5,303	25.07
Blue whale	–	–	–	–	6	6	–	6	0.02	6	0.03
Bowhead whale	–	–	–	–	–	–	3	3	0.01	3	0.01
Fin whale	–	–	–	–	4	4	1	5	0.02	5	0.02
Humpback whale	–	–	53	349	154	556	11	567	1.88	218	0.01
Northern right whale	–	–	4,168	433	143	4,744	127	4,872	16.13	4,439	20.98
Sei whale	–	–	–	–	4	4	–	4	0.01	4	0.02
Sperm whale	–	–	–	–	3	3	–	3	0.01	3	0.01
Total expenditures for listed marine mammal species	**2,901**	**869**	**10,674**	**9,053**	**592**	**24,088**	**6,119**	**30,207**	**100.00**	**21,156**	**100.00**
Total expenditures for all listed species	66,536	6,021	53,029	24,589	273,691	423,866	100,311	524,177			
Marine mammal expenditures as % of expenditures for all listed species	4.4%	14.4%	20.1%	36.8%	0.2%	5.7%	6.1%	5.8%			

Appendix C.4. Federal and state expenditures (in $ thousands) for listed species of marine mammals in 2001
(Source: USFWS 2005f)

Species	FWS	USGS	NMFS	USCG	Other Federal	Total Federal	State	Total State and Federal	% Total By Species	Total State and Federal $ Excl. USCG	% Total By Species Excl. USCG
West Indian manatee	2,363	510	–	480	85	3,438	5,936	9,373	14.15	8,893	16.50
Southern sea otter (except experimental population)	184	868	–	–	7	1,059	35	1,094	1.65	1,094	2.03
Caribbean monk seal	–	–	–	–	8	8	–	8	0.01	8	0.01
Hawaiian monk seal	–	–	2,100	2	5	2,108	14	2,121	3.20	2,119	3.93
Guadalupe fur seal	–	–	–	–	–	–	–	–	–	–	–
Steller sea lion (eastern and western populations)	–	–	33,312	11,067	66	44,445	2,338	46,783	70.62	35,716	66.27
Blue whale	–	–	–	–	1	1	–	1	0.00	1	0.00
Bowhead whale	–	–	–	–	–	–	25	25	0.04	25	0.05
Fin whale	–	–	–	–	22	22	2	24	0.04	24	0.04
Humpback whale	–	–	53	324	352	729	11	740	1.12	416	0.77
Northern right whale	–	–	5,270	474	147	5,891	145	6,036	9.11	5,562	10.32
Sei whale	–	–	–	–	12	12	–	12	0.02	12	0.02
Sperm whale	–	–	–	–	27	27	–	27	0.04	27	0.05
Total expenditures for listed marine mammal species	2,547	1,378	40,735	12,348	732	57,739	8,505	66,244	100.00	53,897	100.00
Total expenditures for all listed species	50,294	11,241	95,879	28,219	388,314	573,976	76,633	647,580			
Marine mammal expenditures as % of expenditures for all listed species	5.1%	12.3%	42.5%	43.8%	0.2%	10.1%	11.1%	10.2%			

Appendix C.5. Federal and state expenditures (in $ thousands) for listed species of marine mammals in 2002
(Source: USFWS 2005e)

Species	FWS	USGS	NMFS	USCG	Other Federal	Total Federal	State	Total State and Federal	% Total By Species	Total State and Federal $ Excl. USCG	% Total By Species Excl. USCG
West Indian manatee	1,710	523	–	228	182	2,643	5,929	8,571	11.11	8,343	16.19
Southern sea otter	170	856	–	–	5	1,031	35	1,066	1.38	1,066	2.07
Caribbean monk seal	–	–	–	–	–	–	–	–	–	–	–
Hawaiian monk seal	–	–	2,100	46	38	2,184	14	2,197	2.85	2,151	4.17
Guadalupe fur seal	–	–	–	–	–	–	–	–	–	–	–
Steller sea lion (eastern and western populations)	–	–	29,295	24,172	35	53,502	2,496	55,998	72.59	31,826	61.75
Blue whale	–	–	–	7	1	8	–	8	0.01	1	0.00
Bowhead whale	–	–	–	7	–	7	–	7	0.01	–	0.00
Fin whale	–	–	–	7	5	13	1	13	0.02	6	0.01
Humpback whale	–	–	150	280	449	879	11	890	1.15	609	1.18
Northern right whale	–	–	7,120	857	136	8,113	280	8,393	10.88	7,536	14.62
Sei whale	–	–	–	–	1	1	–	1	0.00	1	0.00
Sperm whale	–	–	–	–	1	1	–	1	0.00	1	0.00
Total expenditures for listed marine mammal species	1,880	1,379	8,665	25,606	853	68,382	8,765	77,147	100.00	51,540	100.00
Total expenditures for all listed species	76,341	11,878	180,735	27,319	348,339	644,611	74,606	719,218			
Marine mammal expenditures as % of expenditures for all listed species	2.5%	11.6%	4.8%	93.7%	0.2%	10.6%	11.7%	10.7%			

Appendix C.6. Federal and state expenditures (in $ thousands) for listed species of marine mammals in 2003
(Source: USFWS 2005d)

Species	FWS	USGS	NMFS	USCG	Other Federal	Total Federal	State	Total State and Federal	% Total By Species	Total State and Federal $ Excl. USCG	% Total By Species Excl. USCG
West Indian manatee	2,070	971	–	713	75	3,830	5,969	9,799	11.87	9,085	22.93
Southern sea otter (includes experimental population)	156	1,154	–	–	26	1,336	40	1,376	1.67	1,376	3.47
Caribbean monk seal	–	–	–	–	–	–	–	–	–	–	–
Hawaiian monk seal	–	–	2,100	–	30	2,130	15	2,145	2.60	2,145	5.41
Guadalupe fur seal	–	–	–	–	–	–	–	–	–	–	–
Steller sea lion (eastern population)	–	–	4,090	–	4	4,094	1,203	5,297	6.41	5,297	13.37
Steller sea lion (western population)	–	–	8,180	39,940	194	48,314	1,200	49,514	59.97	9,574	24.16
Blue whale	–	–	–	199	4	203	–	203	0.25	4	0.01
Bowhead whale	–	–	–	199	5	204	–	204	0.25	5	0.01
Fin whale	–	–	–	199	6	205	1	206	0.25	7	0.02
Humpback whale	–	–	1,150	199	248	1,597	18	1,615	1.96	1,416	3.57
Northern right whale	–	–	10,270	1,098	312	11,679	123	11,802	14.29	10,705	27.02
Sei whale	–	–	–	199	4	203	–	203	0.25	4	0.01
Sperm whale	–	–	–	199	4	203	–	203	0.25	4	0.01
Total expenditures for listed marine mammal species	2,226	2,125	25,790	42,944	912	73,997	8,570	82,567	100.00	39,623	100.00
Total expenditures for all listed species	92,011	12,167	150,898	47,732	313,875	616,683	68,146	684,829			
Marine mammal expenditures as % of expenditures for all listed species	2.4%	17.5%	17.1%	90.0%	0.3%	12.0%	12.6%	12.1%			

Appendix C.7. Federal and state expenditures (in $ thousands) for listed species of marine mammals in 2004 (Source: USFWS 2006)

Species	FWS	USGS	NMFS	USCG	Other Federal	Total Federal	State	Total State and Federal	% Total By Species	Total State and Federal $ Excl. USCG	% Total By Species Excl. USCG
West Indian manatee	2,432	428	–	831	226	3,917	5,945	9,862	13.86	9,030	18.73
Southern sea otter	134	578	–	–	3	714	20	734	1.03	734	1.52
Caribbean monk seal	–	–	–	–	–	–	–	–	–	–	–
Hawaiian monk seal	–	1	2,164	105	51	2,321	–	2,321	3.26	2,216	4.60
Guadalupe fur seal	–	–	–	–	–	–	1	1	0.00	1	0.00
Steller sea lion (eastern population)	–	–	9,605	–	3	9,608	1,203	10,811	15.19	10,811	22.42
Steller sea lion (western population)	–	–	9,605	20,856	85	30,546	1,200	31,746	44.60	10,890	22.58
Blue whale	–	–	–	60	4	65	2	67	0.09	6	0.01
Bowhead whale	–	–	–	60	13	190	–	190	0.27	130	0.27
Fin whale	0.2	–	–	63	6	69	3	72	0.10	9	0.02
Humpback whale	–	–	–	416	243	659	7	666	0.94	250	0.52
Northern right whale	0.2	–	11,225	444	197	11,866	504	12,370	17.38	11,925	24.73
Sei whale	–	–	–	60	6	66	–	66	0.09	6	0.01
Sperm whale	6	–	–	60	2,203	2,268	2	2,270	3.19	2,210	4.58
Total expenditures for listed marine mammal species	2,571	1,007	32,559	22,956	3,040	62,290	8,887	71,177	100.00	48,221	100.00
Total expenditures for all listed species	128,534	10,940	151,230	33,091	408,359	732,154	60,965	793,120			
Expenditures for listed marine mammal species as % of expenditures for all listed species	2.0%	9.2%	21.5%	69.4%	0.7%	8.5%	14.6%	9.0%			

APPENDIX D

FEDERAL AND STATE EXPENDITURES (IN $ THOUSANDS) FOR LISTED SPECIES OF MARINE MAMMALS BY YEAR: 1998 – 2004

(Source: USFWS 1998, 2003b, 2003c, 2005b, 2005d, 2005f, 2006)

Fiscal Year	FWS	USGS	NMFS	USCG	Other Federal	Total Federal	State	Total State and Federal
West Indian Manatee								
1998	927	526	–	–	99	1,551	13	1,565
1999	1,145	526	–	619	117	2,407	1,945	4,351
2000	2,727	466	–	461	166	3,820	5,923	9,743
2001	2,363	510	–	480	85	3,438	5,936	9,373
2002	1,710	523	–	228	182	2,643	5,929	8,571
2003	2,070	971	–	713	75	3,830	5,969	9,799
2004	2,432	428	–	831	226	3,917	5,945	9,862
Southern Sea Otter								
1998	97	389	–	–	9	495	–	495
1999	95	317	–	–	47	459	156	615
2000	174	403	–	–	13	589	35	624
2001	184	868	–	–	7	1,059	35	1,094
2002	170	856	–	–	5	1,031	35	1,066
2003	156	1,154	–	–	26	1,336	40	1,376
2004	134	578	–	–	3	714	20	734
Caribbean Monk Seal								
1998	–	–	–	–	10	10	–	10
1999	–	–	–	–	–	–	–	–
2000	–	–	–	–	–	–	–	–
2001	–	–	–	–	8	8	–	8
2002	–	–	–	–	–	–	–	–
2003	–	–	–	–	–	–	–	–
2004	–	–	–	–	–	–	–	–

Federal and State Expenditures (in $ thousands) for Listed Species of Marine Mammals by Year: 1998 – 2004 (continued)

Fiscal Year	FWS	USGS	NMFS	USCG	Other Federal	Total Federal	State	Total State and Federal
Hawaiian Monk Seal								
1998	–	–	1,504	–	12	1,516	–	1,516
1999	–	–	1,052	48	4	1,104	0.4	1,105
2000	–	–	1,210	–	43	1,253	14	1,267
2001	–	–	2,100	2	5	2,108	14	2,121
2002	–	–	2,100	46	38	2,184	14	2,197
2003	–	–	2,100	–	30	2,130	15	2,145
2004	–	1	2,164	105	51	2,321	–	2,321
Guadalupe Fur Seal								
1998	–	–	–	–	–	–	–	–
1999	–	–	–	–	2	2	–	2
2000	–	–	–	–	2	2	–	2
2001	–	–	–	–	–	–	–	–
2002	–	–	–	–	–	–	–	–
2003	–	–	–	–	–	–	–	–
2004	–	–	–	–	–	–	1	1
Steller Sea Lion (eastern and western populations)								
1998	–	–	3,040	–	20	3,060	19	3,079
1999	–	–	4,879	2,291	56	7,226	8	7,234
2000	–	–	5,243	7,810	54	13,107	6	13,113
2001	–	–	33,312	11,067	66	44,445	2,338	46,783
2002	–	–	29,295	24,172	35	53,502	2,496	55,998
2003 (eastern)	–	–	4,090	–	4	4,094	1,203	5,297
2003 (western)	–	–	8,180	39,940	194	48,314	1,200	49,514
2004 (eastern)	–	–	9,605	–	3	9,608	1,203	10,811
2004 (western)	–	–	9,605	20,856	85	30,546	1,200	31,746

Federal and State Expenditures (in $ thousands) for Listed Species of Marine Mammals by Year: 1998 – 2004 (continued)

Fiscal Year	FWS	USGS	NMFS	USCG	Other Federal	Total Federal	State	Total State and Federal
Blue Whale								
1998	–	–	–	–	3	3	1	4
1999	120	–	–	–	5	125	–	125
2000	–	–	–	–	6	6	–	6
2001	–	–	–	–	1	1	–	1
2002	–	–	–	7	1	8	–	8
2003	–	–	–	199	4	203	–	203
2004	–	–	–	60	4	65	2	67
Bowhead Whale								
1998	–	–	–	–	–	–	1	1
1999	–	–	–	–	–	–	3	3
2000	–	–	–	–	–	–	3	3
2001	–	–	–	–	–	–	25	25
2002	–	–	–	7	–	7	–	7
2003	–	–	–	199	5	204	–	204
2004	–	–	–	60	130	190	–	190
Fin Whale								
1998	–	–	–	–	4	4	1	5
1999	–	–	–	9	4	13	0.3	13
2000	–	–	–	–	4	4	1	5
2001	–	–	–	–	22	22	2	24
2002	–	–	–	7	5	13	1	13
2003	–	–	–	199	6	205	1	206
2004	0.2	–	–	63	6	69	3	72
Humpback Whale								
1998	–	–	240	–	80	320	41	361
1999	–	–	131	277	76	484	8	492
2000	–	–	53	349	154	556	11	567
2001	–	–	53	324	352	729	11	740
2002	–	–	150	280	449	879	11	890
2003	–	–	1,150	199	248	1,597	18	1,615
2004	–	–	–	416	243	659	7	666

Federal and State Expenditures (in $ thousands) for Listed Species of Marine Mammals by Year: 1998 – 2004 (continued)

Fiscal Year	FWS	USGS	NMFS	USCG	Other Federal	Total Federal	State	Total State and Federal
Northern Right whale								
1998	2	–	1,100	–	357	1,458	1	1,460
1999	–	–	1,542	892	549	2,983	290	3,273
2000	–	–	4,168	433	143	4,744	127	4,872
2001	–	–	5,270	474	147	5,891	145	6,036
2002	–	–	7,120	857	136	8,113	280	8,393
2003	–	–	10,270	1,098	312	11,679	123	11,802
2004	0.2	–	11,225	444	197	11,866	504	12,370
Sei Whale								
1998	–	–	–	–	4	4	1	5
1999	–	–	–	–	4	4	–	4
2000	–	–	–	–	4	4	–	4
2001	–	–	–	–	12	12	–	12
2002	–	–	–	–	1	1	–	1
2003	–	–	–	199	4	203	–	203
2004	–	–	–	60	6	66	–	66
Sperm Whale								
1998	–	–	–	–	4	4	1	5
1999	–	–	–	6	1	7	–	7
2000	–	–	–	–	3	3	–	3
2001	–	–	–	–	27	27	–	27
2002	–	–	–	–	1	1	–	1
2003	–	–	–	199	4	203	–	203
2004	6	–	–	60	2,203	2,268	2	2,270

APPENDIX E

NATIONAL MARINE FISHERIES SERVICE LINE ITEMS RELATED TO ENDANGERED MARINE MAMMAL SPECIES: 2001–2005
(IN $ THOUSANDS)

(Source: NOAA Budget Bluebooks for FY2003 and FY2005)

Budget Line Item	FY2001 Enacted	FY2002 Enacted	FY2003 Enacted	FY2004 Enacted	FY2005 Request
SCIENCE AND TECHNOLOGY					
STELLER SEA LIONS					
Alaska Fisheries Foundation	–	500	994	961	–
Alaska SeaLife Center	5,967	5,000	4,968	5,912	1,400
Recovery Plan: Base	21,952	16,800	4,968	3,562	9,796
North Pacific Universities MM Consortium	798	3,500	2,484	2,465	800
University of Alaska Gulf Apex Predator	998	1,000	994	989	1,000
Endangered Species Act	848	850	844	841	850
Steller sea lion/pollock research	1,996	2,000			
PROTECTED SPECIES MISCELLANEOUS					
Marine mammals, sea turtles, others	9,517	3,500	3,477	3,433	3,500
Right whale activities	1,592	2,250	4,968	10,322	2,250
Right whale NE Consortium	2,894	1,000	–	–	–
Hawaiian monk seals	798	825	820	816	825
Alaska harbor seal research	898	900	894	3,958	900
Manatee: New College	–	–	248	248	–
Marine mammal strandings	3,991	4,000	3,974	3,694	4,000
Bottlenose dolphin research	748	2,000	1,987	3,958	–
North Pacific southern resident killer whales	–	–	746	1,458	–
Recovery of endangered large whales	–	–	994	(10)	1,000

National Marine Fisheries Service Line Items Related to Endangered Marine Mammal Species: 2001– 2005 (continued)
(in $ thousands)

Budget Line Item	FY2001 Enacted	FY2002 Enacted	FY2003 Enacted	FY2004 Enacted	FY2005 Request
CONSERVATION MANAGEMENT					
MARINE MAMMALS					
Cook Inlet beluga	–	150	149	147	150
Right whale activities	503	2,100	4,968	(108)	2,100
Right whale cooperative state plans	–	1,500	–	1,979	1,500
Charleston health and risk assessment	–	800	795	396	–
Alaska Sealife Center	–	–	994	989	–
Steller sea lion recovery plan: state of Alaska	2,495	2,495	1,987	1,964	–
NATIVE ALASKA MARINE MAMMALS					
Alaska Eskimo Whaling Commission	399	400	497	492	400
Alaska Eskimo Whaling Comm: Prt of AEV	–	–	–	99	–
Alaska harbor seals	150	150	149	147	150
Aleut Pacific Marine Resources Observatory	125	125	124	61	125
Beluga Whale Committee	225	225	224	223	225
Bristol Bay Native Association	50	50	50	50	50

APPENDIX F

FEDERAL FUNDING OF RESEARCH ON LISTED MARINE MAMMAL SPECIES BY RESEARCH ISSUE: FY1991–FY2000
(in $ thousands)

(Based on Table 6 in Waring 2002)

Issue	Funding Agency	FY1991	FY1992	FY1993	FY1994	FY1995	FY1996	FY1997	FY1998	FY1999	FY2000
International Whaling Commission											
Assessment of stocks	NMFS				75	184			70	108	393
	MMC			8							
	NSF	49									
	DOS	8	45	72	112	63	12	14	22	8	18
Subtotal		**57**	**45**	**80**	**187**	**247**	**12**	**14**	**92**	**116**	**411**
Fisheries/Sea Otter Interactions											
	FWS	323	205	207	157	157	132				1,181
	USGS							132			132
	MMC					3					3
Subtotal		**323**	**205**	**207**	**157**	**160**	**132**	**132**			**1,316**
Bowhead whale											
Assessment of stocks	NMFS	912	655	499	314	298	315	413	465	400	
	MMS	264	513	549	549	495	482	485	450	450	266
	NSF	55									14
Biology	MMS							625	376	$ 650	
Subtotal		**1,231**	**1,168**	**1,048**	**863**	**793**	**797**	**1,523**	**1,291**	**1,500**	**280**

Federal Funding of Research on Listed Marine Mammal Species by Research Issue: FY1991–FY2000 (continued)
(in $ thousands)

Issue	Funding Agency	FY1991	FY1992	FY1993	FY1994	FY1995	FY1996	FY1997	FY1998	FY1999	FY2000
Humpback whale											
Population assessment	NMFS	45	250	240	388	208		175	136	121	
	MMC	8	2	8		10					
	NPS	21	16	16	20			70	70	60	229
	SERDP				265	45	241				
	NOS					1	2	12	61	2	26
Biology	NPS	13									
	NMFS	20									27
	NOS										60
	NSGCP			43							
	MMC					2					
Subtotal		107	268	307	673	266	243	257	267	183	342

Issue	Funding Agency	FY1991	FY1992	FY1993	FY1994	FY1995	FY1996	FY1997	FY1998	FY1999	FY2000
Northern Right Whale											
Population assessment	NMFS	194	235	324	510	371	827	379	552	869	1,797
	MMC	2	28	20			6			1	
	MMS	196									
	USCG				80					285	
	Navy							970	350	693	611
	NSGCP										57
	DOT										217
Biology	Navy					90	80				197
	NSF	200									
	NMFS	45				228	97	51			212
	MMS	4	13								
	NOS							25	140		
	USCG							80			
Subtotal		641	276	344	590	689	1,010	1,505	1,042	1,848	3,091

Federal Funding of Research on Listed Marine Mammal Species by Research Issue: FY1991–FY2000 (continued)
(in $ thousands)

Issue	Funding Agency	FY1991	FY1992	FY1993	FY1994	FY1995	FY1996	FY1997	FY1998	FY1999	FY2000
Beluga whale											
Population assessment	MMS	80						28			75
	MMC									2	
	NMFS	25	184	276	173	185	205	405	205	199	186
Biology	Navy				172	387	115	5			
	NSF	55	57		107	209	146	106		90	90
Subtotal		160	241	276	452	781	466	544	205	291	351
Bottlenose dolphin											
Population assessment	MMC		4	5					1		
	NMFS	32	105	65	750	845			722	601	443
	EPA		23	10	56	5					
	NSGCP			86	83	83					
	NASA								9	5	
	NPS								10		
Biology	Navy	864	525	677	786	1,504	975	671	634	805	1,398
	DHHS	109					35				
	NSF	100	168				18	151	17	160	162
	NMFS	35	250			20			31		
	NOS									10	252
	NSGCP									13	13
Subtotal		1,140	1,075	843	1,675	2,457	1,028	822	1,424	1,594	2,268
Northern Fur Seal											
Population assessment	NMFS	6	7	9	95	24	24	24	106	603	
Biology	NMFS		4	4					74		1,957
	NSF					$ 138					
Subtotal		6	11	13	95	162	24	24	180	603	1,957

Federal Funding of Research on Listed Marine Mammal Species by Research Issue: FY1991–FY2000 (continued)
(in $ thousands)

Issue	Funding Agency	FY1991	FY1992	FY1993	FY1994	FY1995	FY1996	FY1997	FY1998	FY1999	FY2000
Hawaiian Monk Seal											
Population assessment	NMFS	448	731	717	519	1,109	1,450		769		1,152
	Navy					30	9				
	NPS								5	5	
Biology	NSGCP	25	14	34							
	Army	20									
	NMFS										745
Subtotal		**493**	**745**	**751**	**519**	**1,139**	**1,459**		**774**	**5**	**1,897**
Steller Sea Lion											
Population studies	NMFS		191	101			779	1,580	1,407	1,203	2,560
	NOS										1,100
	MMC	3									
	NPS	1	2		16			20	20		3
	NSGCP		25	20							
Biology	NMFS		690	713	750	591	895	304			
	Navy									15	
	NOS										512
Subtotal		**4**	**908**	**834**	**766**	**591**	**1,674**	**1,904**	**1,427**	**1,218**	**4,175**

Federal Funding of Research on Listed Marine Mammal Species by Research Issue: FY1991–FY2000 (continued)

(in $ thousands)

Issue	Funding Agency	FY1991	FY1992	FY1993	FY1994	FY1995	FY1996	FY1997	FY1998	FY1999	FY2000
Manatees and Dugongs											
Population studies	FWS		23					47	186	1	76
	NASA	10	10	24	24	24	26	24	20	25	25
	MMC		3	13					3		
	USGS								231	232	167
	NPS								11		
	Navy										64
Biology	FWS	437	716	681	594	620	484	152	3	172	32
	USGS							409	234	215	180
	Army	145				282	282				
	MMC	4		6							
	NASA	8	7	7	7	7					
	NSF		50	52							
	Navy					375	330				
Subtotal		**604**	**809**	**783**	**625**	**1,308**	**1,122**	**632**	**688**	**645**	**544**
Sea Otter											
Population studies	FWS	210	24	15	43	124	45	7	116	73	193
	USGS			360				329	599	552	353
	NPS		360								
	MMC	3									
	NOS							9	7		5
	MMC					3					
	NSGCP										150
Biology	FWS	703	690	544	403	409	429	8	71	170	25
	USGS							105	195		483
	NSF	174	122	122							
	NPS									5	180
	MMS	7								68	
	USAF				149						
	NOS						2	5	5	7	
Subtotal		**1,097**	**1,196**	**1,041**	**595**	**536**	**476**	**463**	**993**	**875**	**1,389**

APPENDIX G

SUMMARY OF THE STATUS AND PROTECTION PROGRAMS FOR LISTED MARINE MAMMALS

Species	Legal Status	Best Abund. Estimate	Minimum Population Estimate	Potential Biological Removal	Minimum Annual Mortality Fisheries	Meeting Zero Mortality Goal?	Minimum Annual Mortality Other	Potential Threats	Recovery/ Conservation Plan	Critical Habitat
West Indian manatee	Endangered									Yes
Florida population		3,300	3,300	3	Undeter.	Undeter.	~298	Boat collisions; loss of warm-water refuges; flood gates/navigation locks; habitat degradation	2001 (Update In Process)	1976
Antillean population		121	121	0	Undeter.	Undeter.	Undeter.	Fishery interactions; boat collisions	1986	
Southern sea otter	Threatened	2,735	2735	7	Undeter.	Not available	Undeter.	Oil spills; fishery interactions; disease	2003	None
Northern sea otter, SW Alaska	Threatened	41,865	33,203	830	Undeter.	Not available	Undeter.	Oil spills; predation by killer whales; infectious disease	Draft In Process	
Caribbean monk seal	Endangered	0	0						None	None
Hawaiian monk seal	Endangered	1,252	1,224	Undeter.	Undeter.	No	Undeter.	Prey availability; fishery interactions; debris entanglement; shark predation	1983 (Update In Process)	1986, 1988
Guadalupe fur seal	Threatened	7,408	3,028	104	Undeter.	Yes	Undeter.	Fishery interactions	None	
Northern fur seal										
Eastern Pacific	Depleted	688,028	676,540	14,546	15	Yes	870	Prey availability; fishery interactions; debris entanglement; industrial development	1993	

Summary of the Status and Protection Programs for Listed Marine Mammals (continued)

Species	Legal Status	Best Abund. Estimate	Minimum Population Estimate	Potential Biological Removal	Minimum Annual Mortality Fisheries	Meeting Zero Mortality Goal?	Minimum Annual Mortality Other	Potential Threats	Recovery/Conservation Plan	Critical Habitat
Steller sea lion										
Western population	Endangered	44,916	38,513	231	30.9	No	187.3	Prey availability; fishery interactions; predation by killer whales	1992 (Update In Process)	Yes
Eastern population	Threatened	43,728	43,728	1,967	5.3	Yes	2	Fishery interactions; subsistence hunting		1993
Blue whale	Endangered								1998	None
Western North Atlantic		Undeter.	Undeter.	Undeter.	Undeter.	Undeter.	Undeter.	Ship strikes		
Pacific Coast		1,774	1,384	1.4	0	Yes	0.2	Ship strikes		
Hawaii		Undeter.	Undeter.	Undeter.	Undeter.	Undeter.	Undeter.	Not available		
Bowhead whale	Endangered								None	None
Western Arctic population	Endangered	10,545	9,472	95	0.2	Yes	40	Fishery interaction; oil and gas development; climate change; ship strikes		
Fin whale	Endangered								Draft (2006)	None
Western Atlantic		2,814	2,362	4.7	0.4	No	1	Ship strikes; fishery interactions		
Pacific Coast		3,279	2,541	15	1	Yes	0.4	Fishery interactions; ship strikes		
Northeast Pacific		5,703	5,703	11.4	0.6	Yes	0.2	Fishery interactions; ship strikes		
Hawaii		174	191	0.1	0	Undeter.	Undeter.	Not available		

Summary of the Status and Protection Programs for Listed Marine Mammals (continued)

Species	Legal Status	Best Abund. Estimate	Minimum Population Estimate	Potential Biological Removal	Minimum Annual Mortality Fisheries	Meeting Zero Mortality Goal?	Minimum Annual Mortality Other	Potential Threats	Recovery/ Conservation Plan	Critical Habitat
Humpback whale	Endangered								1991	None
Gulf of Maine		902	647	1.3	2.8	No	0.4	Fish. interactions; ship strikes		
Eastern North Pacific		1,391	1,158	2.3	1.2	No	0.2	Fish. interactions; ship strikes		
Central North Pacific		4,005	3,698	12.9	3.4	No	0.8	Fish. interactions; ship strikes		
Western North Pacific		394	367	1.3	0.69	No	Undeter.	Fish. interactions		
Northern right whale	Endangered								1991	Yes
North Atlantic		299	299	0	1.6	No	1	Fish. interactions; ship strikes	2005	1994
North Pacific		Undeter.	23	Undeter.	Undeter.	Undeter.	Undeter.	Fish. interactions; ship strikes	(1991)	2006
Sei whale	Endangered								Draft (1998)	None
Nova Scotia		Undeter.	Undeter.	Undeter.	Undeter.	Undeter.	Undeter.	Ship strikes; fish. interactions		
Eastern North Pacific		56	35	0.01	0	Yes	0	Ship strikes; fish. interactions		
Hawaii		77	37	0.1	0	Undeter.	Undeter.	Ship strikes; fish. interactions		
Sperm whale	Endangered								Draft (2006)	None
North Atlantic		4,804	3,539	7	0	Yes	0.4	Fish. interactions; ship strikes		
Northern Gulf of Mexico		1,349	1,114	2.2	0	Yes	0	Fish. interactions; ship strikes		
Pacific Coast		1,233	885	1.8	1	No	Not available	Fish. interactions; ship strikes		
Hawaii		7,082	5,531	11	0	Undeter.	0	Fish. interactions; ship strikes		

Summary of the Status and Protection Programs for Listed Marine Mammals (continued)

Species	Legal Status	Best Abund. Estimate	Minimum Pop. Estimate	Potential Biological Removal	Minimum Annual Mortality Fisheries	Meeting Zero Mortality Goal?	Minimum Annual Mortality Other	Potential Threats	Recov/ Cons. Plan	Critical Habitat
Sperm whale	Endangered								Draft (2006)	None
North Pacific		Undeter.	Undeter.	Undeter.	Undeter.	Undeter.	Undeter.	Fishery interaction; ship strikes		
Cook Inlet beluga whale	Depleted	357	366	2	0	Yes	1	Subsistence harvest; fishing interactions; vessel traffic; coastal development	Draft (2005)	None
Mid–Atlantic coastal bottlenose dolphin	Depleted								Draft (2001)	None
Northern Migratory		17,466	14,621	146.2	11	No	Undeter.	Fishery interactions; contaminants		
Northern North Carolina		7,079	4,083	40.8	8	No	Undeter.	Fishery interactions; contaminants		
Southern North Carolina		4,787	1,987	19.9	Undeter.	Yes	Undeter.	Fishery interactions; contaminants		
Winter Mixed		16,913	13,558	135.6	58	No	Undeter.	Fishery interactions; contaminants		
South Carolina		2,325	1,963	19.6	Undeter.	Undeter.	Undeter.	Contaminants		
Georgia		2,195	1,716	17.2	Undeter.	Undeter.	Undeter.			
Northern Florida		448	328	Undeter.	0	Yes	Undeter.			
Central Florida		10,652	7,377	Undeter.	6	Yes	Undeter.	Contaminants		
Southern resident killer whale population	Depleted	84	84	0.8	0	Yes	0	Prey availability; contaminants; oil spills	In Process	Proposed
AT1 Group, killer whale	Depleted	9	9	0	0	Yes	0	Oil spills; contaminants; prey availability; fishery interactions; vessel traffic		None